THE IMPACT OF IMMIGRATION ON AFRICAN AMERICANS

THE IMPACT OF IMMIGRATION ON AFRICAN AMERICANS

Steven Shulman, *editor*

Transaction Publishers
New Brunswick (U.S.A.) and London (U.K.)

Library of Congress Catalog Number: 2004041187
ISBN: 0-7658-0582-0
Printed in the United States of America

Library of Congress Cataloging-in-Publication Data

The impact of immigration on African Americans / Steven Shulman, editor.
    p. cm.
  Includes bibliographical references and index.
  ISBN 0-7658-0582-0 (pbk. : alk. paper)
  1. African Americans—Economic conditions. 2. African Americans—
Politics and government. 3. African Americans—Social conditions—
1975- 4. Working poor—United States. 5. Immigrants—United
States—Economic conditions. 6. Immigrants—United States—Social
conditions. 7. United States—Ethnic relations. 8. United States—
Emigration and immigration—Economic aspects. 9. United States—
Emigration and immigration—Political aspects. 10. United States—
Emigration and immigration—Social aspects. I. Shulman, Steven.

E185.8.I47   2004
330.973'089'96073—dc22   2004041187

This book is dedicated to my mother, Edith.
Her spirit stays with us.

Contents

Introduction   ix
Steven Shulman

1. The Economic Well-Being of Black Americans: 1
The Overarching Influence of U.S. Immigration Policies
Vernon M. Briggs, Jr.

2. Immigration and the Black-White Color Line in   27
the United States
Jennifer Lee, Frank D. Bean, Jeanne Batalova, and Sabeen Sandhu

3. Occupational Context and Wage Competition of New   59
Immigrant Latinos with Minorities and Whites
Lisa Catanzarite

4. Immigration and the Employment of African   77
American Workers
Hannes Johannsson and Steven Shulman

5. Do Blacks Lose When Diversity Replaces   93
Affirmative Action?
Gerald Jaynes and Frederick McKinney

6. Somewhere Over the Rainbow? African Americans,   107
Unauthorized Mexican Immigration, and Coalition Building
Manuel Pastor, Jr. and Enrico A. Marcelli

7. Immigration and Race: What We Think We Know   137
Robert Cherry

About the Contributors   163

Index   167

Introduction

Steven Shulman

Americans are worried about immigration. Polls show that a majority believes that immigration policies should be more restrictive. In large part this is because of the sheer size of immigrant inflows. The Census Bureau estimates that the U.S. population will reach nearly 420 million by the middle of this century—an increase of 50 percent since 2000—and almost all of this population growth is due to immigration. More people means more pollution, more depletion of scarce resources, more congestion, more sprawl, and more pressure on public services. But as the English-only movement shows, the worries about immigration go beyond concerns about the sheer number of people living in the United States. There is a palpable fear that immigration is eroding the cultural commonalities, rooted in a shared if contested history, that give Americans a needed sense of identity and purpose. The majority that wants less immigration wants more cohesion, including more ethnic cohesion. In this view, we have an historical obligation to help our fellow citizens first, especially our fellow African American citizens. Mass immigration (to use Vernon Briggs' apt phrase) creates new ethnic problems and crowds out the resources and attention needed to respond to our own troubled history of ethnic conflict and oppression. Its attendant burdens, such as increased competition for jobs and public services, fall especially hard on African Americans and Hispanic Americans. For this reason, many advocates of ethnic justice, from A. Philip Randolph to Cesar Chavez, have argued in favor of immigration reduction.

There is an alternative perspective, more popular among scholars than the general public, that holds that the association of ethnic justice and immigration reduction is wrong-headed and even dangerous. In this view, immigration brings economic, political, and social benefits to African Americans as well as to America as a whole. Immigration can stimulate economic growth and urban revitalization, which disproportionately benefit African Americans. Because the large majority of immigrants are ethnic minorities in the U.S. context, immigration has the potential to expand the civil rights coalition and to dilute the political hegemony of European Americans. It creates an increased emphasis on diversity and an increased awareness of ethnocentrism. It internationalizes our traditionally parochial and insular nation. It encourages those of us who are European American to recognize that, in the global context, we are the minority. In this view, ethnic cohesion is less a matter of holding on to a Eurocentric past than of accepting a more multicultural future. Limiting immigration just feeds ethnocentrism. Although immigration can create short-run disruptions and dislocations, in the long run it is bound to benefit all Americans and especially African Americans.

The debate about the impact of immigration on African Americans is fundamentally empirical, but it has broad political ramifications. Immigration advocates often say that "we are a nation of immigrants." However, African Americans are the descendants of slaves, not immigrants. Immigration may increase ethnic diversity, but if it does so at the expense of African Americans it is hard to see how it can be justified in terms of historical or social justice. Nor are the political lines clear-cut. The supporters of expanded immigration are a peculiar coalition of low-wage employers, libertarians, multiculturalists, and previous immigrants. Restricted immigration is supported by an equally odd coalition of leftwing and rightwing forces, including environmentalists, nativists, advocates for low-wage workers, and cultural conservatives. Although immigration advocates are fond of comparing themselves to the civil rights movement, it is not at all obvious which side flies with the angels.

Of course, these two positions are not entirely mutually exclusive. Many scholars believe that immigration has a complicated set of effects, some positive and some negative, so that the impact on African Americans is neither simple nor obvious. The chapters in this volume represent an attempt to summarize what is known about the impact of immigration on African Americans, and to add to our knowledge of its economic, social, and political effects. The contributors—well-known scholars of ethnicity and immigration—reflect the debate about immigration both in their analytical differences and in their shared concern for ethnic justice and the well-being of African Americans.

The volume begins with an historical discussion of African American economic circumstances and their interaction with immigration policy. Vernon Briggs argues that African Americans have experienced an expansion of opportunity during periods when immigration was more restrictive, and a restriction of opportunity during periods when immigration was more expansive. From slavery through the post-civil rights period, the impact of immigration has been to increase job competition for African Americans and to provide employers with a low-cost alternative to them. African American history is rarely studied in the context of immigration policy, and Briggs provides a number of interesting insights into the background and interaction of the two. He is clearly concerned with the historical obligation the United States owes to African Americans, and his negative interpretation of immigration will challenge those who wish the read the historical record differently.

The next chapter analyzes the social trends created by immigration and their implications for ethnic relations in the United States. Jennifer Lee et al. explore the transition from a (mostly) biracial society to a multiracial society. As immigration, intermarriage, and multiethnic identifications have increased, the historical division between black and white has reemerged as a division between black and nonblack. Immigrants, in other words, are largely being assimilated into the white majority, a process that continues to elude African Americans. This interpretation reflects the complexity of the subject at hand. Eurocentrism does seem to be on the decline, and this seems to support the positive view of immigration. But it has declined by incorporating immigrants into the traditional ethnic hierarchy that marginalizes African Americans, a trend that supports the more negative view of immigration. Paradoxically, America can become more multicultural without becoming less racist. That cannot be a comforting thought for African Americans.

The chapters by Briggs and Lee et al. provide the historical and social contexts for understanding the economic effects of immigration. Lisa Catanzarite analyzes the impact of immigrants on the wages of natives in "brown collar" occupations (those with an over-representation of Latino immigrants). She finds that immigration lowers wages for all natives, but the wage penalty is largest for African Americans and even larger for previous immigrants. Her interpretation again reflects the complexity of the subject: immigration does have a negative impact on the wages of African Americans, but its even larger negative impact on the wages of previous immigrants shows that structural forces are at work that harm both groups. Employers use whatever means they have to drive down wages; that, and not immigration *per se*, is the common problem facing both African Americans and Latinos.

Johannsson and Shulman focus on the impact of immigration on the employment of African Americans. They show that immigration is associated with a substantial drop in the labor force participation of both African Americans and European Americans. They also show an insignificant impact of immigration on unemployment, suggesting that the drop in participation tends to offset and conceal the negative impact of immigration on employment and earnings (making the findings of Catanzarite and others who have found that immigration lowers the wages of low-skill native workers that much more striking). Johannsson and Shulman explain their findings in terms of job competition effects: large and sustained immigrant inflows, their geographic and skill concentrations, and the integrated nature of labor markets result in job displacement among low-skill and African American workers. The findings in this chapter support the negative view of immigration as a regressive policy that undercuts our historical obligation to help African Americans.

The next two chapters focus on the political effects of immigration, and take a more positive view of its effects on African Americans. Gerald Jaynes and Frederick McKinney analyze the impact of immigration on affirmative action policies. It has often been argued that the emphasis on diversity allows firms to achieve their affirmative action goals by hiring immigrants and European American women instead of African Americans. Jaynes and McKinney suggest that the opposite is equally plausible: as ethnic minorities become an increasingly important part of firms' consumer markets, firms have a greater incentive to transact with all minorities as employees as well as customers. They use EEOC data to show that African American employment prospects are not hurt by the increasing employment of other ethnic minorities or of European American women; in fact, managerial and supervisory opportunities for African Americans may actually be enhanced. These findings are consistent with the positive view of immigration that stresses its expansion of multiculturalism and the resulting benefits that accrue to African Americans.

Manuel Pastor and Enrico Marcelli also focus on the political fallout from immigration. They ask a question that seems so obvious that it is surprising that no one has asked it before: if immigration has negative economic consequences for African Americans, why do surveys show that African Americans are no more opposed to immigration, and often are more supportive of it, than other Americans? Pastor and Marcelli argue that the explanation may be that African Americans perceive potential gains from a political alliance with immigrants that more than offsets the negative effects of immigration on African American employment and earnings. They test this hypothesis with data from the Los Angeles Survey of Urban Inequality, and their results support the hypothesis. Like Jaynes and McKinney, Pastor and Marcelli show that increasing multiculturalism can provide opportunities for African Americans even when they seem to be in competition with other ethnic minorities. This is a complex and nuanced view of the impact of immigration, and will undoubtedly spur further research about the variety of its possible costs and benefits for African Americans.

The volume concludes with a chapter by Robert Cherry that summarizes a large body of research on the economic implications of immigration for African Americans. By stepping back from primary research and asking the broad question "what do we know?", Cherry returns our attention to the big picture. His reading of the literature is largely negative: the results of a wide range of research show that immigration harms the earnings and employment of African Americans. This does not invalidate the more positive view of immigration, but it complicates it. The costs of immigration for African Americans are concrete and immediate. The benefits, as hypothesized by Pastor and Marcelli, are uncertain and off in the future. In that sense the weight of the evidence would seem to be that immigration policy has had ethnically regressive effects.

The immigration reforms passed by Congress in 1965 began a great national experiment, one that is dramatically transforming the quantity and composition of the U.S. population. Unfortunately, as Briggs shows, this policy was adopted with little clear thought as to its consequences. Many (including this author) believe that immigration policy should first and foremost be judged in terms of its concrete impact on the economic opportunities and quality of life of American citizens, especially low-wage workers and African Americans. The evidence in this regard is largely negative: immigration does create some benefits, but its sheer size and concentration in the low-wage sector of the labor market have resulted in economic and fiscal costs that dominate its effects on low-wage and African American workers. In these terms, our lax immigration policy must be judged to be a colossal failure.

Immigration is not inevitable. Most immigration is legal and can be changed by the stroke of a pen. It is also much more feasible to reduce illegal immigration than is commonly believed (for example, employers could be required to check an Internet data base of social security numbers before hiring workers). The issue is not our capacity to reduce immigration, but our political will. Aside from the editorial board of the *Wall Street Journal*, almost no one believes in open borders. The meaningful question is not whether to limit immigration, but at what level to limit it.

Who we should admit and how many we should admit are urgent issues that strike at the heart of our national identity and purpose. In this sense, the well-being of African Americans and our historical obligation to heal the wounds of racism are the first issues that should come to mind as we evaluate and debate immigration.

The idea for this book arose out of a 2002 conference on the theme of "Globalization, the New Economy, and United States Minorities" sponsored by the Social Science Department at City College of San Francisco. The paper I presented at this conference was a rather mundane summary of the research showing that immigration had a negative economic impact on African Americans; nonetheless, it aroused accusations of racism from one member of the panel (who felt no need to present or summarize any research coming to a different conclusion) and heated discussion from the ethnically diverse audience. As a result of this experience, I decided to put together a volume that would deal with these charged issues in an objective and productive fashion. My hope is that readers will be able to use the evidence and interpretations presented in it to come to their own conclusions about the wisdom of sustained, large-scale immigration into the United States.

I am grateful to the chief organizer of the conference, Professor John Whitehead, for encouraging me to present my paper and for his support during and after the conference. I am also grateful to Professor Thomas (Danny) Boston, the former editor of the *Review of Black Political Economy*, whose enthusiasm for this project got it going.

1

The Economic Well-Being of Black Americans: The Overarching Influence of U.S. Immigration Policies

Vernon M. Briggs, Jr.

Of the myriad public policies that have impinged on the economic well being of black Americans over the years, none has had more overarching and continuous effects than those pertaining to immigration. Immigration policies and trends have set the stage that has allowed other outcomes to happen. From the beginning, when blacks were introduced into the British colonies that would later become the United States, to contemporary times, when the nation finds itself in the throes of the largest and longest period of mass immigration in its history, immigration policy has significantly influenced the geographical, occupational, and industrial employment patterns of black Americans.[1]

Given the harrowing experiences of black Americans as the only racial or ethnic group to have ever been collectively subjected to both enforced slavery and *de jure* segregation, no form of public policy should be allowed to do harm to their quest to overcome these imposed handicaps. Unfortunately, U.S. immigration policy has not held to that standard. The burden of this neglect continues to this day.

The Nature of Immigration Policy: A Brief Digression

Before proceeding, it is necessary to mention briefly the special nature of immigration policy. Unlike most types of public policies, immigration policy falls exclusively within the province of the federal government. It is at the local and state levels, however, that immigration exerts its economic, political, and social influences. The governmental bodies at these levels have no say at all as to what the prevailing federal policies should be. They and their residents can only respond to the consequences.

Given the prominent role that immigration has played in the history of the nation, it is surprising that the subject is not mentioned anywhere in the U.S. Constitution. But as its significance was gradually recognized, the federal government—in the latter part of the nineteenth century—sought exclusive responsibility to regulate all aspects of immigration. Through a series of U.S. Supreme Court decisions, such authority was finally formalized.[2] In essence, these decisions state that the power to regulate immigration—while not speci- fied—is a plenary power of the national government that is inherent in the metaphysical concept of "national sovereignty." Being a nation implies a claim of authority to govern a prescribed land area in order to protect and to serve those people who live therein. The U.S. government, therefore, has the duty to set annual admission levels; to establish admission categories; to specify entry requirements; to order entry priorities; and to enforce the restric- tions it imposes. No citizen of a foreign country has a right to reside, visit, enter, work, or seek refuge in the United States simply because of a desire to do so. They may only legally do any of these activities with the expressed permis- sion of policies enacted by the federal government. Accompanying such ex- clusive regulatory power is an implied duty to design an immigration policy that conforms to the best interests of the citizens of the United States.

It is true, of course, that ever since the federal government has sought to screen would-be immigrants and to limit immigration, a significant number of persons have simply ignored the policy restrictions and have illegally entered or overstayed their visas. Thus, immigration policy includes the necessary commitment to enforce the policies that are put in place.

The Pre-Nation Legacy of Immigration

The roots of the influence of immigration on the black experience stem from the nation's lengthy history as a British colony. Shortly after the found- ing of the first permanent British settlement at Jamestown, Virginia in 1607, blacks became part of the settlement movement. The first blacks were brought to the colony in 1619 aboard a Dutch slave ship. As there was no tradition of slavery in British colonies at the time, blacks were initially treated the same as were most white settlers at the time. They and others who followed became indentured servants. They were expected to work to pay off the cost of their transport and, in the process, gain their freedom at some future time. Between 1640 and 1660, however, this system came to and end.[3] Blacks were no longer treated as indentured servants; their servitude would be life long. Thus, racism cannot explain the actual origins of slavery in the English colonies, but it soon became the rationale for its continuance.

For present purposes, the formalization of the use of slave labor and the subsequent importation of tens of thousands of black slaves during the remainder of British rule meant that blacks would be the paramount exception to the labor acquisition process during colonial times. Blacks would enter the colonies as "involuntary immigrants" for over two hundred years.

Although slaves could be found in all thirteen British colonies, the slave system of work was overwhelmingly concentrated in the South. The lasting influence of this process has been that the majority of the nation's black population has to this day always resided in the South. Employment patterns of blacks, therefore, have been disproportionably linked to the industries and occupations associated with the development of the southern economy—especially to its rural sector.

Initially, slavery grew slowly in the South. But in the 1690s the rise of the southern plantation system caused the demand for slaves to increase dramatically. In response, the flow of imported slaves became enormous. By 1710, this influx of more "involuntary immigrants" had reduced the supply of white indentured servants to the South to negligible numbers.[4] The legacy of this regional labor supply policy was that the white indentured servants from Europe and their lineal successors—the European immigrants—became the backbone of the work force of the North and Midwest but not of the South. By the time the colonies won their independence and the United States formally became a nation in 1788 (with the ratification of the U.S. Constitution), slaves made up 20 percent of the U.S. population and 28 percent of the nation's labor force with 96 percent of all slaves being in the southern states.

Nationhood and the Issue of Slave Trading

Following the successful war for independence from English rule, the Treaty of Paris of 1783 ceded all British land claims south of the Great Lakes to the interim confederation created by the former thirteen colonies. Thus, the original landmass of what would become the United States extended from the Atlantic Seaboard (except for Florida, which still belonged to Spain) to the Mississippi River. Becoming the unified nation that would occupy this space, however, was not an easy process. Among the many political issues and regional suspicions that had to be overcome was the issue of slavery.

Slavery was an inherited problem from colonial rule. In the North, slaves were few in number and of little economic importance. Hence, in one state after another slaves were emancipated by statutes until by 1804 they all had done so. But in the South, where virtually all of the slaves were to be found and where the extant agricultural economy was dependant on their use, the issue was far more complex. While few people sought to defend slavery in principle, many of the former southern colonies let it be known that they would not join the proposed union if slavery were prohibited. So resolution of this issue had to be deferred until after the ratification of the U.S. Constitution and the United States itself was established.

Likewise, the issue of slave trading also became involved in the founding of the nation. By the time of the Constitutional Convention, all of the former colonies had banned the importation of slaves from abroad except for Georgia and South Carolina. They threatened to refuse to join the proposed new nation before it was even established if the practice was banned. A compromise was reached by the drafters of the Constitution. Hence, the only provision in the U.S. Constitution that has anything even remotely to say about immigration pertained to the importation of slaves.[5] Namely, slaves could continue to be brought into the country for twenty years—or until 1808—after which time Congress would have to decide the issue. With this compromise, the creation of the country became possible.

Subsequently, in December 1806, President Thomas Jefferson recommended to Congress that the importation of slaves be prohibited as of January 1, 1808 (i.e., the earliest possible date). Congress responded in late 1807 by passing such a ban.

This legislation, however, did not actually end slave trading, nor did it have any immediate impact on the institution of slavery. In fact, the demand for slaves increased markedly in the years after 1808. During the 1820s, cotton became "king" and the modern cotton industry of the South began to develop.[6] The number of slaves in the labor force grew from 893,602 slaves in 1800 to 3,953,760 slaves on the eve of the Civil War in 1860. Most of the growth was the result of the natural reproduction of the slave population. Some was the result of land expansion during this period as slaves were included with the enormous amount of territory associated with the Louisiana Purchase of 1803 and with the annexation of Texas in 1845. But the continual import of slaves was also a factor in the subsequent growth of the South's own slave population. Since it was an illegal act, however, no official data exist as to how many slaves were imported after the practice became illegal in 1808. Ship manifests were regularly falsified to show cargoes other than the slaves that were actually aboard. It has been, however, estimated that at least 270,000 slaves—and probably more—were smuggled into the South from 1808 to 1861.[7]

In other words, slave trading flourished despite the ban on the practice. The governmental agencies given responsibility for enforcing the importation ban (the Department of the Treasury, the U.S. Navy, and then the Department of the Interior) all had multiple duties to perform. Moreover, the funds appropriated by Congress for patrol of the long sea border of the southeastern United States were grossly inadequate. Outside of the South, there was general apathy by the public about the importance of addressing the illegal slave trade issue. It was seen to be a regional concern. As a consequence, slave trading did not end until slavery itself was abolished. This process began when President Abraham Lincoln in 1862 issued the Emancipation Proclamation, which freed the slaves as of January 1, 1863 in those states that seceded from the Union; it was completed after the war with the ratification of the Thirteenth Amendment to the Constitution in 1865, which forbade the practice of slavery everywhere in the nation.

The effect of slavery on the composition of the labor force was, of course, primarily felt in the South. In 1860, the slave population accounted for 21 percent of the nation's labor force with 97 percent of the slave population being in the South. Some of the slaves worked in towns and cities of the South but most were tied to rural plantations. Agriculture remained overwhelmingly the industrial base of the entire southern economy and the dominant occupational source for most of the black labor force.[8]

Mass Immigration Begins: The South is Bypassed

In the thirty years prior to the outbreak of the Civil War (roughly from the early 1830s and lasting until the late 1850s), the "first wave" of mass immigration from Europe began. Five million immigrants arrived over this time span. They were responding to an emerging demand for urban workers. The process of industrial diversification of production had begun earlier in the New England states. It was especially associated with the regional growth of the new manufacturing sector that began in earnest after 1815. Cotton textiles became the nation's first major manufacturing industry. Originally, the employers of these factories sought to use women and children from the local communities as their workers.[9] But by the 1830s, they began to hire immigrants from Ireland and French-speaking Canada. Germany also became a major source of immigrants for the emerging demand for urban labor. Indicative of this industrial transformation is the fact that the percentage of the labor force of the states of the North and West employed in agriculture plummeted from 68 percent in 1800 to 40 percent in 1850.[10]

Thus, as industrialization was taking hold in New England and around the urban fringes of the upper Midwest along the shores of the Great Lakes, blacks still were trapped in the slave system of the South. As mentioned, black slave trading continued during the critical period, albeit illegally, so the "involuntary" immigration of blacks was also part of the "first wave" of mass immigration until the Civil War finally halted the practice.

Largely confined to the South, virtually all blacks were still linked to its regional economy. Although there were isolated instances where some iron, granite, and tobacco manufacturing occurred in the South, which used some slave labor, agriculture remained the mainstay of the southern industrial structure. Cotton farming was the dominant source of production and black employment. But other crops, such as tobacco, rice, and indigo, were also important and, increasingly, hemp and sugarcane became so too. Furthermore, cotton farming (and the use of slaves) shifted during these years from the Carolinas to the richer soil of the bottomlands of the Mississippi and Alabama and, still later, to Arkansas and Texas. In sharp contrast to the experiences of the rest of the country during these early years of the Republic, the percentage of the southern labor force employed in agriculture actually increased from 82 percent in 1800 to 84 percent in 1850.[11]

Thus, during these years prior to the Civil War, slavery was the force that kept blacks regionally confined and occupationally concentrated. Immigration contributed to the growing size of the black population in the South. But elsewhere, immigration served primarily as an alternative to seeking black workers (who could not respond to market forces anyhow due to the restrictive hold of slavery) or relying on native-born white workers (for whom the western frontier often served as a mobility lure).

The Industrialization of the U.S. Economy Takes Hold:
The South is Left Out

The Civil War was not only a turning point in the nation's social history as regards to ending slavery. It was also the economic "break point" between "agricultural America" and "industrial America."[12] The prewar pace of diversification of the economies of the North and the West accelerated during the war and took off in the immediate decades that followed. Major physical improvements were made in transportation systems during and after the war. Large military contracts from the federal government during the war hastened the onset of mass production techniques that enhanced productivity in the years that followed. By the end of the nineteenth century, corporate domination of the business sector had taken hold and, through a wave of mergers, the scale of many production units was dramatically increased. The internal combustion engine was introduced as the twentieth century began, which revolutionized transportation and hastened the development of the petroleum industry. Thus, by 1920, manufacturing had replaced agriculture as the nation's largest employment sector. The preponderance of this vibrant and diverse activity occurred in the North and the West. The South, in sharp contrast, lay in physical ruin after the war and only slowly was it able to reconstruct its infrastructure and its industrial base. Its economy remained bound to agriculture.

In contrast, the North and West needed to enlarge its urban workforce during these years to meet this acceleration of demand for largely unskilled workers. Immigration from Europe and, to a far lesser degree, from Asia, became the chosen course.[13] It was the strength of the "pull" factors of the U.S. economy rather than the "push" factors of conditions in their homelands that set this mass movement of people in motion.[14] Ten million immigrants, mostly from Northern and Western Europe, entered between 1861 and 1890 (the "second wave" of mass immigration) and 16 million more, mostly from Eastern and Southern Europe, entered between 1890 and 1920 (the "third wave" of mass immigration).

It is instructive to note that during all of these years "the greatest direct beneficiary of the flow of immigrant labor was never agriculture though farming was our primary industry."[15] The economy of the South, of course, was still primarily agriculturally based and it was where most black workers were to be found. Throughout the latter half of the nineteenth century, the economic growth in the South was slow. For blacks, little changed in terms of their economic status. Slavery was replaced by sharecropping, which was essentially another form of bondage whereby credit was extended but the borrower's mobility was restricted until all debts were paid off. "Black codes" were enacted that regulated black conduct in day-to-day life. Most blacks in the rural South, therefore, were prevented from being able to leave the plantations where they had previously worked as slaves. As a consequence blacks "tended to be frozen to agriculture" throughout this era.[16] The imposition of the infamous "Jim Crow" segregation laws in the 1890s and their enforcement during the years that followed served to complete the social marginalization process of blacks in the South.

Thus, during these critical transition years of the American economy from its original heritage as a static agricultural society to its new era as a dynamic and industrially diverse economy, most native-born workers (black and white) who populated the nation's vast rural areas were left out. Most of these native born rural workers were living lives of poverty. They were also lacking in human capital endowments. But given the types of unskilled jobs that were being created at the time in the urban sectors outside the South, they were certainly as minimally qualified as were most of the immigrants who became the preferred alternative.

Most of these rural workers nationwide were whites but the most obvious source of surplus labor at the time was the black population who were still trapped in the South. The percentage of the black population living in the South in 1910 (90 percent) was essentially the same as it was on the eve of the Civil War fifty years earlier in 1860 (92 percent). Indeed, the famed black educator of the era, Booker T. Washington, made the status of black labor the central theme of his famous speech at the Atlanta Exposition of 1895. He pleaded with the assembled white industrialists not to look "to the incoming of those of foreign birth and strange tongue and habits."[17] Instead, he asked them to turn to native-born blacks, "who shall stand with you with a devotion that no foreigner can approach" and, by "interlacing our industrial, commercial, civil, and religious life with yours...[we] shall make the interests of both races one."[18] His wise words—while cheered at the time—were ignored in practice. It would not be until immigration was cut off during World War I that blacks could finally migrate and compete for the new array of jobs being created in the urban North and West.

"Open-Door" Immigration Ends; Black Out-Migration Begins

The outbreak of World War I in Europe in 1914 led to a rapid decline in immigration to the United States. It was no longer feasible for Europeans to leave as their governments were recruiting armies and fighting among themselves. Travel in many areas was impossible. Over 80 percent of the 5.7 million immigrants who entered the United States over the decade (i.e., from 1911 to 1920) arrived before the war, from 1911-1914; 10 percent came after the war was over in 1919 and 1920.

The cutoff of immigration from its primary supply source (Europe) and the simultaneous increase in the demand for domestic workers—to fill military orders for the government and to replace workers conscripted into military service—led to the most significant change in economic circumstances that black Americans had yet experienced. Namely, they had the opportunity to move to urban areas outside the South. The chance was seized.

When World War I was over, there were immediate signs that another wave of European immigration was poised to commence. But attitudes and circumstances had changed in the United States. Geographically speaking, the continental frontiers had all been overcome. Moreover, the alleged benefits of mass immigration as a source of cheap and exploitable labor had given way to a recognition that there were also real costs that needed to be balanced off. Uncontrolled immigration had been found to generate unemployment, depress real wages, increase urban poverty, foster slum housing, and contribute to a variety of adverse health and safety conditions.[19] Furthermore, there were widespread concerns that the "third wave" of mass immigration had been so diverse in its ethnic, racial, linguistic, and religious makeup and so immense in its scale that it was proving difficult, if not impossible, for the urban population to meld into a unified citizenry.

With widespread popular support, legislation was enacted to end almost a hundred years of continuous mass immigration. Efforts to screen out some immigrant groups had begun earlier on a small scale, but now legislation was passed to restrict the level of immigration. In 1917, the Immigration Act of 1917 had created the "Asiatic Barred Zone" which, in effect, banned all immigration from Asia; in 1921 legislation established a temporary annual ceiling of 358,000 immigrants from the Eastern Hemisphere (where most "third wave" immigration had originated) with discriminatory country quotas (favoring immigrants from Northern and Western European countries) until a more comprehensive piece of legislation was drafted. These efforts culminated in the enactment of the Immigration Act of 1924 (also known popularly as the National Origins Act). It established the annual ceilings on immigration at an even lower annual level of 154,000 persons from Eastern Hemisphere nations (which was essentially Europe). In addition, the legislation also set individual quotas for each country that was eligible to supply immigrants. These quotas were discriminatory in that much higher quotas applied to countries of Western and Northern Europe while much lower quotas applied to countries of Eastern and Southern Europe. Immigration from Asian countries had been essentially banned entirely by earlier legislation and restrictive agreements. Likewise, blacks were excluded from any computation of the population for the purpose of establishing future quota eligibility because they were considered by legislators to have been "involuntary immigrants."[20] Hence, there would be virtually no future immigration permitted from most African countries (except for token quotas given to some North African nations and some African colonies of European nations).

Clearly, the objective of the national origins system was to eliminate the foreign born as an important future element in the American population. Indeed, as a consequence of its adoption, the percentage of the U.S. population that was foreign born fell consistently from 14.7 percent in 1910 to its all-time historic low of 4.4 percent in 1965 when, as will be discussed, mass immigration (i.e. "the fourth wave") was accidentally revived.

Support for the imposition of these legislative restrictions on immigration in the 1920s came from virtually every quarter—business, labor, academia, and Protestant church leaders. Black leaders also joined in the chorus. A. Philip Randolph, who later would help lead the civil rights movement in the late 1950s and 1960s, was editor of the *Messenger* magazine (which promoted trade unionism and socialism) in the 1920s. In his editorials at this time, he wrote that the United States was suffering from "immigration indigestion" and he favored reducing immigration "to nothing." He not only supported "shutting out the Germans from Germany, the Italians from Italy...the Hindus from India, the Chinese from China," but he also included keeping out "the Negroes from the West Indies."[21]

The response of blacks in the South to the opening was immediate. Black migration out of the South began in earnest in 1915.[22] In 1910, over two-thirds of all black Americans lived in rural areas (almost exclusively in the South). During the decade from 1911 to 1920, 369,000 blacks left the South; between 1921 and 1930 the number more than doubled (see Table 1).[23] By 1930, 20 percent of the nation's black population lived outside the South, with 88 percent of these persons concentrated in large urban centers.[24]

A New Trend is Born: Declining Immigration
Leads to Increasing Black Migration Out of the South

The migration trend that began with World War I became one of the nation's most important economic and social movements of the twentieth century. For black Americans, it was the most significant such trend. As articulated by Raymond Frost and shown in Table 1, "there is a competitive relationship between immigration and black migration out of the South.... [W]hen the rate of immigration declines, black migration to the North and West increases; when the rate of immigration increases, black migration declines."[25]

The reception by those outside the South to the arrival of blacks to their cities was anything but hospitable. As historian Arthur Link described the reception in the North and Midwest of blacks into their already existing urban slums, "they became the object of the suspicion and hatred of white unskilled workers, most of them immigrants themselves."[26] Indeed, full scale racial riots—often pitting recent white immigrants versus recent black migrants—broke out in a number of northern and Midwestern cities beginning in East St. Louis in 1917 and continuing intermittently for several decades.[27]

But with immigration controlled for the first time in American history, black migration soared. In each of the decades of the 1940s, 1950s, and 1960s, black out-migration from the South was greater than that of the entire thirty-year period from 1910 to 1940, when it all began.

The economic effect of out-migration on blacks was to widen their industrial and occupational choices. Rural black workers, whose heritage had largely been farm work, joined with similarly situated rural white workers in a mass movement to the nation's urban economy. Over the decade of the 1920s, 6 million persons moved from the farms to the cities. It was the first decade in the nation's history that the rural population actually sustained a net loss. With mass immigration finally restrained, native-born rural workers were free at last to seek the wider economic opportunities afforded by the rapidly expanding urban labor market. Arthur Link has described this rural to urban migration as "one of the most important changes in the American social fabric."[28] Given their inadequate educational preparation and lack of skill training, most of these newly urbanized blacks had to start on the bottom rung of the job ladder. But at least they could finally enter competition. Fortunately, most of the expanding urban jobs in this era did not require much in the way of job preparation—if one could get hired.

Table 1
Black Migration Out of the South and U.S. Immigration Levels 1911-1980

Years	Black Migration from the South (Thousands)	Immigration to the United States (Millions)
1911-1920	369	5,735
1921-1930	771	4,107
1931-1940	423	528
1941-1950	1,347	1,035
1951-1960	1,255	2,515
1961-1970	1,413	3,321
1971-1980	313	4,493

Source: Raymond Frost, "Immigration vs. Black American Migration," *Challenge: Magazine of Economic Affairs* (November-December 1991), p. 68 and Bureau of the Census, "Historical Census Statistics on the Foreign Born Population of the United States, 1850-1990," *Working Papers* No. 29 (Washington DC: U.S. Government Printing Office 1999), Table 1.

World War II and its Aftermath:
Low Immigration and the Creation of a Window of Opportunity

The depression decade of the 1930s was a staggering blow to the economic well being of American workers of every description. But as shown in Table 1, the number of blacks leaving the South during these years slowed from its pace in the 1920s but it did not stop. The economic consequences of the outbreak of World War II in the early 1940s, on the other hand, shocked the economy out of its doldrums. Black out-migration from the South soared. By 1950, one-third of the black population lived north of the Mason-Dixon line.

With over 11 million men drafted into military service during the war years and with dramatic increases in related military production levels as the result of sharp increases in government spending, it was imperative that civilian workers be found to meet the demand for labor. Immigration levels, which had been low since the late 1920s, continued to be so. Hence, national employment policy was forced to tap domestic reserves that had been hitherto ignored, underutilized, or marginalized. Rural workers were one source of surplus labor and the rural South in particular was a rich pool of potential manpower. Blacks poured out of the South—both into military service and to the domestic job opportunities in the North and West. Others who responded were women, older workers, youths, and disabled workers. Thus, despite the withdrawal of millions of working-age men during the war into military service, the nation's civilian labor force still increased by over 5 million workers between 1941 and 1945.

The tight labor market of the early 1940s provided the chance for black leaders to attack broadside the issue of racial discrimination in employment. A. Philip Randolph and other black leaders threatened in 1940 to organize a "march on Washington" to publicize the issue of employment discrimination in all regions of the country. President Franklin Roosevelt responded in 1941 by issuing executive orders banning discrimination by holders of federal contracts—of whom there were many at the time—and creating a federal committee to investigate charges of employment discrimination. These actions are considered "milestones" in the path that would lead to the passage of the historic Civil Rights Act of 1964 a generation later. Thus, the labor shortages of this period and the lack of an immigrant alternative for employers were both crucial contributors to the launching of the economic plank (i.e. the equal employment opportunity goal) of the broader civil rights agenda that would come to a head in 1964.

The Civil Rights Movement Spills Over to Immigration Reform

In the early 1960s, the major domestic issue was not immigration reform. It was civil rights policy. But their destinies became intertwined. The civil rights movement had evolved into an activist stage that used demonstrations, marches, and boycotts to protest in non-violent manners the perpetuation of overt segregation against black citizens in the South. The primary focus was on the abuses of social dignity (i.e., segregated public facilities) and the denial of political rights (i.e., restrictions on the right to vote).

The culmination of these protests came with the passage of the Civil Rights Act of 1964. In the wake of the assassination of President John F. Kennedy in November 1963, the political logjam that had blocked Kennedy's attempts to address a multitude of domestic policy concerns was finally broken. The new president, Lyndon B. Johnson, was one of the most politically astute men to ever hold the position. After assuming office, he announced his intention to enact a broad social program under the rubric of building "The Great Society." Virtually all of this ambitious domestic reform agenda were subsequently enacted. Moreover, persons dedicated to the accomplishment of these objectives were appointed to head the various government agencies to implement this social agenda.

One of the reforms pertained to the subject of immigration and it was directly linked to another: civil rights. For to invoke in legislation the explicit principle that overt racism could no longer be tolerated in the ways citizens treated each other implicitly meant that there could no longer be overt discrimination in the nation's laws that governed the way future citizens would be considered for immigrant admission. Secretary of State Dean Rusk made this linkage explicit in testimony before Congress in support of immigration reform in August, 1964: "The action we urge…is not to make a drastic departure from the long-established immigration policy, but rather to reconcile our immigration policy as it had developed in recent years with the with the letter of the general law."[29] It was the passage of the Civil Rights Act of 1964, therefore, that created the political climate needed to legislatively end the discriminatory national origins system the following year with the adoption of the Immigration Act of 1965.[30]

There was, however, an ironic twist to the linkage of civil rights legislation to immigration reform. While both issues came to the forefront of the national agenda because of political and social concerns, both also had significant economic consequences with regard to their labor market impacts. The economic aspects, however, were not the focus at the time nor was the possibility foreseen seen that these two policy pursuits could conflict with each other.

The Civil Rights Act of 1964 contained Title VII, which prohibited discrimination in employment on the basis of race, color, gender, religious belief, or national origin. When it actually went into effect on July 1, 1965, its terms applied to employers, labor unions, and private employment services. As opposed to the other sections of the Act that focused on social and political practices largely occurring in the South, equal employment opportunity was an economic issue and it had nationwide implications.

Within months after its enactment, however, a rash of civil disturbances broke out in urban areas across the nation. Over the ensuing years, there were many more. To identify the causes of these riots, the National Advisory Commission on Civil Disorders was established. It issued its historic report in March 1968. It found that the issue of employment discrimination was a far more complex issue than the drafters of the Civil Rights Act had earlier envisioned.[31] Public policies were needed to overcome the past denial of job opportunities and to provide employment preparation. They would entail far more programmatic action and public funds than the mere issuance of a ban on future discriminatory behavior as stated by Title VII.

If past patterns of employment for black Americans were not to be replicated in the future, affirmative action policies would be needed to reach out to *already qualified* blacks for jobs. But in far too many cases, blacks were unqualified for the high-skilled, high-income jobs that were expanding in number. Too many blacks were disproportionately concentrated in the low-skilled, low-income occupations and industries where jobs were declining due to the advent of new computer technology. To change these employment patterns, it would be necessary to address the extensive human capital deficiencies of blacks that were the accumulated legacy of centuries of stifled aspirations, unequal educations, and inadequate training opportunities. The civil disorders, after all, had occurred at a time when full employment prevailed (i.e., the national unemployment rate was in the mid-3 percent range). But, because the black population had become highly urbanized, and disproportionately concentrated in central cities, unemployment in these areas remained much higher than the overall national unemployment rate. Moreover, the black labor force was beset with inordinately high incidences of working poor, discouraged workers, under-employed workers, involuntary part-time workers, and female-headed households. There was no thought at the time that many of these same urban labor markets where blacks were concentrated were about to receive a mass infusion of new immigrants—most of whom would themselves be from minority groups and many of whom also had significant human capital deficiencies.

The Advisory Commission boldly stated that the nation had unfinished business to address if it was serious about fulfilling the ideals of the Civil Rights Act. It was in the national interest to upgrade the capabilities and expand the utilization of the available pool of black workers. Otherwise, many blacks would be condemned to lives in a permanent underclass—with all of the attended hardships of welfare dependency, crime, alcoholism, prostitution, and irregular work habits that scar the individuals involved and burden society. But with respect to blacks, there was also a clear moral imperative that recognized that their collective fate had been greatly influenced by external institutional forces over which they only had marginal control.[32] A programmatic agenda, aimed at bridging the past period of denial of opportunities and a future period of equal opportunity, was required. What was anticipated was that there would be a concerted effort made over the ensuing decade to give priority to the urgent needs of black Americans.

Who could have foreseen that immigration reform was about to become a new example of the institutional policies adversely affecting blacks that the Advisory Commission had condemned? In earlier times, immigration policy had kept blacks in the rural South after slavery ended by providing an alternative source of workers to meet the industrial expansion needs of the North and West. In the late twentieth century, immigration policy once more provided an alternative to providing the momentum for the pursuit of inclusive policies needed to alter the economic status of blacks in U.S. society. It also sparked pressures for blacks to migrate back to the South beginning in the late 1970s.

The Immigration Act of 1965: Intentions Versus Outcomes

The intent of the supporters of immigration changes in the early 1960s was best expressed by President John Kennedy, who initiated the process. He stated that, "the most urgent and fundamental reform I am recommending relates to the national origins system of selecting immigrants."[33] He recommended that it be replaced by a system that would give "the highest priority" to "the skills of the immigrant and their relationship to our need" and it should not "matter where they are born."[34] His proposal did not call for any significant increase in the level of immigration. In contrast to earlier times, he specifically pointed out that "we no longer need settlers for virgin lands."[35] Thus, he reiterated that, "the clash of opinion arises not over the number of immigrants admitted, but over the test for admission."[36]

On July 23, 1963, the administration formally forwarded its immigration reform proposal to Congress. It sought to change the character of existing immigration policy and was *not* intended to increase the level of immigration. Indeed, there were widespread fears in Congress at this time that increasing the number of immigrants in general would lead to adverse employment and wage effects in the labor market.

Following the assassination of President Kennedy, as previously indicated, President Johnson took up the immigration reform banner. It was not until early 1965, however, that Congress responded to the administration's proposals. The original bill had called for a five-year phase-out of the national origins system and the immediate termination of the last traces of discrimination against Asian immigration. In place of the use of national origin as the primary admission criteria, the bill proposed that 50 percent of admissions would be based on the preferences given to immigrants who had skills and work experience that were currently in need by the U.S. economy. The other half would be granted on the basis of various adult family relationships of would-be immigrants to U.S. citizens or permanent resident aliens. As before, the preferences would only apply to Eastern Hemisphere immigrants.

Given the times, political agreement to end the overt racism of the national origins system was relatively easy. Finding common ground for a replacement criterion was much more difficult. From the onset, Congress let it be known to the Johnson administration that any new legislation in this area must contain two new components.

First, there must also be a ceiling on Western Hemisphere immigration. Congress feared that with the extraordinarily high population-growth rates in Latin America, the absence of a limit would lead to an uncontrolled influx of immigrants from this region in the near future. Hence, the inclusion of a ceiling on the Western Hemisphere in the enacted bill "was a necessary *quid pro quo* in exchange for abolishment of the national origins quota system."[37] Thus, an annual ceiling of 120,000 immigrants from the Western Hemisphere was included in the final version of the legislation.

Secondly, congressional leaders felt that the labor certification requirements for non-family related immigrants had to strengthened. Thus, under the Immigration Act of 1965, immigrants from Eastern Hemisphere nations who were admitted on any basis other than family reunification or refugee status must receive certification in advance from the U.S. Department of Labor that their presence would not adversely affect employment opportunities or the prevailing wage and working conditions of citizen workers.

Under other provisions of the Immigration Act of 1965, an annual ceiling of 170,000 visas was imposed on immigration from all the nations of the Eastern Hemisphere. This figure was slightly higher than the hemispheric limit in effect since the 1920s.

To determine which individuals were to be admitted within the framework of the numerical ceiling set for the Eastern Hemisphere, a seven-category preference system was created. The new preference system relied largely on family reunification as its priority concern. "Immediate family" relatives (i.e., persons defined under the Act as being spouses and minor children although it did add parents of U.S. citizens over the age of twenty-one to this category) were not counted as part of the hemispheric or the individual country ceilings. Thus, the term "family reunification" in this case referred to the admission of adult children of U.S. citizens over the age of twenty-one; spouses and unmarried children of permanent resident aliens; and adult brothers and sisters of U.S. citizens. Collectively, they accounted for 74 percent of the annually available visas. Thus, family reunification became the "cornerstone" of U.S. immigration policy and it has remained so ever since.[38] During the legislative process, Congress reduced the occupational preferences share of the annually available visas to no more than 20 percent. The remaining visas, 6 percent, were reserved for a new admission category: refugees.

These changes in the priorities of the admission system were made in response to the lobbying of groups that were strongly opposed to abolition of the national origins system. Recognizing that they could not block the reform drive on this fundamental issue, they sought to make the changes in the admissions criteria more symbolic than real. These groups and their congressional sympathizers believed that by stressing family reunification it would be possible to retain essentially the same racial and ethnic priorities that the national origins system had fostered even if this mechanism itself was abolished. It seemed unlikely, for instance, that many persons from Asia, Africa, or from southern or eastern Europe would be admitted under the new system because the prohibitions imposed during the national origins era had prevented the entry of many of their relatives for the past forty years. Conversely, those favored over the past forty years would most likely have the most living family relatives who could use their citizenship status to admit others like them.

Thus, the principle of family reunification, which political supporters have strongly defended in subsequent years, does not rest on a strong moral foundation. It should not be overlooked that, aside from making nepotism the dominant admission criterion of the legal immigration system, family reunification was based on the nefarious belief that it would perpetuate past discrimination into the future but under a more politically acceptable mantle. As Congressman Emanuel Celler (D-N.Y.)—the co-sponsor of the legislation—stated on the floor of Congress during the final debate on the bill in which he urged passage, "there will not be, comparatively, many Asians or Africans entering the country…since the people of Africa and Asia have very few relatives here, comparatively few could immigrate from those countries because they have no family ties to the U.S."[39] Thus, it was clearly understood by Congress that immigration reform was not intended to increase the size of the nation's black population.

Likewise, there were other things that were promised that would not happen if this bill passed. Senator Edward M. Kennedy (D-Mass.), floor manager of the bill in the Senate, reiterated during the final debate on the pending legislation: "this bill is not concerned with increasing immigration to this country, nor will it lower any of the high standards we apply in the selection of immigrants."[40] Earlier, in a committee session, he stated that "our cities will not be flooded with a million immigrants annually;" that "the ethnic mix of this country will not be upset;" and "it [the pending bill] would not cause American workers to lose their jobs."[41] But, as will be seen, the new law did, in fact, set into motion the process over the ensuing years whereby none of his assumptions proved to be valid.

In the 1970s, two important amendments were added to the Immigration Act of 1965. Following the imposition of the ceiling on Western Hemisphere immigration, a massive backlog of applications for visas quickly developed from persons living in Latin American nations (especially Mexico). Accordingly, in 1976 an amendment was adopted that extended the seven-category preference system and the labor certification requirements to would-be applicants from Western Hemisphere nations as well. The effect of this extension was that, for the first time, it would be difficult for any person from the Western Hemisphere who did not fit into one of the seven preference categories to enter legally. Another amendment in 1976 extended the annual ceiling of 20,000 immigrants from any single nation in the Western Hemisphere that had been applied to nations in the Eastern Hemisphere in 1965.

In 1978 another amendment was added to the Immigration Act of 1965, which finally gave the United States the unified immigration system that reformers had sought for over three decades. The two separate hemispheric ceilings were merged to give the nation a single worldwide quota that was set at 290,000 visas a year.

The Revival of Mass Immigration

Despite assurances that the phenomenon of mass immigration would not be revived from the nation's distant past, the Immigration Act of 1965 had precisely this result. As can be seen from Table 2, the "fourth wave" of mass immigration can be dated to its passage. From 1930 until 1965, the foreign-born population level declined in absolute numbers; as a percentage of the population, the foreign born had been declining since 1910. In 1965 there was

Table 2
Foreign-Born Population of the United States and the Percent of Population Foreign Born 1900-2002

Year	Foreign Born Population (millions)	Percent of Population Foreign Born
1900	10,300	13.6
1910	13,500	14.7
1920	13,920	13.2
1930	14,204	11.6
1940	11,594	8.8
1950	10,347	6.9
1960	9,738	5.4
1965	8,549	4.4
1970	9,619	4.7
1980	14,079	6.2
1990	19,767	7.9
2000	31,100	11.1
2002	32,500	11.5

Sources: U.S. Bureau of the Census (except for 1965); for 1965 the data are from Jeffery Passel, "30 Years of Immigration and U.S. Population Growth," paper presented at the Annual Meetings of the Association for Public Policy Analysis and Management, Washington D.C. (November 1995), un-numbered chart.

no reason to expect that either of these dominant trends would be reversed. But, as Table 2 shows, they were—and significantly so.

The precise factors that led to that accidental revival of mass immigration are too complex to describe here.[42] In a nutshell, however, they are: an explosion in illegal immigration; refugee entries have soared far beyond anticipated levels as has the arrival of tens of thousands of political asylum applicants each year after an asylum policy was added in 1980; the emphasis on family preference admission has led to far greater numbers of "immediate relatives" (whose numbers are not restricted) than anticipated; and the liberalization of various non-immigrant (i.e., temporary foreign worker) visa provisions has led to far more such foreign job seekers than was predicted. As these unexpected results have been revealed, the responses of subsequent Congresses has been either to ignore these outcomes; or to pass half-hearted and ineffective restrictive measures (as in the case of attempts to address illegal immigration); or to take counter-productive steps based on false premises (i.e., the expansion of legal immigration in 1990 based on the assumption that illegal immigration has been significantly reduced by legislation in 1986).

The impact of the "fourth wave," however, is far more than the mere increase in numbers. Unlike the previous three "waves" where the preponderance of the immigrants was from Europe, the "fourth wave" is unique in that most of the immigrants are non-European and non-Africans. In 2000, 51 percent of the foreign born population of the United States were from Latin America; 25.5 percent from Asia. In sharp contrast, only 15.3 percent were from Europe and 2.5 percent were from Africa.[43] Given these shifts in the countries of origin, it is not surprising that the racial composition of the foreign born population in 2000 has been dramatically altered.[44] Blacks were 13.5 percent of the native-born population but only 7.8 percent of the foreign-born population while non-Hispanic whites were 75.9 percent of the native population but 24.8 percent of the foreign population. On the other hand, the major gainers were the Hispanic population (of any race) who were only 8.1 percent of the native born population but 45.2 percent of the foreign-born population; and the Asian population who were only 1.7 percent of the native-born population but 23.6 percent of the foreign-born population.

No racial group, therefore, has been more adversely affected than has the black population by the shift in source countries that has occurred since 1965. Black immigration (mainly from Africa and the Caribbean Islands) represents the smallest component by far of the foreign-born population. Indeed, primarily as a consequence of post-1965 immigration, Hispanics (of any race) became in 2003 the nation's largest and the most rapidly growing minority group. But the issue is more than one of numbers; it also pertains to qualitative labor force characteristics in a post-1965 U.S. labor market convulsive with change.

Mass Immigration and the "New" Economy

While immigration policy in the post-1965 years has affected the size and composition of the supply of labor, the demand for labor has also sustained a metamorphosis these same years from anything ever experienced before. In the three earlier "waves" of mass immigration, the economy needed large numbers of essentially manual workers. It made little difference whether they had skills, were educated, or spoke English. In most cases, the immigrants had few human capital attributes. But in the post-1965 era, the advent of computer technology and the globalization of trade have caused a diminishment in the demand for low-skilled workers while the supply of low-skill jobs (especially in manufacturing) has been reduced. Conversely, the economy has entered a new developmental phase in which the expanding employment opportunities have been predominantly in the information and service producing sectors.[44] By 2001, 81 percent of the non-agricultural labor force of the nation was employed in service sector industries. The manufacturing sector, which was the largest employment sector from the 1920s until the mid-1950s, had fallen to fourth place (out of a total of nine non-agricultural industrial groupings) by 2001 in terms of employment. These industrial shifts have also affected occupational changes (a shift in white collar jobs) and geographic shifts (a decentralization of service jobs as opposed to the tendency to the concentrate jobs when goods producing dominated). Thus, the labor force since 1965 has been in a state of radical transformation. Over these same years the supply of labor has grown dramatically due to the demographic positioning of the "baby boom" generation, the unexpected mass entry of women into the paid-sectors of the economy and, of course, the return of mass immigration to the American experience. Against this backdrop of extensive changes, the new era of equal employment opportunity for blacks was also launched in 1965.

It is unfortunate that the only one of these forces of change that is totally subject to public policy determination—mass immigration—has been allowed to evolve since 1965 without any accountability for its economic consequences. Immigration policy over these years has been the product of an on-going series of dubious political compromises. As a consequence, it now consists of a hodgepodge of ineffective, counter–productive, and special interest provisions. In 1997, the U.S. Commission on Immigration Reform (CIR), chaired by the late Barbara Jordan for most of its life, concluded, "our current immigration system must undergo major reform" and it requires "a significant redefinition of priorities."[45] Among CIR's many recommendations were that the annual level of immigration be reduced by over one-third; that all of the extended family admission categories be eliminated; that no unskilled adults be admitted as legal immigrants; that refugee admissions be capped in number; and that every effort be made to stop the entry of illegal immigrants.

For present purposes, the significance of the nation's prevailing immigration policies has been to produce an influx of disproportionately unskilled and poorly educated into many of the nations largest urban labor markets (and, in selective cases into certain rural labor markets.) In the year 2000, one-third of the adult foreign-born population had less than a high school diploma and another one-quarter had only a high school degree.[46] Moreover, 95 percent of the foreign-born population lived in metropolitan areas (as opposed to 79 percent of the native born) with 50 percent living in central cities in 2000.[47] As for the jobs that immigrants hold, they are disproportionately employed in service occupations (19.2 percent); operators, fabricators, and laborers (18.7 percent); and farms, forestry, and fishing (4.5 percent).[48]

The "Fourth Wave" of Immigration: Its Relevance to Black Americans

In far too many ways, the indicators describing the foreign-born population closely resemble those of black Americans, which suggest the probability of competition in the labor market. For the black population too is disproportionately unskilled, concentrated in the central cities of metropolitan areas, and employed in low-skilled occupations. In 2001, 20.6 percent of adult blacks over the age of twenty-five were without a high school diploma; in addition, another 34.4 percent of blacks had only a high school degree.[49] As for urban concentration, 87.5 percent of the black population lived in metropolitan areas with 52 percent of all blacks living in central cities.[50] With respect to occupational patterns, 21.5 percent of blacks were employed in service occupations; 18.1 percent were operators, fabricators, and laborers (almost one-third of all black males were employed in this occupation); and 1.1 percent in farming, forestry, and fishing.

In terms of geographic concentration in 2000, 26 percent of the foreign-born population resided in the South (the highest such percentage in U.S. history—with most of this increase occurring since 1990) while 55 percent of the black population did so.[51] Unlike the earlier waves of mass immigration, a substantial number of the "fourth wave" is now living and working in the South. Indeed, Florida and Texas rank third (18.4 percent) and fifth (12.2 percent) respectively in terms of the proportion of their population who were foreign born in 2000. But the foreign-born population is also rapidly increasing in North Carolina, South Carolina, Georgia, and Alabama, which is without precedent.[52]

By the same token, the greatest growth in size of the foreign-born population has been outside the South, which is once more affecting the internal migration patterns of the black population. As discussed earlier, the black population did not migrate out of the South until the end of the "third wave" of mass immigration (i.e., the outbreak of World War I). Throughout the rest of the twentieth century (as shown in Table 1), there was a net migration out of the South up until the 1980s (when the "fourth wave" of mass immigration was in high gear). But beginning in the late 1970s, the pattern reversed itself.[53] Between 1990 and 1996, for instance, the net migration of blacks to the South was 368,000.[54]

There are, of course, many factors that influence internal migration of the nation's domestic population. But that does not lessen the fact that international immigration into specific labor markets affects the internal mobility decisions of native-born workers. Indeed, research on contemporary labor mobility has found that native-born workers are less likely to migrate to urban areas where immigrants are concentrated.[55] Furthermore, foreign-born workers are less likely to move out of states where they are concentrated than are native born.[56] Both features cause an accentuation of the impact of immigration in those urban labor markets where immigrants are concentrated. As economist Lawrence Katz has found, "there is now evidence that where immigrants are going, natives are leaving," because the arrival of more unskilled immigrant workers means lower wages and fewer low-end jobs for those who were originally there.[57] In those urban cities in California that have experienced significant increases in immigration, for example, there has been a "flight" of low-income, poorly educated citizen workers out of their former communities to the outer fringes of their metropolitan areas or to other states.[58]

It is likely, therefore, that the fact that more blacks are migrating to the South as the twenty-first century begins than are moving out is due to the extensive immigration into urban labor markets in the North and into the coastal states of the South since 1965. But as immigrants have since the 1990s also been moving into the South, there is now nowhere else for blacks to go. They too will have to confront the reality of the consequences of the nation's unguided and largely unregulated flow of mass immigration. But at least in the South, the black population is significant in size and well established in its presence to meet the challenge.

Lastly, there is the issue of employment discrimination by the new immigrants against black Americans. With the inordinate emphasis given to family reunification in the post-1965 legal immigration system, it is not surprising that most of the new immigrants settle in the same geographic labor markets as have their relatives whose family ties were the basis for their admission. Kinship, therefore, rather than labor market needs, is the primary basis for locational settlement. The effect is that most new immigrants settle in central cities of a selected number of metropolitan areas where earlier immigrants from the same ethnic background have established enclaves.[59] The result is that ethnic networking is often a major feature of the hiring process in these labor markets.[60]

Ethnic network hiring was a distinguishing feature of the urban labor markets of the earlier three waves of mass immigration. Since the passage of the Civil Rights Act of 1964, hiring practices are supposed to be changed so that it is illegal to hire (or to exclude) job applicants on the basis of their national origin. But such practices have again become common in those urban labor markets where immigrants have congregated. The casualties often are the native-born citizens who also reside in these cities (especially black Americans) who are denied the opportunity to compete for such jobs on an equal access basis. As one study in New York City found, "there are tens of thousands of jobs in New York City for which the native born are not candidates."[61] The reason, according to the study, is that "ethnic hiring networks and the proliferation of immigrant-owned small businesses in the city have cut off open-market competition for jobs."[62] New York City, it should be noted, has the largest black population (2.3 million persons in 2000) of any city in the country.

Likewise an investigative report by the *Wall Street Journal* in 1995 found that in Los Angeles "many immigrant bosses are refusing to hire the nation's largest minority" (i.e., American-born blacks) for entry-level jobs in their enterprises.[63] These immigrant entrepreneurs feel that immigrants are "more dependable" because they are "not inclined to complain about low wages and lousy working conditions;" they are "unaware of labor laws;" and that blacks "don't mix well with workers of other backgrounds."[64] It was reported that "it's like an unwritten law:" immigrant employers "won't hire blacks."[65] With immigrant-owned enterprises accounting for about one-quarter of all low-wage jobs in these cities, a significant portion of the entry-level jobs in these cities are essentially off-limits to native-born black job seekers. The report found that the same pattern of exclusionary hiring practices characterized the behavior of other immigrant-owned enterprises in higher paying industries—like electronics.[66]

The research in rural labor markets where immigrant labor is found has also noted widespread use of ethnic networking in the hiring process.[67] As in urban areas, the practice limits job opportunities for native-born workers for these rural jobs.

Given the racial tensions in many communities between citizens (especially black Americans) and post-1965 immigrants, the need for corrective equal employment opportunity enforcement is long overdue.

Concluding Observations

In terms of immigration policy, the United States began the twenty-first century just as it did the twentieth century: in the throes of another period of mass immigration. As a consequence, immigration is once again a significant influence on the nation's labor market in general and the well being of black Americans in particular.

The most obvious impact is the direct effect. No racial grouping receives fewer immigrants than does the black community. Consequently, in relative terms, other groups increase in number disproportionately to blacks—a fact that has significant political implications. Furthermore, the tendency of the black population and the foreign-born population to both concentrate in a select number of metropolitan areas (e.g., New York, Chicago, Detroit, Los Angeles, Philadelphia, Houston, Miami, Washington D.C.) means that for about one-third of the black population there is direct economic competition, for jobs, housing, and social services.

But there are also indirect effects that are the cumulative consequences of four decades of mass immigration. Most of the foreign-born population who have entered since 1965 are also minority group members themselves. Since so many recent immigrants are unskilled, policymakers no longer seem to feel any urgency about the special problems faced by unskilled black workers . The consequences have been unfortunate. Black politicians and community leaders, who in the past were in the vanguard of advocating for restrictive and enforceable immigration policies, are not critics of the *status quo* of the contemporary era. They have felt the need to form alliances with these other groups who favor large-scale and loosely enforced immigration policies. Immigration expert David North has explained the seeming paradox. Focusing on the U.S. Congress—since immigration policy is exclusively a federal responsibility—North has observed

> Black members of Congress, who might be expected to defend the interests of their often low-income constituents against competition with newly-arrived illegal immigrant worker, do not do so. The members of the Black Caucus, identifying with the members of the Hispanics Caucus, routinely support the Hispanics position on immigration issues. The politics of the chamber, in short, are more important to these Black Congressmen than the politics of the constituency.[68]

Thus, the politics associated with the "rainbow coalition" have led most black politicians to remain silent on the chronic need for comprehensive immigration reform in hope of gaining support for pet programs and of receiving influential appointments. But immigration policy has long-term implications that have been shown to be adverse to the economic interests of black Americans. Unless policy changes are forthcoming—such as those suggested by the Jordan Commission—the pace of progress for black citizens and workers will be hampered. For as the Emperor Napoleon wisely said, "policy is destiny."

Notes

1. For an overview of the issue of mass immigration—its characteristics, causes, and consequences—see Vernon M. Briggs, Jr., *Mass Immigration and the National Interest: Policy Direction for a New Century*, third edition (Armonk, N.Y.: M.E. Shape, Inc., 2003).
2. See *Ekiu v. United States*, 142 U.S. 651 (1892); *Henderson v. Mayor of the City of N.Y.*, 92 U.S. 259 (1876); *Lung v. Freeman*, 92 U.S. 276 (1876).
3. Stanley M. Elkins, *Slavery*, (New York: Grosset and Dunlop, 1959), p. 38.
4. Ibid., p. 49.
5. U.S. Constitution Article I, Section 9, Subsection 1.
6. W.E.B. DuBois, *The Suppression of the African Slave Trade to the United States* (New York: Schocken Books, 1969), pp. 152-153.

7. Stanley Lebergott, *Manpower in Economic Growth* (New York: McGraw Hill, 1964), p. 20.
8. Ibid,, p. 102.
9. Barbara Tucker, *Samuel Slater and the Origins of the American Textile Industry* (Ithaca: Cornell University Press, 1984).
10. Lebergott, op. cit., p. 102.
11. Ibid.
12. Vernon L. Parrington, *The Beginning of Critical Realism in America* (New York: Harcourt, Brace, (1930), p. 7.
13. See Briggs, op. cit., chapters 6 and 7; and Lebergott, op. cit., pp. 24-29.
14. Lebergott, op. cit., p. 40.
15. Ibid. p. 28.
16. Ray Marshall, *The Negro Worker* (New York: Randon House, 1967), p. 11.
17. Booker T. Washington, "The Atlanta Exposition Address," in *Three Negro Classics* (New York: Avon Books, 1965), p. 147.
18. Ibid., p. 148.
19. For a summary of these findings, see U.S. Immigration Commission, *Abstracts of the Reports of the U.S. Immigration Commission* (Washington D.C.: U.S. Government Printing Office, 1911), Volume 1; see also discussion of the Report in Briggs, op. cit., pp. 81-82.
20. Desmond King, *Making Americans: Immigration, Race, and the Origins of the Diverse Democracy* (Cambridge, Harvard University Press, 2000), pp. 39-49, 152, and 163-164.
21. See quotations contained in Daryl Scot, "Immigration Indigestion: A. Phillip Randolph, Radical and Restrictionist," *Backgrounder* (Washington D.C.: Center for Immigration Studies, 1999), p. 3.
22. Arthur S. Link, *American Epoch* (New York: Alfred A. Knoff, 1956), p. 297.
23. Raymond Frost, "Immigration vs. Black American Migration," *Challenge: A Magazine of Economic Affairs* (November-December, 1991), p. 68.
24. Link, op. cit., p. 297.
25. Frost, op. cit., p. 28.
26. Link, op. cit., p. 244.
27. Hugh D. Graham and Ted R. Gurr, *Violence in America* (New York: Bantam Books, 1969), pp. 401-406.
28. Link, op. cit., p. 297.
29. "Statement by Secretary of State Dean Rusk before the Subcommittee on Immigration of the U.S. Senate Committee on the Judiciary," as reprinted in the *Department of State Bulletin*, "Department Urges Congress to Revise Immigration Laws" (August 24, 1965), p. 276.
30. U.S. Congress, House of Representatives, Committee on the Judiciary, 104th Congress, 1st Session, *Immigration and Nationality Act*, tenth edition (Washington, D.C.: U.S. Government Printing Office, 1989), p. 589.
31. National Advisory Commission on Civil Disorders, *Report of the National Advisory Commission on Civil Disorders* (New York: Bantam Books, 1968).
32. Ibid., p. 203.
33. John F. Kennedy, *A Nation of Immigrants*, Revised Edition with an Introduction by Robert F. Kennedy (New York: Harper and Row, 1964), p. 102.
34. Ibid., p. 103.
35. Ibid., p. 80.
36. Ibid.

37. U.S. Congress, Senate Committee on the Judiciary, 96th Congress, 1st Session, *U.S. Immigration Law and Policy: 1952-79* (Washington, D.C.: U.S. Government Printing Office, 1979), pp. 234-42.
38. U.S. Congress, U.S. House of Representatives Select Committee on Population, 95th Congress, 2nd Session, *Legal and Illegal Immigration to the United States* (Washington D.C.: Government Printing Office, 1978), p. 10.
39. U.S. Congress, House of Representatives, *Congressional Record*, 89th Congress, 1st Session (August 25, 1965) (Washington D.C.: U.S. Government Printing Office, 1965), pp. 21, 758.
40. U.S. Congress, Senate, *Congressional Record*, 89th Congress, 1st Session (September 17, 1965) (Washington D.C.: U.S. Government Printing Office, 1965), pp. 24, 225.
41. "Statement of Senator Edward Kennedy," *Hearings on S. 500*, 89th Congress, 1st Session, (August 25, 1965) (Washington D.C.: U.S. Government Printing Office, 1965), pp. 1-3.
42. For detailed discussion of the factors that triggered the revival of mass immigration, see Briggs, op. cit., chapter 10.
43. U.S. Bureau of the Census, *Profile of the Foreign-Born Population in the United States: 2000* (Washington D.C.: U.S. Bureau of the Census, 2001), pp. 23-206; 10. (The remainder of the foreign born were from North America, Australia Oceania.)
44. For elaboration, see Briggs, op. cit., chapter 11.
45. U.S. Commission on Immigration Reform, *Legal Immigration: Setting Priorities* (Washington D.C.: U.S. Commission on Immigration Reform, 1994), p. i of letter of transmittal.
46. U.S. Bureau of the Census, op. cit., p. 36.
47. Ibid., p. 17.
48. Ibid., p. 40.
49. U.S. Bureau of the Census, *The Black Population in the United States: March 2002* (Washington D.C.: U.S. Government Printing Office, 2003), p. 4.
50. U.S. Department of Labor, *Employment and Earnings* (Washington D.C.: U.S. Government Printing Office, 2002), p. 172.
51. Ibid., p. 175.
52. U.S. Bureau of the Census, *Migration of Nations and the Foreign Born: 1995-2000* (Washington D.C.: U.S. Government Printing Office, 2003), p. 5.
53. Kenneth R. Weiss, "Migration of Blacks from the South Turns Around," *New York Times* (June 11, 1989), p. 36; "Blacks in Decline in Northern Cities," *New York Times* (July 6, 1991), p. A-7.
54. William H. Frey, "Black Migration to the South Reaches Record Highs in 1990s," *Population Today* (February, 1998), p. 3.
55. Robert Walker, Mark Ellis, and Richard Barff, "Linked Migration Systems: Immigration and Internal Labor Flows in the United States," *Economic Geography* (July, 1992), pp. 234-248.
56. Mary Kritz and June Marie Nogle, "Nativity Concentration and Internal Migration Among the Foreign Born," *Demography* (August, 1994) p. 1-16.
57. Quoted in Peter Passell, "A Job-Wage Conundrum," *New York Times* (September 6, 1994), p. D-1; see also Richard Freeman and Lawrence F. Katz, "Industrial Wage and Employment Determination in an Open Economy," *Immigration, Trade and the Labor Market*, edited by John M. Abowd and Richard B. Freeman (Chicago: The University of Chicago Press, 1991), p. 241-246.

58. William H. Frey, "Immigration and Internal Migration Flight: A California Case Study," *Population and Environment* (March 1995), pp. 353-375; see also, William A. Frey, "Black Migration to the South ..." op. cit., pp. 1-3.
59. Alejandro Portes and Ruben G. Rumbaut, *Immigrant America: A Portrait* (Berkeley, University of California Press, 1990), chapter 2.
60. Philip Martin, " Network Recruitment and Labor Displacement," *U.S. Immigration Policy in the 1980s*, edited by David E. Simcox (Boulder: Westview Press, 1988), pp. 67-91. See also Donatella Lorch, "Ethnic Niches Creating Jobs that Fuel Immigrant Growth," *New York Times* (January 12, 1992), pp. A-1, A-20.
61. Elizabeth Bogen, *Immigration in New York* (New York: Praeger Publishers, 1987), p. 91.
62. Ibid.
63. Jonathan Kaufman, "Help Unwanted: Immigrant Businesses Often Refuse to Hire Blacks in Inner City," *Wall Street Journal* (June 6, 1995), p. 1.
64. Ibid.
65. Ibid.
66. Ibid.
67. Martin, op. cit.; see also Richard Mines and Philip Martin, "Immigrant Workers and the California Citrus Industry," *Industrial Relations* (Spring, 1984), pp. 139-149.
68. David North, "Why Democratic Governments Cannot Cope with Illegal Immigrants," paper presented at the International Conference on Immigration, Rome, Italy, March 13, 1991, sponsored by the Organization for Economic Co-Operation and Development, Paris, 1991, p. 5 of xerox copy of the paper.

2

Immigration and the Black-White
Color Line in the United States[*]

*Jennifer Lee, Frank D. Bean, Jeanne Batalova,
and Sabeen Sandhu*

Owing to the practice of slavery, its legacy of discrimination, and the history of black social and economic disadvantage, the central organizing principle of racial/ethnic relations in the United States has revolved around the axis of the black-white color line (Bobo 1997; Clark 1965; Drake and Cayton [1945] 1993; Farley and Allen 1987; Myrdal 1944). The unique deprivations blacks have suffered and the history of black-white relations in this country provide stark reminders of the strength of the divide—a delineation that assigns and consigns blacks and whites to different positions in the social order and attaches a different set of rights and privileges to each group (Blumer 1965). In numerous ways, many Americans have viewed the black-white gulf in categorical and absolute terms, as reflected in the legal adoption of the "one-drop" rule in U.S. southern states (Davis 1991; Wright 1994) and in the color line's long discriminatory life in the United States. The enduring nature of the fault line, of course, was famously forecast in 1903 by the prominent African American social theorist W.E.B. Du Bois when he prophesied that the

* The authors would like to thank the Russell Sage Foundation and the Center for Immigration, Population and Public Policy at the University of California, Irvine for generous research support on which this chapter is based. This chapter was partially completed while Frank D. Bean was a Visiting Scholar at the Russell Sage Foundation and Jennifer Lee was a Fellow at the Center for Advanced Study in the Behavioral Sciences with generous financial support provided by the William and Flora Hewlett Foundation, Grant #2000-5633. A previous version of this chapter was presented as a paper at the Center for Comparative Studies in Race and Ethnicity at Stanford University in April 2002.

"problem of the twentieth-century is the problem of the color line" ([1903] 1997: 45).

Now, many observers in the United States think problems of race are beginning to recede into the background. Nearly one hundred years after the end of the Civil War, the Civil Rights laws of the 1960s eradicated the last vestiges of legal discrimination on the basis of race. In part as a result, by the end of the 1970s, considerable, if not complete, progress had been achieved in closing black-white economic gaps (Jaynes and Williams 1989; Farley 1996). But disparities remained, and the gains of the 1970s subsequently stalled, or in some instances even reversed themselves (Danziger and Gottschalk 1995; Smelser, Wilson, and Mitchell 2001; Wilson 1987). Some public intellectuals and commentators see grounds for optimism in these patterns and emphasize the progress that has occurred (e.g., Thernstrom and Thernstrom 1997), embracing a positive perspective on race relations in the country and suggesting the beginnings of the disappearance of the black-white color line. Others see grounds for pessimism and emphasize the continuing nature and degree of the gulf between blacks and whites (Bobo 1997, 1999; Hacker 1992; Massey and Denton 1993; Oliver and Shapiro 1995; Schuman, Steeh, and Bobo 1985).

Other trends have increasingly transformed questions about race relations in the United States into questions about racial/ethnic relations. The biggest, of course, is immigration, which over the past four decades has added complex new dimensions to the matter. Because of the vast number of newcomers, America is no longer merely a black and white society, and as a result, questions are now being raised about the current placement and meaning of America's racial/ethnic color lines (Gans 1999; Sanjek 1994; Skrentny 2001; Waters 1999). In fact, the use of the term "color" itself now introduces ambiguities into the matter of racial/ethnic terminology. Sometimes the word has been used to designate persons who are nonwhite, whereas at others, it has been used more traditionally to refer only to blacks. Such multiplicities of usage, while assuredly not new, reflect transformations in the country that are currently broader and deeper than at any time since the first part of the twentieth century. Even in 1903, during a time of substantial immigration, it seems unlikely that Du Bois could have anticipated that America's new immigrants in the late twentieth century would so drastically modify the racial and ethnic makeup of the United States, perhaps either changing or obscuring the nature of the color line in the process.

Today's immigrants are notable because they are mainly non-European. By the 1980s, only 12 percent of legal immigrants originated in Europe or Canada, whereas nearly 85 percent reported origins in Asia, Latin America, or the Caribbean (U.S. Immigration and Naturalization Service 2002; Waldinger and Lee 2001). America's newcomers have made an indelible mark on the nation's racial/ethnic scene, and in the year 2002, immigrants and their children accounted for almost 66 million people, or about 23 percent of the U.S. population (Fix, Passel, and Sucher 2003; Smith and Edmonston 1997; U.S. Bureau of Census 2002). And according to National Research Council projections, by the year 2050, America's Latino and Asian populations are expected to triple and constitute about 25 and 8 percent of the U.S. population, respectively (Smith and Edmonston 1997).

Along with the increased racial/ethnic diversity brought about by changes in immigration over the past four decades are the dramatic rises in racial/ethnic intermarriage. Within the thirty-year period between 1960 and 1990, a time coinciding with the rise of the new immigration, the intermarriage rate between whites and Asians and whites and Latinos increased tenfold, now exceeding 50 percent among the third-generation Asians and Latinos (Jacoby 2001; Waters 1999). The increase in interracial marriage has also led to a growing multiracial population. Currently, one in forty persons identifies himself or herself as multiracial, and by the year 2050, this ratio could rise to one in five (Farley 2001; Smith and Edmonston 1997).

What does current thinking and evidence about the new immigration, race/ethnicity, intermarriage, and multiracial reporting imply about America's racial/ethnic divides? At first glance, these changes seem to indicate that race has become a less prominent social marker in the United States, pointing to the erosion of racial/ethnic boundaries. However, this may not be the case; or it may be the case for only some groups and not others. While increases in intermarriage, properly interpreted, may indicate the loosening of racial/ethnic boundaries, a crucial question is whether such increases are evenly distributed across all groups. If the evidence points to a substantial loosening of boundaries for only some groups, this would suggest that while boundary crossing may be more common, it is not unconditional, suggesting the birth of a new racial/ethnic divide.

Although America's landscape has changed to one that is far more multiracial and multiethnic, theory and research in the fields of race and ethnicity have often not kept pace with the nation's vastly changing demographic scene, often pursuing the study of immigration and race/ethnicity as separate topics (Bean and Bell-Rose 1999). Thus, much theorizing about race and ethnicity continues to be couched in terms of the traditional black-white framework. For example, scholars often treat today's new immigrant groups as if they were racialized minorities who are subject to mobility barriers and levels of discrimination sufficiently strong to create the beginnings of a new rainbow underclass by the second generation (Portes and Rumbaut 2001). However, unlike African Americans who were forcefully brought to this country as slaves, today's Latino and Asian newcomers are voluntary migrants, and consequently, their experiences may be qualitatively distinct from those of African Americans. Hence, it may be inaccurate to treat them as racialized minorities who incur barriers to mobility and suffer discrimination, similar to that of African Americans. Instead, the newest immigrants may be more akin to the earlier

European immigrants who initially experienced discrimination but eventually became indistinguishable from and part of the larger white racial category. Which of these possibilities is more nearly correct bears direct relevance to the way we think and interpret evidence about changes in America's color lines.

One important contingency in resolving this question concerns whether the members of immigrant groups see themselves and are treated by others primarily as racialized minorities. For instance, if one adopts the perspective that Latinos and Asians are racialized minorities (that is, as persons whose race or ethnicity constitutes a basis for substantial discrimination), and thus persons falling closer to blacks than whites along some scale of social disadvantage, then the high levels of intermarriage and multiracial reporting occurring among these groups suggest that boundaries are not only fading for these groups, but also for all nonwhites, including blacks. Such a conclusion would support the sanguine view that the old black-white divide is breaking down and that racial prejudice and boundaries are fading altogether. However, this interpretation may attribute signs of incorporation to all nonwhites that are in fact more the province of Latinos and Asians than blacks, thus risking overly optimistic conclusions about the breadth of boundary dissolution.

If, on the other hand, Latinos and Asians more represent new immigrant groups, whose members' disadvantage derives from their not yet having had time to join the economic and social mainstream, but many of whom soon will, then their high levels of intermarriage and multiracial reporting signal that their experience may be different from that of blacks altogether. Such a conclusion would support a more pessimistic view that the experiences and situations of Latinos and Asians do not necessarily imply that similar improvements can be expected among blacks. Thus, what may at first glance appear to suggest a dissolution of color lines for all racial/ethnic groups may simply be a loosening of boundaries for new immigrant groups who are undergoing the transitional phases of immigrant incorporation. This distinction is critical, and helps us to differentiate whether color lines are shifting for all racial/ethnic groups, or whether they are changing mainly to accommodate new nonblack immigrant groups.

In this chapter, we thus inquire into the theoretical and empirical bases for drawing conclusions about the placement and strength of color lines in the United States given the new immigration, including an assessment of what this suggests about the strength and salience of America's traditional black-white color line. We begin by focusing on extant theories concerning immigration and immigrant incorporation, the declining significance of race, and group position in the United States. Then, we present recent data on intermarriage and multiracial identification and examine differences among whites, blacks, Latinos, and Asians. We note that the higher rates of intermarriage and multiracial identification for Latinos and Asians compared to blacks suggest that the boundaries may be less salient for these groups. These patterns reveal that the color line may not be as strong (or may be shifting more rapidly) for these newer immigrant groups compared to blacks. Based on these patterns, we find evidence of a new color line that is no longer divided by black and white (and by implication white and nonwhite) but rather by black and nonblack. Finally, we return to debates about the declining significance of race and group position theory. Based on our theoretical syntheses and examinations of recent data, we suggest that little ground may exist to claim that major changes have occurred in the country that signify a notably reduced significance of race or an unconditional fading of racial/ethnic boundaries, especially for blacks.

Theory and Evidence

This study falls at the intersection of the literature on race/ethnicity and immigrant incorporation. First, we review previous research and theory on immigration and immigrant incorporation and then examine the tenets of theories of the declining significance of race and group position. While scholars have developed and debated both the race/ethnicity and immigrant incorporation literatures, these bodies of literature have rarely been considered together, even though each has implications for patterns of intermarriage, multiracial identification, and changing color lines. In fact, each of these theoretical frameworks provides rationales for expecting higher levels of intermarriage and multiracial reporting among Asians and Latinos than among blacks.

Immigration and the Construction of Race/Ethnicity

In the conclusion to her book *Black Identities*, Waters (1999: 339) raises the following questions about immigration and America's color lines: "How will this wave of immigration affect American race relations? Where will the color line be drawn in the twenty-first century?" A number of social scientists have suggested that today's racial/ethnic hierarchy could be replaced by a dual hierarchy consisting of "blacks and nonblacks" or "whites and non-whites" (Bean and Stevens 2003; Gans 1999; Gitlin 1995; Lee and Bean 2003, 2004; Sanjek 1994; Waters 1999). Higher rates of intermarriage and multiracial identification for Latinos and Asians indicate that the racial/ethnic hierarchy may be changing once again with race declining in significance for these groups, especially compared to blacks.

Social scientists generally agree that race is a social rather than biological category, and have documented the processes by which racial categories have undergone reconceptualization throughout our nation's history. For instance, previously "nonwhite" ethnic groups such as Irish, Italians, and Jews became "white," often by deliberately distinguishing themselves from blacks (Alba

1985, 1990; Brodkin 1998; Foner 2000; Gerstle 1999; Igantiev 1995; Roediger 1991). Even Asian ethnic groups such as the Chinese in Mississippi have changed their lowly racial status from almost black to almost white by achieving economic mobility, emulating the cultural practices of whites, intentionally distancing themselves from blacks, and rejecting fellow ethnics who married blacks, as well as their Chinese-black multiracial children (Loewen 1971). The change in racial classification among ethnic groups from nonwhite to white or almost white illustrates that race is a cultural rather than biological category that has expanded over time to incorporate new immigrant groups (Alba 1985, 1990; Gerstle 1999; Omi and Winant 1994; Tuan 1998; Waters 1990, 1999). As Gerstle (1999: 289) explains, whiteness as a category "has survived by stretching its boundaries to include Americans—the Irish, eastern and southern Europeans—who had been deemed nonwhite. Contemporary evidence suggests that the boundaries are again being stretched as Latinos and Asians pursue whiteness much as the Irish, Italians, and Poles did before them."

However, many social scientists caution that the very fact that Irish, Italians, and Jews were not subject to the same type of systematic legal discrimination as African Americans illustrates that they were on a different plane from blacks to begin with, a standing that facilitated their eventual racial treatment as whites (Alba 1985; Foner 2000; Lieberson 1980). Moreover, the disappearance of national origin differences among European ethnics and the discontinuation of tendencies to view such differences not only in racial terms, but in fact in rigid black-white terms, contributed to the development of the idea that, for many European immigrants, race was an achieved rather than an ascribed status (Alba 1990; Gans 1979; Perlmann and Waldinger 1997; Waters 1990). But this in all likelihood was because such persons were viewed as nonwhite rather than black. In that time period's rigidly compartmentalized black-white world governed by the "one-drop" rule (which emphasized pure whiteness versus everything else), not being white did not necessarily involve actually being black, but it was *like* being black. Thus, it is not surprising that these national origin groups were treated as black. Perhaps because in fact they were *not* black, their status was eventually allowed to change, thus hastening the evolution and acceptance of the idea that at least some racial categories—maybe all except black—could in fact be changed.

Furthermore, because the construction of racial identities is a dialectical process—one that involves both internal and external opinions and processes— the way in which the native-born population categorizes immigrant ethnic groups is a crucial component of determining the group's racial and ethnic boundaries (Loewen 1971; Nagel 1994; Portes and MacLeod 1996; Portes and Rumbaut 2001). Unlike the traditional "one-drop" rule that has historically imposed a racial identity on blacks (Davis 1991; Nobles 2000; Wright 1994), the U.S. native-born population seems less concerned with constraining the identification of Latinos and Asians. In addition, the very size and socioeconomic diversity of the Latino and Asian immigrant streams make it more difficult for the native-born to categorize them so easily. Thus, the sheer racial, ethnic, and socioeconomic diversity among contemporary Latino and Asian immigrants may render racial and ethnic boundaries less constrained and more negotiable than for blacks. Moreover, like earlier European immigrants, today's immigrants have not undergone the social history of slavery of African Americans, out of which the pernicious black-white color line was born and cemented. Hence, the bipolar racial divide may be less relevant to the historical and contemporary experiences of today's Latino and Asian immigrants (Lopez and Espiritu 1990; Rodriguez 2000). By contrast, the unique history and experience of black Americans in this country, especially with regard to slavery and *de jure* segregation, make the black-white racial divide qualitatively different from the Latino-white or Asian-white racial divides (Bailey 2001). All of these reasons provide bases for expecting higher rates of intermarriage and multiracial reporting among Latinos and Asians than among blacks.

Immigrant Incorporation

Given that immigrants and their children account for 23 percent of the U.S. population, it is also important to consider how their process of incorporation may affect changes in the nation's color lines. Different racial/ethnic minority groups in the United States have had different historical experiences before they came to the United States and a variety of incorporation experiences after they have arrived (Bean et al. 1997; Bean and Stevens 2003; Portes and Rumbaut 1990; Portes and Zhou 1993). These experiences have led to the formulation of three main perspectives about the processes and outcomes of incorporation: straight-line assimilation, segmented assimilation, and ethnic pluralism. The first two have been very influential in the debates about immigrant incorporation, but ethnic pluralism less so. A key difference among these views concerns their implicit or explicit treatment of the relationship between structural and cultural incorporation—a matter that has implications for the persistence and reformation of racial/ethnic identities and America's color lines.

The first is the classic "straight-line" model of assimilation (Gordon 1964), with its many variants (Alba 1990; Crispino 1980; Gans 1992; Waters 1990). The straight-line model predicts that newcomers will both affect and be affected by the fabric of American life so that, in the long run, the immigrant minorities and the majority become ever more indistinguishable from one another, at least after several generations. Born of the predominantly European-origin migration taking place at the beginning of the twentieth century, this model emerged out of the experience and strategy of incorporation adopted by European immigrants for establishing a foothold and gaining economic mobility in the United States. This view was canonized by Gordon (1964), who postulated that acculturation not only preceded but was also necessary for structural incorporation.

The failure of the model had partly to do with its imperfections in depicting the experiences of European migrants, but also partly with its inability to explain the experience of African Americans (Glazer and Moynihan 1963). While African American customs, practices, ideals, and values by the early 1960s had come to mirror those of the larger population to a considerable degree, what was missing was satisfactory African American structural incorporation. The prevailing view was that the removal of legal barriers would in fairly short order lead to substantial structural incorporation among African Americans. The elimination of such barriers to blacks, however, resulted in only slight improvements in black economic situations, a consequence that could readily be discerned by the mid-1970s (Bean and Bell-Rose 1999; Glazer 1997; Wilson 1987).

At about the same time, it was also becoming increasingly clear that many white European groups continued to manifest aspects of ethnic distinctiveness despite their substantial structural incorporation. Researchers have demonstrated, however, that much of the ethnic revival of this period was symbolic, giving rise to the concept of "symbolic ethnicity" for white ethnics (Alba 1990; Gans 1979; Waters 1990). Both of these trends, however, contributed to the development of an ethnic pluralist model of incorporation that was predicated on the idea that cultural incorporation was neither inevitable nor necessary for structural incorporation (Greeley 1974). In the end, both the straight-line and pluralist models promoted the preservation and distinctiveness of sharp racial/ethnic boundaries.

The difficulty with both the straight-line and pluralist models is that the historical experiences that have helped give rise to them (i.e., those of European immigrants and African Americans) seem inadequate to describe the situations and experiences of the new Asian and Latino immigrants in the later part of the twentieth century. Today's newest immigrants to America's shores are neither black nor white but appear to occupy a position in between, at least in terms of skin color. Moreover, Latinos—especially Mexicans, who are by far the largest immigrant group—have come mostly from "hybrid" or "mestizo" backgrounds where racial boundaries are not as sharply drawn (Glazer 2003; Rodríguez 2000; Rodriguez 2003). Moreover, if cultural accommodation facilitated structural incorporation in the past, this has not seemed apparent or necessary for many of today's newcomers, illustrating the frequent decoupling of the traditional linkages thought to exist between acculturation and economic mobility (Neckerman, Carter, and Lee 1999; Portes and Zhou 1993). Rather, many of today's new Asian and Latino immigrants seem to have adopted a path of "selective acculturation" (Portes and Rumbaut 2001; Portes and Zhou 1993; Zhou and Bankston 1998) or "accommodation without as-similation" (Gibson 1988). In the path of selective assimilation, ethnicity acts as a resource to upward mobility and appears less constraining than previ-ously presumed, becoming more useful, flexible, and non-constraining than emphasized by the straight-line model. As a result, we would expect that inter-racial marriage and multiracial identification to be more likely among Asian and Latino immigrants than among blacks because racial/ethnic boundaries are not as constrained for the newer immigrant groups compared to native-born blacks.

The Declining Significance of Race

Two separate strands of thinking about race provide further bases for expec-tations about changing color lines. The first is represented in Wilson's seminal work *The Declining Significance of Race* (1980), the basic thesis of which is that the direct effects of race on economic opportunities and outcomes have diminished significantly since the 1960s. According to Wilson's argument, race per se and the racial characteristics of one's parents matter less in deter-mining one's life chances than class. Thus, racial differences in earnings may persist, but they are now more likely to stem from racial differences in educa-tion rather than from direct racial discrimination (Sakamoto, Wu, and Tzeng 2000). Hence, according to Wilson (1980) and Sakamoto et al. (2000), the color line between majority whites and nonwhite minorities in the United States has become much less sharply drawn.

This reasoning and evidence can be applied to the likelihood of interracial marriage between whites and nonwhites and multiracial identification. At least in those cases involving a white partner or one of the identities being white among multiracial individuals (which according to the results of the 2000 Census made up 80.1 percent of the multiracial identities), Wilson's thesis implies that the likelihood of white-nonwhite interracial marriage and the likelihood of multiracial identification will be similar among all racial/ethnic groups. The greatest variance would be across class lines. Hence, according to the major idea in the declining significance of race thesis, the factors that produce and reflect racial mixing, intermarriage, and multiracial reporting should be equally evident among all racial/ethnic groups, with perhaps lower levels of interracial marriage and multiracial reporting among blacks for whom Sakamoto et al. (2000) find somewhat higher unexplained earnings disadvantages.

Wilson's ideas, while highly influential, have not gone without criticism. One major line of critique is that societal progress in reducing the perniciously negative direct effects of discrimination has been substantially less successful in reducing the indirect effects of race. This is especially the case in regard to effects connected to racial residential segregation between whites and blacks, and its resultant consequences in limiting opportunities and labor market outcomes for African Americans (Farley and Frey 1994; Massey and Denton 1993; Neckerman and Kirschenman 1991; Newman 1999; Pattillo-McCoy 1999). In a similar vein, although not one that emphasizes the spatial aspects of black disadvantage, Patterson (1998a; 1998b) argues that black economic progress has been concentrated among those with high education. Blacks with lower levels of education continue to experience severe disadvantages.

While research points to the continued disadvantage experienced by many blacks (Smelser, Wilson, and Mitchell 2001), America's newest nonwhite immigrant groups evince quite different patterns. Recent scholarship on immigrant incorporation reveals that such handicaps among less well-educated Latinos and Asians do not appear to persist much beyond the first generation (Bean and Stevens 2003; Bean et al. 2000; Gibson 1988; Kao and Tienda 1995; Portes and Rumbaut 2001; Zhou and Bankston 1998). Hence, we may find evidence of the emergence of a new color line at the beginning of the twenty-first century, namely a black-nonblack line that will persist with greater strength than a white-nonwhite line or the black-white color line. Furthermore, we would expect that the black-nonblack line is much stronger in the case of blacks with lower levels of education than it is in the case of blacks of higher education. Therefore, we would expect less intermarriage and multiracial reporting among blacks than among the other major racial/ethnic groups, with most of the deficit concentrated among blacks at lower levels of education and income.

Group Position Theory

The ideas advanced by group position theory are also relevant for understanding differential rates of intermarriage and multiracial identification and their implications for America's changing color lines. Introduced by Blumer (1958) and extended and elaborated by Bobo and his colleagues (Bobo 1997, 1999, 2001; Bobo and Hutchings 1996; Bobo, Kluegel, and Smith 1997), group position theory holds that the major impetus for racial prejudice is not individuals' likes or dislikes, but instead, the manifest attempts by the dominant group (exercised both directly and indirectly), to protect the dominant group's position vis-à-vis others in a racialized hierarchy, especially when this position is perceived as threatened. As Bobo (2001: 206) succinctly articulates,

> To be sure, group position theory is directly concerned with hierarchical social arrangements: systematic and long-standing advantage and disadvantage, privilege and disprivilege allocated along racial lines. Yet, group position theory is also expressly historized…. Once a set of arrangements and practices is well institutionalized and rationalized, the dominant groups' privilege is readily maintained by defending "the system" and reacting against threats to it posed by members of subordinate groups.

According to group position theory, racial attitudes are not simply expressions of individual prejudice, but rather, are reflections about preferences regarding the status arrangements of racial groups in relation to one another. In essence, acts of racial prejudice stem from group concerns about entitlements, privileges, and threats (Bobo and Johnson 2000).

Associated with group position theory is the emergence of a new form of racism—best described as "laissez-faire racism"—which involves a tendency to see the situations of racial groups as deriving from their own efforts (or lack thereof) rather than from historical factors or systemic constraints. If outcomes are only the product of individual efforts (thus the use of the term "laissez-faire"), then individuals are responsible for their own lack of success. This perspective views blacks themselves, not prejudice on the part of whites, as responsible for blacks' position in the socioeconomic hierarchy, thus denying any white responsibility for the social condition of African Americans (Bobo, Kluegel, and Smith 1997). According to group position theory, laissez-faire racism functions effectively to defend white privilege, group entitlement, and group position vis-à-vis blacks, consequently serving to widen the gap between whites and blacks. Defending the sense of group position in a racialized order is central to understanding the persistence of the black-white color line, which has been and continues to be historically, culturally, and structurally entrenched (Bobo 1997, 1999).

While debates about the declining significance of race and group position depict the nature and nuances of the black-white model of race relations and the black-white color line, for the most part, this debate has rarely extended to include the experiences of other groups such as Latinos and Asians (see Bobo et al. 2000; Lee 2002a, 2002b for exceptions). Also curiously missing in the debates about race and group position is the attention to recent patterns of immigration, intermarriage, and multiracial identification that may have a profound affect on today's racial hierarchy. While group position theory would suggest that patterns of black-white intermarriage and multiracial reporting would be low because whites seek to secure their sense of privilege and position vis-à-vis blacks, the implications of group position theory for Latinos and Asians are ambiguous. They are ambiguous precisely because it is unclear whether these groups are racialized minorities or new immigrants who have not fully completed processes of incorporation. If Latinos and Asians are treated as racial minorities as some research posits (e.g., Bobo et al. 2000), then we would expect similarly low rates of intermarriage and multiracial reporting among Latinos, Asians, and blacks. By contrast, if Latinos and Asians are treated as new, albeit ethnically distinct, immigrant groups, we would expect to find higher rates of interracial marriage and multiracial reporting for these groups compared to blacks.

Intermarriage in the United States

At the beginning of the twentieth century, intermarriage between white ethnics was rare and nearly caste-like, especially between "old" white ethnics and newer arrivals from Eastern and Southern Europe (Pagnini and Morgan 1990). Today, white ethnics intermarry at such high rates that only one-fifth of whites has a spouse with an identical ethnic background, reflecting the virtual disappearance of boundaries among white ethnic groups (Alba 1990; Lieberson and Waters 1988, 1993; Waters 1990). By contrast, marriage across racial/ ethnic groups, while on the rise, is still relatively uncommon between some groups, and all groups continue to intermarry at rates lower than would be predicted at random (Moran 2001). For example, only 4.7 percent of white and 8.4 percent of black marriages were exogamous in 1990, while 31.5 percent of Asian and 32.5 percent of Latino marriages were. While these percentages increased in 2000, they remained relatively low. Only 7.0 percent of white and 12.6 percent of black marriages were exogamous compared to 30.9 percent of Asian and 29.3 percent of Latino marriages (see Table 1).

In one sense, that intermarriage is not as common as white interethnic marriage should come as little surprise given that it was illegal in sixteen states as recently as 1967 until the Supreme Court ruling *Loving v. Commonwealth of Virginia* overturned the last remaining anti-miscegenation laws. The ruling had an enormous impact on the rise in interracial marriage, which increased tenfold within a thirty-year period from 150,000 in 1960 to 1.6 million in 1990 (Jacoby 2001; Waters 2000b), far beyond what would be predicted by population growth alone. Trends in exogamy are significant because social scientists conceive of racial/ethnic intermarriage as a measure of decreasing social distance, declining prejudice, and changing group boundaries (Davis 1941; Fu 2001; Gilbertson, Fitzpatrick, and Yang 1996; Gordon 1964; Kalmijn 1993; Lee and Fernandez 1998; Lieberson and Waters 1988; Merton 1941; Rosenfeld 2002; Tucker and Mitchell-Kernan 1990). Given its theoretical significance, we review recent findings on intermarriage between whites and nonwhites and explore their implications for America's color lines.

While the tenfold rise in intermarriage over the past thirty years might initially appear to indicate that boundaries are fading for all groups, the different rates of intermarriage between white and nonwhite groups speak volumes about where the boundaries are eroding most rapidly. For instance, the intermarriage rate for Asians and Latinos is nearly three times as high as the black intermarriage rate, and these rates rose between 1990 and 2000. In addition,

Table 1
Rates of Exogamy among Marriages Containing at Least One Member of the Racial/Ethnic Group in the United States, 1990 and 2000

United States	Total	White	Black	Asian	Latino	Other
1990	4.4	4.7	8.4	31.5	32.5	74.8
2000	6.4	7.0	12.6	30.9	29.3	70.7

Source: IPUMS, 2003

among the native-born Asians and Latinos, the rate of intermarriage is even higher; in the year 2000, 55.7 percent of marriages containing a native-born Asian and 41.5 percent of marriages containing a native-born Latino were exogamous (see Table 2). Among young (25-34 years of age) native-born Asians and Latinos, the intermarriage figures are higher still; nearly two-thirds of married Asians and two-fifths of Latinos out-marry, mostly with whites (Qian 1997). The comparatively higher rates of intermarriage among native-born Asians and Latinos indicate that as these groups incorporate into the United States, not only do they become receptive to intermarriage, but whites also perceive them as suitable marriage partners (Moran 2001). By contrast, less than one-tenth of young blacks marry someone of a different racial background (Perlmann 2000). While the rate of black-white intermarriage more than doubled in the 1970s and 1980s (Kalmijn 1993), on the whole, the intermarriage rate for whites and blacks remains relatively low (see Table 1).

In sum, there appear to be three distinct trends in interracial marriage in the United States. First, intermarriage for all racial groups has increased dramatically over the last thirty-five years and will probably continue to rise. Second, intermarriage is not uncommon in the cases of newer immigrant groups such as Asians and Latinos (particularly among the young, native-born populations). Third, compared to Asians, Latinos, and American Indians, intermarriage is still relatively uncommon among blacks. The differential rates of intermarriage among nonwhite racial groups suggest that racial/ethnic boundaries are more prominent for some groups than for others. The significantly higher rates of intermarriage among Asians and Latinos indicate that racial/ethnic boundaries are more fluid and flexible, and racial/ethnic prejudice less salient for these groups. By contrast, the lower rates of intermarriage among blacks suggest that racial boundaries are more prominent, and the black-white divide more salient than the Asian-white or Latino-white divides. Hence, while boundaries are fading, boundary crossing among racial groups is *not* unconditional, and race is not declining in significance at the same pace for all groups.

Table 2

Rates of Exogamy among Marriages Containing at Least One Native-born Member of the Racial or Ethnic Group, 1990 and 2000

	1990		2000	
	Count	Percent	Count	Percent
Asian	365,866	45.5	590,666	55.7
Latino	2,348,427	40.3	3,087,771	41.5

Source: IPUMS, 2003

Multiracial Identification

The rise in intermarriage has resulted in the growth of the multiracial population in the United States. This population became highly visible especially when, for the first time in the nation's history, the 2000 Census allowed Americans to select "one or more races" to indicate their racial identification. Brought about by a small but highly influential multiracial movement, this landmark change in the way the United States measures racial identification reflects the view that race is no longer conceived as a bounded category (DaCosta 2000; Farley 2001; Hirschman, Alba, and Farley 2000; Waters 2000a; Williams 2001). In 2000, 6.8 million persons, or 2.4 percent of Americans identified themselves as multiracial, that is, about one in every forty people. While these figures may not appear large, a recent National Academy of Science study noted that the multiracial population could rise to 21 percent by the year 2050 when—because of rising patterns in intermarriage—as many as 35 percent of Asians and 45 percent of Hispanics might claim a multiracial background (Smith and Edmonston 1997). The growth of the multiracial population provides a new reflection on the nation's changing racial/ethnic boundaries.

Of those who reported a multiracial background, 93 percent reported exactly two races, 6 percent reported three races, and only 1 percent reported four or more races. While most individuals who report a multiracial identification list exactly two races, the selection of these races is not evenly distributed across all racial groups. As Table 3 illustrates, the groups with a high percentage of multiracial persons as a percentage of the total group include "Native Hawaiian or Other Pacific Islander," "American Indian and Alaska Native," "Other," and "Asian." While "Latino" or "Hispanic" was not a racial category on the 2000 Census, the Office of Management and Budget directive about the change in the race questions mandated two distinct questions regarding a person's racial/ethnic background: one about race and a second about whether a person was of Spanish-origin in order to identify the Latino population of the United States. In both 1990 and 2000, slightly more than 97 percent of those who checked "Other" were Latinos (Anderson and Fienberg 1999; U.S. Bureau of the Census 2001).

As illustrated in Table 3, the groups with the lowest proportion of persons claiming a multiracial background in 2000 are "Whites" and "Blacks." However, because whites account for 77 percent of the total U.S. population, most individuals who report a multiracial identity also claim a white background. More specifically, while 5.1 million whites report a multiracial background, this accounts for only 2.3 percent of the total white population. Like whites, the proportion of blacks who claim a multiracial background is also quite small, accounting for only 4.2 percent of the total black population. These figures stand in sharp contrast to those among American Indian/Alaska Natives and Native Hawaiian or Other Pacific Islanders who show the highest

Table 3
Multiracial Identification by Census Racial Categories

	Racial Identification[1] (millions)	Multiracial Identification[2] (millions)	Percent Multiracial
White	216.5	5.1	2.3
Black	36.2	1.5	4.2
Asian	11.7	1.4	12.4
Other	18.4	3.0	16.4
American Indian and Alaska Native	3.9	1.4	36.4
Native Hawaiian or Other Pacific Islander	0.7	0.3	44.8

Source: U.S. Census 2000

[1] Racial/Ethnic group totals do not sum to the total U.S. population because multiracial persons are counted here in more than one group.

[2] Multiracial persons are counted for each race category mentioned.

percentage of multiracial reporting as a proportion of their populations at 36.4 and 44.8 percent, respectively. Asians and Latinos fall in between with significantly higher rates of multiracial reporting than blacks and whites at 12.4 and 16.4 percent, respectively, but lower rates compared to American Indian/Alaska Natives and Native Hawaiian/Other Pacific Islanders.

If we examine the rates of black-white, Asian-white, and Latino-white multiracial combinations as a percent of the total black, Asian, and Latino populations (Table 4), we find these figures equal 1.9, 7.0, and 4.9 percent, respectively. Among Asians, the Asian-white multiracial combination is about *three and a half times* more likely to occur, and among Latinos, the Latino-white combination *more than two and a half times* more to occur, as the black-white combination among blacks. Mirroring trends in intermarriage, there appear to be three distinct patterns in multiracial identification. First, the multiracial population seems likely to continue to grow in the foreseeable future as a result of increasing intermarriage. Second, multiracial identification is not uncommon among the members of new immigrant groups such as Asians and Latinos (particularly for those under the age of eighteen). Third, at only 4.2 percent, multiracial identification remains relatively uncommon among blacks compared to Asians and Latinos.

Why blacks are far less likely to report a multiracial background is particularly noteworthy considering that the U.S. Census Bureau estimates that at least three-quarters of the black population in the United States is ancestrally multiracial (Davis 1991; Spencer 1997). In other words, while at least 75

Table 4
Percent of Various Racial/Ethnic Groups Reporting a Multiracial Identity in Combination with Selected Additional Racial Identities

Group	White	Black	Asian	Native American	Other
			Second Racial Identity		
Whites[1]	—	0.3	0.4	0.5	1.1
Blacks[1]	1.9	—	0.3	0.6	1.1
Asians[1]	7.0	0.8	—	1.5	2.2
Native Americans[1]	25.5	4.6	4.1	—	2.4
Others[2]	11.9	2.2	1.3	0.5	—
Latinos[3]	4.9	0.8	0.4	0.5	5.1

[1]Defined as non-Hispanics of the given category reported alone or in combination.

[2]Can be either Hispanic or non-Hispanics reporting the "other" racial category alone or in combination with the white, black, Asian, or Native American categories.

[3]Consists of Latino respondents reporting multiracial identities involving the column race and one or more other races.

percent of black Americans have some alternative ancestry (mostly white) and thus could claim multiracial identities on that basis, just over 4 percent choose to do so, although recent studies reveal that younger black/white multiracials feel less constrained to adopt an exclusively black monoracial identity. For example, Korgen's (1998) study of forty black/white adults reveals that only one-third of her sample under the age of thirty exclusively identifies as black. Moreover, Harris and Sim's (2002) study of multiracial youth shows that 17.1 percent of black/white adolescents choose white as the single race that best describes them. While younger blacks are less likely to report an exclusively black monoracial identity than older black cohorts, blacks overall are still far less likely to report multiracial backgrounds compared to Asians and Latinos.

The tendency of black Americans to be less likely to report multiracial identifications undoubtedly owes to the legacy of slavery, including lasting discrimination and the formerly *de jure* and now *de facto* invocation of the "one-drop rule" of hypodescent (Davis 1991; Haney Lopez 1996; Nobles 2000). For no other racial or ethnic group in the United States and in no other country does the one-drop rule so tightly circumscribe a group's identity choices (Harris et al. 1993). Unlike the "one-drop rule" of hypodescent that has historically constrained racial identity options for multiracial blacks, the absence of such a traditional practice of labeling among multiracial Asians, Latinos, and American Indians leaves room for exercising discretion in the selection of racial/ethnic identities (Bean and Stevens 2003; Eschbach 1995; Harris and Sim 2002; Lee and Bean 2003, 2004; Stephan and Stephan 1989; Xie and Goyette 1997). The higher rates of multiracial reporting among Latinos and

Asians, both as a proportion of the total Latino and Asian populations, and vis-à-vis blacks, indicate that racial boundaries are less constraining for these groups compared to blacks. While boundary crossing may be more common for all groups, it appears that the legacy of institutional racism in the country, as exemplified in such practices as the informal rule of hypodescent, more forcefully constrains the identity options for blacks compared to other non-white groups.

In addition, because a significant proportion of Latinos and Asians in the United States are either immigrants or the children of immigrants, their understanding of race, racial boundaries, and the black-white color divide is shaped by a different set of circumstances than those of African Americans. Most importantly, what sets Latinos and Asians apart is that their experiences are not rooted in the same historical legacy of slavery with its systematic and persistent patterns of legal and institutional discrimination and inequality from which the tenacious black-white divide was born and cemented. Unlike African Americans who were forcefully brought to this country as slaves, today's Latino and Asian newcomers are voluntary migrants, and consequently, their experiences are distinct from those of African Americans. The unique history and experience of black Americans in this country make the black-white racial gap qualitatively and quantitatively different from the Latino-white or Asian-white racial divides. For these reasons, racial/ethnic boundaries appear more fluid for the newest immigrants than for native-born blacks, consequently providing multiracial Asians and Latinos more racial options than their black counterparts.

The Geography of Multiracial Identities

Another way of measuring America's changing boundaries is to unearth where these boundaries are shifting most rapidly. While differences in multiracial reporting across racial groups are readily apparent, also noteworthy is that rates of multiracial identification are not uniform across the country. Patterns of multiracial identification reveal that areas with high immigrant populations evince greater rates of multiracial reporting. Immigration researchers have long noted that the foreign-born population is clustered in several cities and states (Bean et al. 1997; Waldinger and Lee 2001), and like the immigrant population, those who report multiracial backgrounds are similarly clustered. In fact, 64 percent or nearly two-thirds of those who report a multiracial identification reside in just ten states—California, New York, Texas, Florida, Hawaii, Illinois, New Jersey, Washington, Michigan, and Ohio—all of which have relatively high immigrant populations (see Table 5). Moreover, 40 percent of all those who report a multiracial identification reside in the West, a region of the country that has demonstrated substantially more tolerance for racial/ethnic diversity than other parts of the country (Baldassare 2000, 1981;

Godfrey 1988). As Table 5 indicates, California leads as the state with the highest number of multiracial persons and is the only state with a multiracial population that exceeds one million. The multiracial population accounts for 4.7 percent of California's population, or one in every twenty-one Californians, compared to one in every forty Americas for the country as a whole.

In essence, states and metropolitan areas with higher levels of racial/ethnic diversity (as reflected in the percent of the population that is *not* non-Hispanic white or non-Hispanic black) boast much larger multiracial populations than states that are less racially diverse. On the opposite end of the diversity spectrum are states like West Virginia and Maine that have low racial minority populations, and thereby exhibit very low levels of multiracial reporting. States like Mississippi, Alabama, South Carolina, and Louisiana, however,

Table 5
State Summaries: Most and Least Multiracial States, 2000

Rank	State	Number of Multiracial Persons	Multiracial Population (percent)	Percent not Blackor White*
1	Hawaii	259,343	21.4	75.4
2	Alaska	34,146	5.4	29.0
3	California	1,607,646	4.7	46.9
4	Oklahoma	155,985	4.5	18.4
5	Nevada	76,428	3.8	28.2
6	New Mexico	66,327	3.6	53.6
7	Washington	213,519	3.6	17.9
8	New York	590,182	3.1	23.2
9	Oregon	104,745	3.1	14.9
10	Arizona	146,526	2.9	33.3
.				
.				
.				
42	Tennessee	63,109	1.1	4.5
43	Iowa	31,778	1.1	5.3
44	Louisiana	48,265	1.1	5.2
45	New Hampshire	13,214	1.1	4.2
46	Kentucky	42,443	1.1	3.5
47	South Carolina	39,950	1.0	4.5
48	Alabama	44,179	1.0	3.8
49	Maine	12,647	1.0	3.0
50	West Virginia	15,788	0.9	2.3
51	Mississippi	20,021	0.7	3.1

Source: U.S. Census 2000

* Percent *not* non-Hispanic White or non-Hispanic Black.

have relatively large black populations yet evince low levels of multiracial reporting. In these southern states, the strong traditional dividing line between blacks and whites appears to constrain multiracial identification, leading persons to identify monoracially as either white or black rather than adopting a multiracial identity (Bean and Stevens 2003; Davis 1991; Farley 2001; Harris and Sim 2002). We see similar patterns emerge at the metropolitan level as well; areas with greater levels of racial/ethnic diversity evince higher rates of multiracial reporting (see Table 6).

Table 6
U.S. Metro Areas: Top and Bottom Twenty Most and Least
Multiracial Metro Areas, 2000

Metropolitan Area	Number of Multiracial Persons	Percentage Multiracial	Percentage Non-White	Diversity
Honolulu, HI	96,793	16.7	78.3	47.8
Stockton, CA	34,566	6.1	52.9	66.4
Jersey City, NJ	35,697	5.9	63.9	68.6
Oakland, CA	134,331	5.6	52.7	68.7
San Francisco-Oakland-Vallejo, CA	81,209	5.5	53.9	67.3
Tacoma, WA	38,832	5.5	25.0	42.0
Vallejo-Fairfield-Napa, CA	28,429	5.5	46.6	64.5
Modesto, CA	23,731	5.4	42.8	56.7
Sacramento, CA	88,898	5.4	35.9	54.9
San Jose, CA	90,598	5.4	56.8	67.5
Los Angeles-Long Beach, CA	490,587	5.2	68.9	68.0
New York-Northeastern NJ	441,079	5.1	63.5	72.2
Riverside-San Bernadino, CA	136,235	5.1	54.5	63.6
San Diego, CA	143,087	5.0	45.5	61.3
Tulsa, OK	34,585	5.0	25.4	42.3
Fresno, CA	37,585	4.8	60.1	64.9
Colorado Springs, CO	20,139	4.8	25.5	42.3
Orange County, CA	135,743	4.8	49.6	62.7
Bakersfield, CA	32,725	4.8	50.9	60.3
Oklahoma City, OK	23,680	4.7	35.4	54.1
…	…	…	…	…
Charleston-N.Charleston,SC	6,761	1.5	36.3	49.2
Columbia, SC	7,810	1.5	37.6	50.4
St. Louis, MO-IL	37,763	1.5	22.6	36.6
Lancaster, PA	7,042	1.5	11.4	20.9
Sarasota, FL	8,234	1.4	14.9	26.7
Melbourne-Titusville-Cocoa-Palm Bay, FL	6,351	1.4	15.1	27.1

Table 6 (cont.)

Canton, OH	5,441	1.3	9.1	16.9
Richmond-Petersburg, VA	7,534	1.3	38.5	51.3
Cincinnati OH/KY/IN	10,639	1.3	28.5	42.4
Pittsburgh-Beaver Valley, PA	18,142	1.2	14.0	24.8
Charlotte-Gastonia-Rock Hill, SC	8,551	1.2	38.2	53.3
Buffalo-Niagara Falls, NY	14,362	1.2	17.2	29.9
Harrisburg-Lebanon-Carlisle, PA	7,620	1.2	13.6	24.5
Greensboro-Winston Salem-High Point, NC	14,903	1.2	28.1	44.0
Dayton-Springfield, OH	6,199	1.1	23.2	37.0
Scranton-Wilkes-Barre, PA	6,599	1.1	4.9	9.6
Baton Rouge, LA	6,158	1.0	36.0	48.6
Birmingham, AL	5,294	1.0	45.1	52.7
Memphis, TN/AR/MS	4,923	0.9	67.4	51.0
Jackson, MS	2,705	0.6	46.9	52.1
Non-metro areas	2,367,456	1.9	20.3	35.0

Source: IPUMS, 2003

These patterns suggest that multiracial reporting is more likely in areas with greater levels of racial/ethnic diversity, which in turn have largely been brought about by the influx of post-1965 wave of immigrants, particularly Latinos and Asians. By racial/ethnic diversity we mean both the presence of multiple racial/ethnic groups and the relative absence of statistical predominance on the part of any single group. Thus, the more a single racial/ethnic group makes up all of the population of some social, political, economic, or geographic group or area, the less the diversity; conversely, the greater the number of groups and the more equally they are distributed within an area, the greater the diversity. Basically, as used here for racial/ethnic groups, diversity is equivalent to the idea of heterogeneity as often more broadly invoked in sociology (e.g., Blau 1977; Blau and Schwartz 1984; Laumann 1973).

All else equal, we expect greater diversity to lead to increased multiracial reporting because increased diversity (or heterogeneity, more broadly) tends to promote more frequent intergroup associations and greater tolerance, results often noted in the sociological literature (Allport 1954; Blalock 1967; Blau 1977; Massey, Hodson, and Sekulic 1999). In fact, it is precisely the lack of racial/ethnic tolerance in the Deep South that has tended to constrain the reporting of multiracial mixing, as noted above. In general, we expect increased tolerance and flexibility to generate increased multiracial reporting. Immigration increases the likelihood of multiracial identification because the greater diversity it fosters leads to the loosening of racial/ethnic boundaries, and consequently allows more flexibility in the identity options for multiracial persons.

The geography of multiracial reporting clearly indicates that the rate varies widely across the country, with the highest levels in states and metropolitan areas that exhibit the greatest racial/ethnic diversity brought about by the arrival of new immigrants to these areas. Hence, while national patterns in interracial marriage and multiracial identification indicate a loosening of racial boundaries, particularly for Latinos and Asians, these shifts appear to be taking place more rapidly in certain parts of the country and among certain groups.

Linking Diversity to Multiracial Identification and Group Position

Noting that a few areas with greater diversity appear to have higher multiracial reporting, however, does not provide as strong a basis for establishing a connection between growing diversity and the breakdown of racial/ethnic color lines. What is needed are research results demonstrating more systematically bases for such linkage. We have argued that the multiracial population is likely to continue to increase, and that its existence and growth may have broader implications. We have also argued that multiracial reporting is more likely among Asians and Latinos than among blacks, as a consequence of both higher rates of intermarriage and greater tendencies for the members of these groups to see themselves in multiracial terms. Places that have experienced more immigration may also reveal larger relative sizes of racial/ethnic minority groups (at least in the cases of Latinos and Asians) and increased diversity, with the latter in turn loosening racial/ethnic boundaries and increasing the likelihood of multiracial reporting.

But a countervailing tendency is suggested by the literature on minority group size. An appreciable body of research indicates that larger relative minority group size increases perceptions of threat to the majority group (Blalock 1967; Blumer 1958; Cohen 1999; Forbes 1999; Fossett and Kiecolt 1989; Schuman, Steeh, and Bobo 1985). Furthermore, under conditions of continuing immigration, a constant influx of new members of a given racial/ethnic group into areas containing concentrations of group members will not only add to the group's relative size, it may also reinforce the group's distinctive behavioral and cultural patterns (Massey 1995). In turn, this may increase and heighten the group's distinctive sense of ethnicity, foster ethnic insularity, and tighten racial/ethnic boundaries. As a result, increased relative racial/ethnic and immigrant group size, in addition to fostering diversity in a broad sense, may also make it less likely that the members of such groups will either come from multiracial backgrounds (due to declines in intermarriage) or come to perceive themselves in multiracial terms. In short, while larger relative group size may foster multiracial identification through one pathway, it may diminish intermarriage and multiracial identification through others.

Here we examine metropolitan-level data on multiracial identification available to provide an assessment of the effects of relative group size and diversity on multiracial reporting. For example, Table 6 presents basic data for metropolitan areas on multiracial identification and racial/ethnic composition. We should note that we exclude in our measure of multiracial reporting those Latinos who report in response to the U.S. Census question on race that they possess both "white" and "other" racial backgrounds. Some scholars have suggested that such persons should not be included as multiracials because they are Latinos whose responses may reflect confusion about what the race question meant. Alternatively, we would suggest that among many Latinos, the categories "white" and "other" reflect "white" and "mestizo" backgrounds (Rodríguez 2000; Rodgriguez 2003), suggesting, we would argue, that they indicate actual multiracial backgrounds. Whatever the case, we also reran the results we present below to include these persons and found that this did not affect the pattern of our findings.

We present in Figure 1 the estimates of a simple model of the effects of relative group size on diversity and multiracial identification focusing on three major racial/ethnic groups: blacks, Latinos, and Asians. The sizes of two of these, Latinos and Asians, have been substantially affected by immigration during the past decade. We use data from the 2000 Census, and we construct from these data a simple measure of diversity, defined as one minus the Herfindahl Index of Concentration. This index indicates the degree to which the members of a population are concentrated in one of several sub-groups. Thus, a high score on the Herfindahl Index indicates that one racial/ethnic group predominates in an area. A high score on the complement of the index signifies that no single group predominates.

The findings make clear that metropolitan areas with relatively larger racial/ethnic groups (resulting in large part from immigration) have higher diversity scores and higher levels of multiracial identification. However, this positive effect of relative group size through diversity is partially offset to some extent by negative direct effects from relative group size in the cases of the Latino and (especially) black populations. But summing these direct and indirect effects together reveals that relative group size exerts an overall positive effect on multiracial identification for Asians and Latinos, with much of this effect operating through increases in diversity, but an overall negative effect for blacks. In other words, the Asian and Latino positive effect of relative group size through diversity is more than large enough to make up for the negative direct effect of relative group size. This pattern of findings thus provides further confirmation that the larger racial/ethnic groups resulting from higher immigration and generating greater racial/ethnic diversity appear also to lead to rising multiracial identification, lending additional weight to

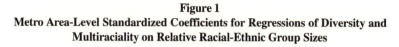

Figure 1
Metro Area-Level Standardized Coefficients for Regressions of Diversity and
Multiraciality on Relative Racial-Ethnic Group Sizes

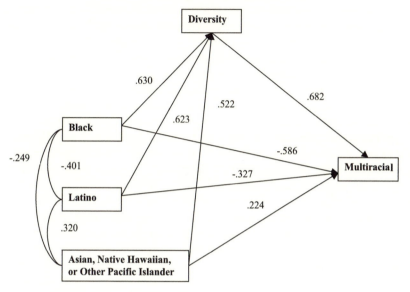

the idea that increasing diversity is operating to loosen traditional racial/
ethnic group boundaries in the United States, but more so for Asians and
Latinos than blacks.

The findings in the model also have implications for group position theory,
which holds that the major impetus for racial prejudice is the manifest attempts by the dominant group to protect their group position vis-à-vis others
in a racialized hierarchy, especially when this position is perceived as threatened. That the larger group size of Latinos and blacks has a negative direct
effect on multiracial reporting suggests that the larger these populations (especially in the case of blacks), the more constrained these groups may be in
adopting a multiracial identification. The more rigid racial/ethnic boundaries
in these cases suggests that whites may feel more threatened and thereby may
be more guarded about defending their sense of group position in metropolitan areas with relatively large black and Latino populations. However, when
group size operates through diversity, not only do these findings suggest a
loosening of racial/ethnic boundaries, but also a relaxing of group position.
The findings imply that whites are less likely to feel threatened or feel a need
to defend their group position in areas that exhibit high levels of racial/ethnic
diversity, even if they have relatively large Latino and black populations
(although more so in the case for Latinos than for blacks). In the case of Asians,

higher levels of racial/ethnic diversity further operate to loosen whites' sense of group position and lead to greater levels of multiracial reporting.

In sum, greater levels of racial/ethnic diversity brought about by increased immigration in certain parts of the country loosens the reign of whites' sense of group position vis-à-vis all racial/ethnic groups, and especially in the case of Asians and Latinos and to a lesser extent in the case of blacks. However, before we reach overly optimistic conclusions about fading racial/ethnic boundaries for all groups and a waning of group position, it is important to underscore that increased diversity exerts a far greater effect on multiracial reporting for Asians and Latinos than for blacks. While increased diversity also leads to greater multiracial reporting among blacks, the effect is far less pronounced, indicating that the color lines are fading more rapidly for Asians and Latinos than for blacks.

Conclusion and Discussion

How do current debates about immigration and race/ethnicity inform our interpretations of the rise in intermarriage and the patterns of multiracial identification? And what are the implications of these patterns for America's color lines? Over the past few decades, the rate of intermarriage between whites and nonwhites increased tenfold, and its increase went hand in hand with the growth in the multiracial population. Recognizing the growth of America's multiracial population, the 2000 U.S. Census allowed Americans the option to mark more than one race to self-identify, reflecting the view that race is no longer conceived as a bounded category. Coinciding with rising intermarriage between whites and nonwhites was a new immigrant stream from Latin America and Asia, creating a nation that has moved from a largely black and white society to one that is more racially and ethnically diverse. Changes brought about by increasing immigration, intermarriage, and multiracial identification beg the question of how relevant the traditional black-white color line and the existing theories of race/ethnic relations and immigrant incorporation are for understanding today's multiracial and multiethnic America. If the black-white color line no longer characterizes America's multiethnic society, where will the line be drawn in the twenty-first century, and what are the implications of these changes for theories that are founded on the black-white model of race relations?

Rates of intermarriage between whites and nonwhites have risen dramatically, and as a consequence, the multiracial population has also increased. Because intermarriage and multiracial reporting indicate a reduction in social distance and racial prejudice, these patterns provide evidence of loosening racial/ethnic boundaries. At first glance, these patterns offer an optimistic portrait of a declining significance of race and a relaxing of group position. However, upon closer examination, we find that changes in intermarriage and multiracial identification are not proceeding apace for all groups. While the rate of intermarriage between whites and nonwhites has increased, the rate is substantially higher for Latinos and Asians than for blacks. Correlatively, the findings on multiracial identification mirror the patterns on intermarriage: Latinos and Asians are much more likely to report a multiracial identification than are blacks.

What is crucial here is how we interpret the findings for Latinos and Asians. For example, if we consider Latinos and Asians as racialized minorities, and thus on the black side of the traditional black-white divide, the patterns of intermarriage and multiracial identification offer an optimistic portrait of the declining significance of race and relaxing of group position. However, if we treat Latinos and Asians as new immigrants who have not completed their path of incorporation, the implications for changing color lines and race/ethnic relations is far less sanguine. This critical distinction helps us to differentiate whether color lines are shifting for all racial/ethnic minorities, or whether they are changing to mainly accommodate new immigrant groups.

Because a significant proportion of the Latinos and Asians in the United States are either immigrants or the children of immigrants, their understanding of race, racial/ethnic boundaries, and the black-white color divide is shaped by a different set of circumstances than those of African Americans. Moreover, their process of incorporation does not dictate full acculturation to achieve structural incorporation, meaning that Latino and Asian immigrants have more leeway in retaining cultural and ethnic distinctiveness than even their European counterparts of yore. Most importantly, what marks the experiences of Latinos and Asians apart from African Americans is that they are not rooted in the same historical legacy of slavery with its systematic and persistent patterns of legal and institutional discrimination and inequality from which the tenacious black-white divide was born and cemented. For these reasons, the racial/ethnic boundaries appear more fluid for the newest immigrants than for native-born blacks. Moreover, gauging from patterns of intermarriage and multiracial reporting, whites also seem less concerned with constraining Latino and Asian identities and boundaries. Hence, the black-white model of race relations does not appropriately capture the incorporation processes of the new immigrant groups, and to therefore make conclusions about the declining significance of race or group position for all racial/ethnic groups based on the patterns for Latinos and Asians would be a grave mistake.

The color line is shifting more readily to accommodate newer immigrant groups such as Latinos and Asians, and while the color line is also shifting for blacks, this shift is occurring much more slowly. Where do Asians and Latinos fit in this divide? At this time, America's changing color lines point to the emergence of a new split that replaces the old black-white divide with one that appears to separate blacks from nonblacks (Bean and Stevens 2003; Gans 1999; Lee and Bean 2003, 2004; Waters 1999). The emergence of a black-nonblack separation is even evident in areas with high concentrations of immigrants, high levels of racial/ethnic diversity, and high levels of multiracial reporting, although not to as strong a degree. But even in these high diversity states and metropolitan areas, a black-nonblack divide is emerging, with Latinos and Asians falling into the nonblack category. Hence, while America's color lines are breaking down, they are not fading at the same pace for all groups, nor are they fading in all areas of the country.

The emergence of a black-nonblack divide could be a disastrous outcome for many African Americans. Once again, they would find that newer nonwhite immigrant groups are able to jump ahead of them in a racialized hierarchy in which blacks, or at least those with less than a college degree, find themselves at the bottom. Based on patterns in immigration, intermarriage, and multiracial identification, however, it appears that Latinos and Asians may have the option to become almost white or even white, and consequently, participate in a new color line that continues to separate blacks from other groups. Hence, America's changing color lines could involve a new racial/ethnic divide that may continue to consign many blacks to disadvantaged positions that are not qualitatively different from those perpetuated by the traditional black-white divide. While rising rates of intermarriage and patterns of multiracial identification clearly indicate that boundaries are breaking down, that the erosion of boundaries is neither uniform nor unconditional indicates little basis for complacency about the degree to which opportunities are improving for *all* racial/ethnic groups in America, even though they be for many of the new immigrant groups.

References

Alba, Richard D. 1985. *Italian Americans: Into the Twilight of Ethnicity*. Engelwood Cliffs, NJ: Prentice Hall.
_____. 1990. *Ethnic Identity: The Transformation of White America*. New Haven, CT: Yale University Press.
Allport, Gordon W. 1954. *The Nature of Prejudice*. Reading, MA: Addison-Wesley.
Anderson, Margo J. and Steven E. Fienberg. 1999. *Who Counts? The Politics of Census-Taking in Contemporary America*. New York: Russell Sage Foundation.
Bailey, Benjamin. 2001. "Dominican-American Ethnic/Racial Identities and United States Social Categories." *International Migration Review* 35 (3): 677-708.
Baldassare, Mark. 2000. *California in the New Millennium: The Changing Social and Political Landscape*. Berkeley: University of California Press.
_____. 1981. *The Growth Dilemma: Residents' Views and Local Population Change in the United States*. Berkeley: University of California Press.
Bean, Frank D. and Stephanie Bell-Rose, eds. 1999. *Immigration and Opportunity: Race, Ethnicity, and Employment in the United States*. New York: Russell Sage Foundation.
Bean, Frank D., Leo Chávez, and Min Zhou. 2000. "Immigration: Proposition 187, Five Years Later." *Bulletin of the American Academy of Arts and Sciences* LIII, (May/June): 28-50.
Bean, Frank D., Robert G. Cushing, Charles Haynes, and Jennifer Van Hook. 1997. "Immigration and the Social Contract." *Social Science Quarterly* 78: 249-68.

Bean Frank D. and Gillian Stevens. 2003. *America's Newcomers and the Dynamics of Diversity*. New York: Russell Sage Foundation.

Blalock Hubert M. 1967. *Toward a Theory of Minority Group Relations*. New York: Wiley.

Blau Peter M. 1977. *Inequality and Heterogeneity*. New York: The Free Press.

Blau Peter M. and Joseph E. Schwartz. 1984. *Crosscutting Social Circles: Testing a Macrostructural Theory of Intergroup Relations*. Orlando: Academic Press.

Blumer, Herbert. 1965. "The Future of the Color Line." Pp. 322-336 in *The South in Continuity and Change*, edited by John C. McKinney and Edgar T. Thompson. Durham, North Carolina: Duke University Press.

_____. 1958. "Race Prejudice as a Sense of Group Position." *Pacific Sociological Review* 1: 3-7.

Bobo, Lawrence. 2001. "Race, Interests, and Beliefs about Affirmative Action: Unanswered Questions and New Directions." Pp. 191-213 in *Color Lines: Affirmative Action, Immigration, and Civil Rights Options for America*, edited by John David Skrentny. Chicago: University of Chicago Press.

_____. 1999. "Prejudice as Group Position: Microfoundations of a Sociological Approach to Racism and Race Relations." *Journal of Social Issues* 55 (3): 445-472.

_____. 1997. "The Color Line, the Dilemma, and the Dream: Race Relations in America at the Close of the Twentieth Century." Pp. 31-55 in *Civil Rights and Social Wrongs: Black-White Relations Since World War II*, edited by John Higham. University Park, PA: Pennsylvania State University Press.

Bobo, Lawrence and Vincent Hutchings. 1996. "Perceptions of Racial Group Competition: Extending Blumer's Theory of Group Position to a Multiracial Social Context." *American Sociological Review* 61: 951-972.

Bobo, Lawrence and Devon Johnson. 2000. "Racial Attitudes in a Prismatic Metropolis: Mapping Identity, Stereotypes, Competition, and Views on Affirmative Action." Pp. 81-163 in *Prismatic Metropolis: Inequality in Los Angeles*, edited by Lawrence Bobo, Melvin Oliver, James Johnson, and Abel Valenzuela. New York: Russell Sage Foundation.

Bobo, Lawrence, James R. Kluegel, and Ryan A. Smith. 1997. "Laissez-Faire Racism: The Crystallization of a Kinder, Gentler, Antiblack Ideology." Pp. 15-42 in *Racial Attitudes in the 1990s: Continuity and Change*, edited by Steven A. Tuch and Jack K. Martin. Westport, CT: Praeger.

Bobo, Lawrence, Melvin Oliver, James Johnson, and Abel Valenzuela, eds. 2000. *Prismatic Metropolis: Inequality in Los Angeles*. New York: Russell Sage Foundation.

Brodkin, Karen. 1998. *How Jews Became White Folks and What That says about Race in America*. New Brunswick, NJ: Rutgers University Press.

Clark, Kenneth. 1965. *Dark Ghetto: Dilemmas of Social Power*. New York: Harper and Row.

Cohen, Philip N. 2001. "Race, Class, and Labor Markets: The White Working Class and Racial Composition of U.S. Metropolitan Areas." *Social Science Research* 30: 146-169.

Crispino, James. 1980. *The Assimilation of Ethnic Groups*. Staten Island, NY: Center for Migration Studies.

DaCosta, Kimberly. 2000. *Remaking the Color Line: Social Bases and Implications of the Multiracial Movement*. Unpublished Dissertation, University of California, Berkeley.

Danziger, Sheldon and Peter Gottschalk. 1995. *America Unequal*. New York and Cambridge: Russell Sage Foundation and Harvard University Press.

Davis, F. James. 1991. *Who is Black?* University Park: Pennsylvania State University Press.

Davis, Kingsley. 1941. "Intermarriage in Caste Societies." *American Anthropologist* 43: 376-395.

Drake, St. Clair and Horace R. Cayton. [1945] 1993. *Black Metropolis: A Study of Negro Life in a Northern City.* Chicago: University of Chicago Press.

Du Bois, W.E.B. [1903] 1997. *The Souls of Black Folk.* Edited by David W. Blight and Robert Gooding-Williams. Boston: Bedford Books.

Eschbach, Karl. 1995. "The Enduring and Vanishing American Indian: American Indian Population Growth and Intermarriage in 1980." *Ethnic and Racial Studies* 18 (1): 89-108.

Farley, Reynolds. 2001. "Identifying with Multiple Races: A Social Movement that Succeeded but Failed?" Research Report No. 01-491. Ann Arbor, MI: Population Studies Center, University of Michigan.

_____. 1996. *The New American Reality: Who We Are, How We Got Here, Where We Are Going.* New York: Russell Sage Foundation.

Farley, Reynolds and Walter R. Allen. 1987. *The Color Line and the Quality of Life in America.* New York: Russell Sage Foundation.

Farley, Reynolds and William H. Frey. 1994. "Changes in the Segregation of Whites from Blacks During the 1980s: Small Steps Toward a More Integrated Society." *American Sociological Review* 59: 23-45.

Fix, Michael, Jeffrey Passel, and K. Sucher. 2003. *Trends in Naturalization.* Washington D.C.: Urban Institute.

Foner, Nancy. 2000. *From Ellis Island to JFK: New York's Two Great Waves of Immigration.* New Haven, CT and New York: Yale University Press and Russell Sage Foundation.

Forbes, H.D. 1997. *Ethnic Conflict.* New Haven, CT: Yale University Press.

Fossett, Mark A. and K. Jill Kiecolt. 1989. "The Relative Size of Minority Populations and White Racial Attitudes." *Social Science Quarterly* 70: 820-835.

Fu, Vincent. 2001. "Racial Intermarriage Pairing." *Demography* 38 (2): 147-160.

Gans, Herbert J. 1999. "The Possibility of a New Racial Hierarchy in the Twenty-first Century United States." Pp. 371-390 in *The Cultural Territories of Race*, edited by Michèle Lamont. Chicago and New York: University of Chicago Press and Russell Sage Foundation.

_____. 1992. "Second-Generation Decline: Scenarios for the Economic and Ethnic Futures of the Post-1965 American Immigrants." *Ethnic and Racial Studies* 15: 173-192.

_____. 1979. "Symbolic Ethnicity: The Future of Ethnic Groups and Cultures in America." *Ethnic and Racial Studies* 2: 1-20.

Gerstle, Gary. 1999. "Liberty, Coercion, and the Making of Americans." Pp. 275-293 in *The Handbook of International Migration*, edited by Charles Hirschman, Philip Kasinitz, and Josh DeWind. New York: Russell Sage Foundation.

Gibson, Margaret. 1988. *Accommodation without Assimilation.* Ithaca, NY: Cornell University Press.

Gilbertson, Greta, Joseph F. Fitzpatrick, and Lijun Yang. 1996. "Hispanic Intermarriage in New York City: New Evidence from 1991." *International Migration Review* 30: 445-459.

Gitlin, Todd. 1995. *The Twilight of Common Dreams.* New York: Metropolitan.

Glazer, Nathan. 2003. "Assimilation Today: Is One Identity Enough?" Pp. 31-43 in *Reinventing the Melting Pot: The New Immigrants and What It Means to Be American*, edited by Tamar Jacoby. New York: Basic Books.

_____. 1997. *We are all Multiculturalists Now.* Cambridge: Harvard University Press.

Glazer, Nathan and Daniel Patrick Moynihan. 1963. *Beyond the Melting Pot.* Cambridge: MIT Press.

Godfrey, Brian J. 1988. *Neighborhoods in Transition: The Making of San Francisco's Ethnic and Nonconformist Communities*. Berkeley: University of California Press.

Gordon, Milton. 1964. *Assimilation in American Life*. New York: Oxford University Press.

Greeley, Andrew. 1974. *Ethnicity in the United States*. New York: Wiley.

Grieco, Elizabeth M. and Rachel C. Cassidy. 2001. "Overview of Race and Hispanic Origin." *Census 2000 Brief*. U.S. Department of Commerce, Economics and Statistics Administration: U.S. Census Bureau.

Hacker, Andrew. 1992. *Two Nations: Black and White, Separate, Hostile, Unequal*. New York: Ballatine Books.

Harris, David R. and Jeremiah Joseph Sim. 2002. "Who Is Multiracial? Assessing the Complexity of Lived Race." *American Sociological Review* 67 (4): 614-627.

Hirschman, Charles, Richard Alba, and Reynolds Farley. 2000. "The Meaning and Measurement of Race in the U.S. Census: Glimpses into the Future." *Demography* 37: 381-393.

Ignatiev, Noel. 1995. *How the Irish Became White*. New York: Routledge.

Jacoby, Tamar. 2001. "An End to Counting Race?" *Commentary* 111, 6 (June): 37-40.

Jaynes, Gerald D. and Robin M. Williams, Jr., eds. 1989. *A Common Destiny: Blacks and American Society*. Washington, D.C.: National Academy Press.

Kalmijn, Matthijs. 1993. "Patterns in Black/White Intermarriage." *Social Forces* 72 (1): 119-146.

Kao, Grace and Marta Tienda. 1995. "Optimism and Achievement: The Educational Performance of Immigrant Youth." *Social Science Quarterly* 76 (1): 1-19.

Korgen, Kathleen O. 1998. *From Black to Biracial: Transforming Racial Identity Among Americans*. Westport, CT: Praeger.

Laumann, Edward O. 1973. *Bonds of Pluralism: The Form and Substance of Urban Social Networks*. New York: Wiley.

Lee, Jennifer. 2002a. *Civility in the City: Blacks, Jews, and Koreans in Urban America*. Cambridge, MA: Harvard University Press.

_____. 2000b. "From Civil Relations to Racial Conflict: Merchant-Customer Interactions in Urban America." *American Sociological Review* 67 (1): 77-98.

Lee, Jennifer and Frank D. Bean. 2004. "America's Changing Color Lines: Immigration, Race/Ethnicity, and Multiracial Identification." *Annual Review of Sociology* 30.

_____. 2003. "Beyond Black and White: Remaking Race in America." *Contexts* 2 (3): 26-33.

Lee, Sharon M. and Marilyn Fernandez. 1998. "Patterns in Asian American Racial/Ethnic Intermarriage: A Comparison of 1980 and 1990 Census Data." *Sociological Perspectives* 41 (2): 323-342.

Lieberson, Stanley and Mary C. Waters. 1988. *From Many Strands: Ethnic and Racial Groups in Contemporary America*. New York: Russell Sage Foundation.

Loewen, James. 1971. *The Mississippi Chinese: Between Black and White*. Cambridge: Harvard University Press.

Lopez, David and Yen Espiritu. 1990. "Pan-ethnicity in the United States." *Ethnic and Racial Studies* 13: 198-223.

Massey, Douglas S. and Nancy A. Denton. 1993. *American Apartheid: Segregation and the Making of the Underclass*. Cambridge: Harvard University Press.

Massey, Garth, Randy Hodson, and Dusko Sekulic. 1999. "Ethnic Enclaves and Intolerance: The Case of Yugoslavia. *Social Forces* 78 (2): 669-93.

Merton, Robert K. 1941. "Intermarriage and the Social Structure: Fact and Theory." *Psychiatry* 4: 361-374.

Moran, Rachel F. 2001. *Interracial Intimacy: The Regulation of Race and Romance*. Chicago: University of Chicago Press.

Nagel, Joane. 1994. "Constructing Ethnicity: Creating and Recreating Ethnic Identity and Culture." *Social Problems* 41: 152-176.

Neckerman, Kathryn M., Prudence Carter, and Jennifer Lee. 1999. "Segmented Assimilation and Minority Cultures of Mobility." *Ethnic and Racial Studies* 22: 945-965.

Neckerman, Kathryn M. and Joleen Kirschenman. 1991. "Hiring Strategies, Racial Bias, and Inner-city Workers." *Social Problems* 38 (4): 433-447.

Newman, Katherine S. 1999. *No Shame in My Game: The Working Poor in the Inner City*. New York: Alfred A. Knopf and Russell Sage Foundation.

Nobles, Melissa. 2000. *Shades of Citizenship: Race and the Census in Modern Politics*. Stanford: Stanford University Press.

Oliver, Melvin and Thomas Shapiro. 1995. *Black Wealth/White Wealth: A New Perspective on Racial Inequality*. New York: Routledge.

Omi, Michael and Howard Winant. 1994. *Racial Formation in the United States: From the 1960s to the 1980s*. New York: Routledge.

Pagnini, Deanna L. and S. Philip Morgan. 1990. "Intermarriage and Social Distance Among U.S. Immigrants at the Turn of the Century." *American Journal of Sociology* 96 (2): 405-32.

Patterson, Orlando. 1998. *The Ordeal of Integration*. Washington, D.C.: Civitas.

———. 1998. *Rituals of Blood*. Washington, D.C.: Civitas.

Pattillo-McCoy, Mary. 1999. *Black Picket Fences: Privilege and Peril among the Black Middle Class*. Chicago: University of Chicago Press.

Perlmann, Joel. 2000. "Reflecting the Changing Face of America: Multiracials, Racial Classification, and American Intermarriage." Pp. 506-533 in *Interracialism: Black-White Intermarriage in American History, Literature, and Law*, edited by Werner Sollars. New York: Oxford University Press.

Perlmann, Joel and Roger Waldinger. 1997. "Second Generation Decline? Children of Immigrants, Past and Present—A Reconsideration. *International Migration Review* 31 (4): 893-922.

Portes, Alejandro and Dag Macleod. 1996. "What Shall I Call Myself? Hispanic Identity Formation in the Second Generation." *Ethnic and Racial Studies* 19 (3): 523-547.

Portes, Alejandro and Rubén G. Rumbaut. 2001. *Legacies: The Story of the Immigrant Second Generation*. Berkeley: University of California Press.

Portes, Alejandro and Min Zhou. 1993. "The New Second Generation: Segmented Assimilation and its Variants." *Annals of the American Political and Social Sciences* 530: 74-96.

Qian, Zhenchao. 1997. "Breaking the Racial Barriers: Variations in Interracial Marriage Between 1980 and 1990." *Demography* 34 (2): 263-276.

Rodriguez Gregory. 2003. "Mexican-Americans and the Mestizo Melting Pot." Pp. 95-108 in *Reinventing the Melting Pot: The New Immigrants and What It Means to Be American*, edited by Tamar Jacoby. New York: Basic Books.

Rodríguez, Clara E. 2000. *Changing Race: Latinos, the Census, and the History of Ethnicity in the United States*. New York: New York University Press.

Roediger, David. 1991. *The Wages of Whiteness*. New York: Verso.

Rosenfeld, Michael J. 2002. "Measures of Assimilation in the Marriage Market: Mexican Americans 1970-1990." *Journal of Marriage and Family* 64: 152-162.

Sakamoto, Arthur, Huei-Hsai Wu, and Jessie M. Tzeng. 2000. "The Declining Significance of Race among American Men During the Latter Half of the Twentieth Century." *Demography* 37: 41-51.

Sanjek, Roger. 1994. "Intermarriage and the Future of the Races." Pp. 103-130 in *Race*, edited by Steven Gregory and Roger Sanjek. New Brunswick, NJ: Rutgers University Press.

Schuman, Howard, Charlotte Steeh, and Lawrence Bobo. 1985. *Racial Attitudes in America: Trends and Interpretations*. Cambridge: Harvard University Press.

Skrentny, John D., ed. 2001. *Color Lines: Affirmative Action, Immigration, and Civil Rights Options for America*. Chicago: University of Chicago Press.

Smelser, Neil, William Julius Wilson, and Faith Mitchell. 2001. *America Becoming: Racial Patterns and their Consequences*. Washington, D.C.: National Academy Press.

Smith, James P. and Barry Edmonston. 1997. *The New Americans*. Washington, D.C.: National Academy Press.

Stephan, Cookie White and Walter G. Stephan. 1989. "After Intermarriage: Ethnic Identity among Mixed-Heritage Japanese-Americans and Hispanics." *Journal of Marriage and Family* 51: 507-519.

Thernstrom, Stephan and Abigail Thernstrom. 1997. *America in Black and White: One Nation, Indivisible*. New York: Simon & Schuster.

Tuan, Mia. 1998. *Forever Foreigners or Honorary Whites? The Asian Ethnic Experience Today*. New Brunswick, NJ: Rutgers University Press.

Tucker, M. Belinda and Claudia Mitchell-Kernan. 1990. "New Patterns in Black American Interracial Marriage: The Social Structural Context." *Journal of Marriage and the Family* 52: 209-218.

U.S. Bureau of Census. 2001. *United States Census 2000.* http://www.census.gov/popest/estimates.php

U.S. Immigration and Naturalization Service. 1998. *1997 Statistical Yearbook of the Immigration and Naturalization Service*. Washington, D.C.: U.S. Government Printing Office.

Waldinger, Roger and Jennifer Lee. 2001. "New Immigrants in Urban America." Pp.30-79 in *Strangers at the Gates: New Immigrants in Urban America*, edited by Roger Waldinger. Berkeley: University of California Press.

Waters, Mary C. 2000. "Immigration, Intermarriage, and the Challenges of Measuring Racial/Ethnic Identities." *American Journal of Public Health* 90: 1735-1737.

_____. 1999. *Black Identities: West Indian Immigrant Dreams and American Realities*. Cambridge: Harvard University Press.

_____. 1990. *Ethnic Options: Choosing Identities in America*. Berkeley: University of California Press.

Williams, Kim. 2001. *Boxed In: The United States Multiracial Movement*. Unpublished Dissertation, Cornell University.

Wilson, William Julius. 1987. *The Truly Disadvantaged: The Inner City, the Underclass, and Public Policy*. Chicago: University of Chicago Press.

_____. 1980. *The Declining Significance of Race*. Second Edition. Chicago: University of Chicago Press.

Wright, Lawrence. 1994. "One Drop of Blood." *New Yorker* 70, 22 (July 25): 46-54.

Xie, Yu and Kimberly Goyette. 1997. "The Racial Identification of Bicracial Children with One Asian Parent: Evidence from the 1990 Census." *Social Forces* 76 (2): 547-570.

Zhou, Min and Carl L. Bankston III. 1998. *Growing Up American: How Vietnamese Children Adapt to Life in the United States*. New York: Russell Sage Foundation.

3

Occupational Context and Wage Competition of New Immigrant Latinos with Minorities and Whites

Lisa Catanzarite

The continuing in-migration of less-skilled workers to the United States has triggered mounting concern regarding the impact of immigration on natives. Scholars and laypeople alike are keenly interested in whether immigrants dampen wages for U.S. natives, particularly for minorities, who are thought to experience greater labor market competition with less-skilled immigrants than do whites.

Research has provided limited evidence that immigration depresses native pay in general (see Smith and Edmonston 1997; and Borjas 1999 for reviews). Findings regarding wage costs of immigration to native-born minorities or less-skilled workers have been inconsistent: analyses suggest that negative wage effects may obtain for the less-skilled (e.g., Johnson 1998) and for some racial/ethnic groups among native workers (Howell and Mueller 2000; Reimers 1998). However, research also suggests that immigration may positively influence wages for particular minority groups (Reimers 1998; Ong and Valenzuela 1996).

Notably, research on immigrant-native wage competition has been dominated by so-called "area studies," which compare aggregate wages across metropolitan areas (MAs). Borjas (1999) suggests moving beyond this approach. Others argue specifically that research on immigrant-native wage competition should more directly attend to (1) the wage consequences of occupational segregation and (2) occupations within local labor markets (Catanzarite 1998; Tienda 1998; Howell and Mueller 2000).

A focus on occupations or jobs provides greater detail and more closely approximates the locus of wage setting than is true of studies that compare aggregate wages across metropolitan areas. Rosenfeld and Tienda's (1999) work on select, local occupations offers suggestive evidence. And, case studies of less-skilled jobs offer important insights into potential competition between immigrants and less-skilled native workers (Waldinger 1999; Waters 1999). Yet, such research does not provide systematic analyses of wages over an array of potentially susceptible occupations.

Recent investigations across a range of fields underscore the importance of occupational context and provide evidence of pay penalties for natives in heavily immigrant occupations-by-industries in New York (Howell and Mueller 2000) and for natives and earlier-immigrant Latinos in occupations with overrepresentations of recent-immigrant Latinos in Los Angeles (Catanzarite 1998). Additionally, analyses of Los Angeles provide evidence of longitudinal pay erosion in *brown-collar* occupations (Catanzarite 2002) (fields with a large share of recent-immigrant Latino men). While these studies are each restricted to a single local labor market, a more comprehensive analysis is provided by Catanzarite's (2003) work on occupations in thirty-eight immigrant-receiving MAs. That investigation yields evidence of substantial wage penalties for native-born and earlier-immigrant Latino men in brown-collar occupations-in-MAs and discerns larger penalties for minorities than for native whites. However, it does not compare penalties for different groups of minority workers.

This chapter examines *differences* in brown-collar wage penalties for native white, native black, native Latino, and earlier-immigrant Latino men across multiple local labor markets. The study employs multi-level modeling to analyze wage determination for different groups of native-born men as well as for earlier-immigrant Latino men in local brown-collar occupations.[1] The data are for a set of eighteen immigrant-receiving metropolitan areas that are heterogeneous with respect to race, ethnicity, and immigration. That is, these MAs (1) are destinations for new immigrant Latinos and (2) have substantial numbers of native blacks, native Latinos, native whites, and earlier-immigrant Latinos. Using data from the 1990 5% Census Public Use Microdata Sample (PUMS), I investigate racial/ethnic/immigrant differences in the magnitude of pay penalties associated with brown-collar occupations. How do brown-collar penalties differ for native whites vs. native Latinos and native blacks; for native minorities vs. earlier-immigrant Latinos?

Framework

Following Catanzarite (2003; 1998), I argue that substantial pay penalties exist for individuals employed in brown-collar occupations. The approach is grounded in: literature on the potential impact of immigrant workers on native earnings; and research on the effects of minority occupational composition on pay. (See Catanzarite 2003 for more detail.)

Brown-Collar Pay Penalties

Potential reasons for wage suppression in minority occupations—and more specifically, brown-collar occupations—are multiple. They include devaluation of work done by low-status groups (Piore 1979; also see England, Herbert, Kilbourne, Reid, and Megdal 1994; Tomaskovic-Devey 1993), poor market position of labor-intensive occupations (Catanzarite 2002; Cohn 1985), limited political power of low-status workers (Catanzarite 2002), labeling of "brown-collar" occupations (Catanzarite 2000; also see Oppenheimer 1985 on female-dominated fields), and willingness of low-status workers to accept poor wages (Hodge and Hodge 1965; Bonacich 1972). Two commonalities of these arguments are notable: (1) Each hinges on social status, where low-status incumbents make an occupation susceptible to wage suppression; and (2) wage effects are expected to obtain for *all* workers (both high status and low status) in vulnerable fields.

Minority: White Differences in Pay Penalties

Because of greater job and occupational similarity with newcomer Latinos, native minorities are likely to be more susceptible to brown-collar pay penalties than are whites.[2] Catanzarite's (1998) research on Los Angeles demonstrates smaller wage penalties for native white men than for native minority men, and the largest penalties for earlier-immigrant Latinos. Based on these findings, she suggests that groups least segregated from recent-immigrant Latinos are likely to suffer the largest wage penalties.

Data and Methods

The analyses employ the 1990 5% PUMS.[3] The individual-level data are for men who are U.S.-born whites, blacks, or Latinos, or earlier-immigrant Latinos (arrived at least five years ago). The age range is eighteen to sixty-four; individuals must have worked in the prior year and lived in one of eighteen select, ethnically heterogeneous immigrant-receiving metropolitan areas. (Criteria for inclusion of MAs are discussed below.) Multi-level models, discussed in detail further on, predict workers' earnings as a function of individual and occupation-within-MA characteristics.

Level-1 independent variables include: years of education, potential labor force experience (age minus education minus 6), potential experience squared, marital status, the natural logarithm of hours worked per week last year, the natural log of weeks worked, and dummy variables distinguishing native blacks, native Latinos, and earlier-immigrant Latinos (with native whites the omitted category). The dependent variable is the natural logarithm of annual earnings in the prior year.

At level 2, I constructed an occupation-by-MA dataset for each of eighteen metropolitan areas. Areas selected for inclusion are moderate-to-large sized, ethnically heterogeneous MAs where recent-immigrant Latinos comprised at least 1 percent of the local labor force.[4] (A list of the MAs is included as Appendix A.) Recent immigrants are defined as those who came to the United States within the previous five years.

The level-2 dataset is aggregated from information on all individuals at least sixteen years of age who worked in the prior year. It contains data on the demographic composition of occupations within each MA (%recent-immigrant Latino men, %women). It also includes aggregate indicators of skills in the occupation-by-MA (natives' mean education, natives' mean potential labor force experience). Because recent-immigrant Latinos tend to pile up in occupations that are low-skill (Catanzarite 2002), I control for these skill proxies to avoid spurious effects. To further guard against possible spurious effects associated with contingent work, I include controls for proportion of part-time and proportion in the public sector.

I use a set of 119 collapsed occupational categories in order to avoid estimation problems associated with small cell sizes. These are based on the Census 3-digit occupation codes. Occupations that are roughly similar in job content and have few incumbents in the sample populations are collapsed (e.g., various types of engineers are merged, judges are pooled with lawyers, crafts apprentices are combined.) Most of the collapsed categories correspond to subcategories of the Census' detailed classifica-tions. The collapse is also informed by descriptions of occupations in the *Occupational Outlook Handbook* (U.S. Department of Labor, Bureau of Labor Statistics 1980) and the *Dictionary of Occupational Titles* (U.S. Department of Labor, Employment and Training Administration 1977). The 119 occupations are cross-tabulated by the eighteen MAs. Hence, the level-2 dataset has 2142 units (119 *18).

I employ hierarchical modeling (Bryk and Raudenbush, 1992; Wong and Mason, 1991), predicting individuals' annual earnings as a function of both individual-level and occupation-by-MA level characteristics. The key effect of interest is the influence of the proportion of recent-immigrant Latino men (RILM) in the occupation-by-MA on other men's earnings. I investigate the magnitude of pay penalties associated with brown-collar occupations for native-born whites, native blacks, native Latinos, and earlier-immigrant Latinos (estimating the effect of %RILM on the slopes for a set of ethnic/immigrant dummy variables).

Models account for the importance of other local occupation factors on the earnings determination process. Level-2 controls include proportion women, the skill proxies (mean of natives' education, and mean of natives' potential experience), and employment regularity (proportion part-time, proportion public sector) in the occupation-by-MA.

The full models take the following form and are simultaneously estimated.

$$y_{ij} = b_{0j} + b_{1j}\text{Native Black} + b_{2j}\text{Native Latino} + b_{3j}\text{Earlier-Immigrant Latino} + \mathbf{BX} \quad (1)$$

where y_{ij} is the earnings of individual i in occupation-by-MA j; $\mathbf{X}$ is a vector of individual characteristics, and $\mathbf{B}$ is a vector of their coefficients.

The occupation-by-MA models use the intercept, b_{0j}, and the parameters for the ethnic/immigrant dummies, b_{1j}, b_{2j}, and b_{3j}, as dependent variables:

$$B_{0j} = a_{00} + \mathbf{ZO} \quad (2a)$$
$$B_{1j} = a_{1o} + \mathbf{ZO} \quad (2b)$$
$$B_{2j} = a_{2o} + \mathbf{ZO} \quad (2c)$$
$$B_{3j} = a_{3o} + \mathbf{ZO} \quad (2d)$$

where $\mathbf{O}$ is a vector of occupation-by-MA characteristics and $\mathbf{Z}$ is a vector of their coefficients.

All variables are grand-mean centered, except for the binary ethnic/immigrant dummy variables and the term for %recent-immigrant Latino men. Thus, the intercept reflects annual earnings for native whites (the omitted group), with average individual-level characteristics, employed in occupation-MAs with 0% recent-immigrant Latino men, and otherwise average characteristics of occupation-MAs.

Results

Descriptive Investigations

Table 1 provides descriptive statistics at both the individual and MA-occupation levels. The level-1 sample used for analysis is comprised of 575,483 men in the eighteen MAs. The grand mean of annual earnings is $33,642. Education averages 13.2 years (s.d. = 3.3); the mean of potential labor force experience is 18 years (s.d. = 12). Fifty-nine percent of the sample is married. The mean of hours per week is 41; mean weeks worked is 43. The sample is comprised of 70 percent native-born whites, 10 percent native blacks, 8 percent native Latinos, and 12 percent earlier-immigrant Latino men.

Descriptive statistics on the level-2 variables are as follows. The percentage of recent-immigrant Latino men in occupations-by-MA ranges from 0 to 29 percent; the distribution is highly skewed (mean=2 percent, s.d. = 3 percent). The representation of women varies from 0 to 99 percent, with a mean of 44 percent (s.d. = 27 percent). Descriptives on the proxies for occupational skill show: mean natives' education ranges from 9 to 19 years, with a mean of 13 (s.d. = 1.6); mean natives' experience averages 19 years (s.d. = 4, range = 2-36). The share of part-time workers in the occupation-MA averages 20 percent and ranges from 0 to 72 percent; percent public-employed has a mean of 16 percent and a full range of 0-100 percent.

Table 1
Descriptive Statistics at Levels 1 and 2, Ethnically Heterogeneous, Immigrant-Receiving Metropolitan Areas

Variable	Mean	Standard Deviation
Level 1: Individuals		
Log of Annual Earnings	9.98	1.11
Annual Earnings	$33,642	—
Log of Hours per Week	3.71	.11
Hours per Week	40.85	—
Log of Weeks Worked	3.77	.32
Weeks Worked	43.38	—
Years of Education	13.21	3.27
Married	.59	—
Native-born White	.70	—
Native-born Non-Latino Black	.10	—
Native-born Latino	.08	—
Earlier-immigrant Latino	.12	—
Potential Experience	18.37	12.16

N=575,483 Individual Men

	Mean	Standard Deviation	Minimum	Maximum
Level 2: Occupations-within-MAs				
Proportion Recent-Immigrant Latino Men	.02	.03	0	.29
Proportion Female	.44	.27	0	.99
Natives' Mean Education	13.26	1.60	8.7	19.0
Natives' Mean Potential Experience	18.68	3.60	1.8	36.1
Proportion Part-Time	.20	.14	0	.72
Proportion Public Employed	.16	.21	0	1.00

N=2142 Occupations-within-MAs

Labor Force Representation and Occupational Segregation

The labor force representation of recent-immigrant Latino men is extremely low in the MAs under investigation. Figure 1 provides data on median labor force share for the different groups of men. The denominator for these percentages is total (male and female) labor force. Recent-immigrant Latino men

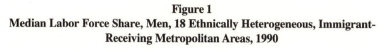

Figure 1
Median Labor Force Share, Men, 18 Ethnically Heterogeneous, Immigrant-Receiving Metropolitan Areas, 1990

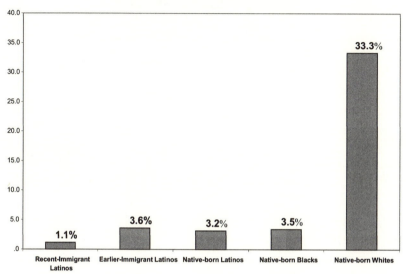

constitute on average, only 1 percent of the local labor force (median = 1.1 percent), with a maximum of 4.6 percent. The median representation of earlier-immigrant Latino men is 3.6 percent, for native-born Latinos is 3.2 percent, for native-born blacks is 3.5 percent, and 33.3 percent for native-born white men.

Despite their very small share of the total labor force, recent-immigrant Latino men are vastly overrepresented in a set of brown-collar occupations in these metropolitan areas, where their representation ranges up to 29 percent of workers in particular local occupations. (Appendix B provides a list of those occupation-MAs with the most pronounced representation of recent-immigrant Latino men.) Many of these fields are upwards of 40 or 50 percent immigrant Latino (combined women and men, earlier- and recent-arrivals), with a maximum of 71 percent. Brown-collar occupations are largely in low-level service, manufacturing, construction, and agriculture.

By aggregate measures, newcomer Latinos are highly segregated from native workers, especially native whites, followed by native blacks, native Latinos, then earlier-immigrant Latinos. The commonly used Duncan and Duncan (1955) Dissimilarity Index (DI) is provided in Figure 2. The DI, averaged across the eighteen cities, has a median of 69 for native whites, 57 for native blacks, 52 for native Latinos, and only 33 for earlier-immigrant Latinos, indicating severe segregation of newcomer Latino men from native-born workers and lower, but still substantial, segregation from earlier-immigrant co-ethnics.[5]

Figure 2
Occupational Segregation from Recent-Immigrant Latino Men,
Median Duncan & Duncan Index, Ethnically Heterogeneous
Immigrant-Receiving Metropolitan Areas, 1990

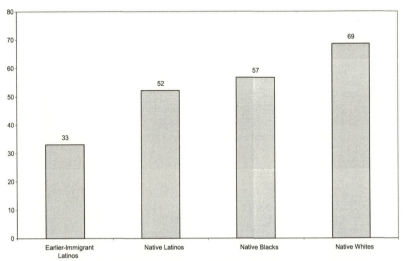

0=complete integration 100=complete segregation

Multi-Level Models

A baseline model, with no variables, but with an intercept that varies by MA-occupation, provides information on the variance of earnings within vs. between level-2 units. This analysis yields an intraclass correlation coefficient of .26, indicating that 26 percent of the variance in earnings is between occupation-MAs. The contextual effects, included in the model presented in Table 2, explain 89 percent of this between-context variation.

Ethnic/Immigrant Differences in Pay Penalties

The multi-level models provide evidence that men experience a substantial brown-collar wage penalty. That is, native-born white, black, and Latino men and earlier-immigrant Latino men employed in brown-collar fields earn less than other workers with similar labor force characteristics and in comparable occupations-within-MAs. Inclusion of the level-2 control variables indicates that brown-collar occupations pay less than other fields similar in terms of %female, employment regularity, and average skills.[6]

How do penalties differ for the various ethnic/immigrant groups? Table 2 provides level-2 results from the multi-level model predicting the level-1 intercept and the slopes on the ethnic/immigrant dummy variables as a function of occupation-by-MA characteristics.

Table 2
Occupation-by-MA Level Effects on Individual-Level Coefficients from Between-Context Hierarchical Linear Model Regression

Independent Variables: Occupation-Level Effects	Dependent Variables			
	Intercept	Native Black Slope	Native Latino Slope	Earlier-Imm Latino Slope
Intercept	10.046 *** (.005)	-.133 *** (.005)	-.080 *** (.004)	-.142 *** (.005)
Proportion Recent-Immigrant Latino Men	-.208 * (.119)	-.260 * (.138)	-.101 (.103)	-.768 *** (.101)
Proportion Female	-.122 *** (.018)	.003 (.020)	-.045 * (.019)	-.083 *** (.021)
Natives' Mean Education	.082 *** (.003)	-.003 (.004)	-.005 (.003)	-.014 ** (.004)
Natives' Mean Potential Experience	.004 ** (.001)	-.005 ** (.001)	-.004 ** (.001)	-.007 *** (.001)
Proportion Public Employed	-.190 *** (.027)	.203 *** (.021)	.117 *** (.018)	.225 *** (.026)
Proportion Part-Time	-.755 *** (.042)	.158 *** (.042)	.140 *** (.041)	.266 *** (.045)

*p < .05; ** p < .01; *** p < .001, one-tailed

Results in Table 2 show a negative effect of %RILM on the intercept (-.208, s.e. = .119, p<.05), and negative effects on the parameters for the native black dummy variable (-.260, s.e. = .138, p<.05) and the earlier-immigrant Latino men dummy (-.760, s.e.= .101, p>.001). The cross-level interaction for native Latinos does not reach statistical significance (-.101, s.e. = .103). The findings provide evidence that brown-collar wage penalties are substantially larger for earlier-immigrant Latino men and African American men than for native white men. By contrast, the penalty for native Latinos does not appear to differ significantly from that for native whites. An alternative model, with native blacks as the omitted category, showed no statistically significant difference in penalties for native Latinos vs. native blacks. I interpret these findings cautiously and suggest that further research is warranted to investigate penalties for native Latinos vs. other groups. The results may be due in part to the relatively small numbers of native minority groups in some occupation-MA cells, and particularly, the smaller numbers of native Latinos than other minority groups in most of the metropolitan areas under investigation.

For heuristic purposes, divergent brown-collar penalties for the four ethnic/immigrant groups are depicted graphically in Figure 3, at the mean of earnings; this corresponds roughly to penalties for the average worker.[7] While brown-collar wage penalties for whites are substantial (and statistically significant), they are much smaller than are penalties for other groups. Earlier-immigrant Latinos clearly suffer the largest wage discount in brown-collar fields, followed by native blacks. For example, at 15 percent RILM, earlier-immigrant Latino men earn $4584 less per year than their counterparts in other, similar occupations, and native blacks earn $2280 less than otherwise comparable

Figure 3
Wage Penalties in Brown-Collar Occupations-in-MAs, for "Average"[a] Male

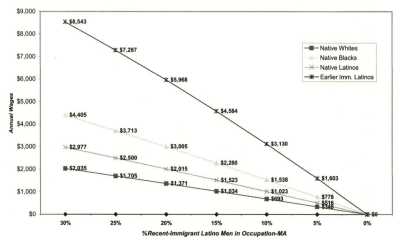

a. Computed at the mean of annual earnings, which is $33,642.

workers. For whites, by contrast, the annual penalty is only $1034; for native Latinos it is $1523.[8] These are substantial wage discounts, given that annual earnings averaged $33,642 in 1989. Thus, earlier-immigrant Latinos, followed by native-born blacks, apparently bear the brunt of wage penalties in brown-collar occupations. Recall that minorities, particularly earlier-immigrant co-ethnics, are more likely to be in brown-collar occupations than are whites, and within occupations they are more likely to be employed in similar jobs.

Discussion

The analyses demonstrate that, across eighteen, ethnically heterogeneous immigrant-receiving local labor markets, employment in brown-collar occupations carries substantial wage disadvantages for both U.S.-born workers and earlier-immigrant Latinos. Relevant to the immigrant-native competition debate, brown-collar wage disadvantages are one avenue by which immigrant employment appears to adversely influence natives' pay. Importantly, among natives, blacks appear to suffer disproportionately from employment in brown-collar jobs: they incur significantly larger penalties than do whites.[9] Further, the findings demonstrate far higher brown-collar wage penalties for earlier-immigrant co-ethnics than for native workers.

The larger wage discounts for earlier-immigrant Latinos and native blacks than for native white men, *ceteris paribus*, are consistent with past research showing that whites are buffered from the most severe pay penalties (Catanzarite 1998). More generally, the results support the notion that minority workers are more likely than whites to bear negative consequences of immigration (also see Altonji and Card 1991; Borjas 1998; Grossman 1982; Smith and Edmonston 1997). Earlier-immigrant Latinos and blacks experience greater competition with recent-immigrant Latinos than do whites. Not only do they suffer larger pay penalties, but they are also more likely than whites to be located in brown-collar fields. Further, whites are more likely than minorities to benefit directly from immigrant labor, as they are more often owners of capital and employers of personal service workers.

Of course, the findings do not support a sweeping conclusion that immigrant employment is generally harmful to native workers or to native minorities. Many brown-collar fields thrive precisely because of the availability of immigrant labor. For example, if cheap immigrant labor were not abundant, many labor-intensive manufacturing operations would relocate overseas, and private household cleaning and gardening occupations would be performed by family members. (See Milkman, Reese and Roth 1998, on the positive relationship between the incidence of domestic service employment and cities' immigrant presence.) Further, the population growth associated with immigration creates a broad range of job opportunities for native-born workers, and thus provides many potential avenues for employment outside of brown-collar fields.

The findings here do demonstrate one important mechanism by which less-skilled immigration appears to lower natives' pay. Native-born men employed in brown-collar occupations suffer a substantial wage discount relative to their counterparts in other fields without overrepresentations of recent-immigrant Latinos. Immigration clearly does not affect all workers equally. Native blacks suffer significantly larger pay losses than do native whites. Undoubtedly, some disadvantaged natives move out of brown-collar occupations. To the degree that these shifts imply occupational mobility into better positions, such workers complement immigrants and benefit from their influx. However, others may be pushed out of the labor force entirely if employers prefer newcomer Latinos in particular jobs, and thus prompt occupational succession, where immigrants flood fields that in the past represented strongholds of other less-skilled workers.

Conclusions

The analysis of occupation-related wage penalties across multiple labor markets contributes to knowledge and understanding of the effects of immigration on the wages of U.S.-born minority and white workers, as well as impacts on earlier-immigrant Latino workers and the marginal economic position of Latino immigrants. Investigation of pay penalties for different ethnic/immigrant groups at the level of local occupations serves to disentangle consequences of immigration, providing evidence of substantial divergence in penalties for different groups of workers.

Note that because wage penalties for whites are significantly smaller than those for African Americans, (and whites constitute the sizeable majority of workers), aggregate measures combining effects for these groups will understate pay penalties in general, and the impact of immigration on natives' wages, in particular. This will be problematic for understanding the effects of less-skilled immigration on wages not just for native minorities, but also for earlier-immigrant co-ethnics.

While the focus of these analyses is largely on U.S. natives, it is earlier-immigrant Latinos who take the hardest hit. They suffer the largest pay penalties. They are *far* more likely to be employed in brown-collar fields than are natives. And, they are least segregated from newcomers across occupations, which suggests they also are less- segregated at the level of jobs (occupations-within-establishments). Thus, the pronounced wage penalties in brown-collar fields indicate not only (1) that immigration lowers wages for particular native workers, but also (2) that, in the absence of proactive policy, wage gains for immigrant Latinos—both recent arrivals and long-term residents—will remain elusive. Pronounced wage penalties in brown-collar fields imply that policies to improve immigrants' wages must move beyond prescriptions for enhancing immigrants' human capital and attend to structural features of labor markets. Catanzarite and Aguilera's (2002) study of pay penalties associated with Latino *jobsite* composition also support this interpretation. In their analyses, legalized immigrant Latinos working at predominantly Latino jobsites incurred penalties equivalent to seven years of education (their median level).

On their face, the findings provide support for the popular perception that native blacks suffer disproportionately from immigration. Indeed, native blacks experience larger wage discounts than do native whites. However, the lack of a statistically significant difference between native Latinos' and native whites' penalties should not be over-interpreted, particularly in light of the finding that native Latinos' penalties also did not differ significantly from those for native blacks. I have suggested that these findings may be an artifact of small sample sizes for native-born Latino men (who are far outnumbered by immigrant co-ethnics in the labor force), and that further research is warranted before drawing definitive conclusions regarding brown-collar wage discounts for this group.

The literature suggests that wage penalties are caused by: the devaluation of work performed by low-status groups; the poor market position of labor-intensive occupations; the limited political power of low-status workers; and the willingness of low-status workers to accept poor wages. In other words, low-status incumbents—and not immigration in and of itself—make an occupation susceptible to wage suppression. If, as I argue, wage suppression is fundamentally tied to low status and power, then policy to subvert occupational pay dynamics should address the problem at its root, and policies that further marginalize newcomers (e.g., a sub-minimum wage) should be assiduously avoided for the benefit of both immigrants *and* natives. This suggests, somewhat paradoxically, that policies aimed at raising the social status of immigrants (e.g., extending worker protections, providing an amnesty for the unauthorized) would protect *native* workers, particularly the less- skilled and minorities, from immigrant competition and brown-collar wage penalties.[10] A similar recognition prompted the AFL-CIO's recent, unprecedented call for a new immigrant amnesty. More generally, perhaps this fundamental recognition—that protection of weaker groups benefits other disadvantaged groups—is what drives the greater sympathy for immigrants among native minorities than among native whites.

Notes

1. Catanzarite's (2000) original usage of the term "brown-collar" occupations refers to those with a large share of immigrant Latinos. Occupations with a large share of recent-immigrant Latino men constitute a subset of the larger group of brown-collar fields and are consonant with the original usage of the term, as newcomer Latinos tend to find employment in the same fields as their co-ethnic predecessors.
2. "Job" refers to occupations-within-firms. These are expected to be more segregated than are the more aggregated occupation categories. For example, recent-immigrant Latinos make up a large share of construction laborers; however, they are not randomly distributed across firms, but tend to work for smaller contractors. Other workers who are in the same firms as newcomer Latinos are likely to suffer larger pay penalties than employees of firms where native-born workers predominate.

3. Data are weighted by the Census weighting field divided by the mean weight; thus, the sample size is still 5 percent of the population.
4. In preliminary analyses with the 1/1000 Census PUMS, I identified metropolitan areas for potential inclusion based on population size and the labor force share of recent-immigrant Latinos. Casting a broad net, I included areas with a minimum of 100,000 workers and 1 percent recent-immigrant Latinos. After compiling the 5 percent data on these candidate MAs, I eliminated several that had less than 1 percent recent-immigrant Latinos in this larger dataset. After examining occupation cell-sizes, I further eliminated relatively small MAs and those with highly skewed occupational distributions (e.g., the heavily agricultural labor market of Brownsville-Harlingen-San Benito). This netted thirty-eight MAs. I then made a further cut to eighteen ethnically heterogeneous MAs. These met the criterion of at least 400 native white men, native black men, native Latino men, and earlier-immigrant Latino men with nonzero earnings, in order to allow comparisons of wage penalties for these groups.
5. The Association Index (Charles and Grusky 1995) also shows a similar pattern of pronounced segregation from native workers and far less from earlier-immigrant Latinos.
6. Recall that the skill proxies are based on average education and experience data for native workers; thus, they are unaffected by the relatively low average human capital of newcomer Latinos.
7. The effects are multiplicative; thus, penalties vary for workers at different points of the wage distribution (i.e., with divergent individual and occupational characteristics). Note also that the graph is truncated at 30 percent because no occupation has more than 29% RILM.
8. At 25% RILM, these penalties are $7287 for earlier-immigrant Latinos, $3713 for native blacks, $2500 for native Latinos, and $1705 for native whites.
9. The findings regarding native Latinos are less conclusive. While native Latino men do suffer substantial brown-collar pay penalties, the wage discounts for this group are not significantly different from those for native whites or native blacks.
10. Native workers would also be protected from immigration-related wage suppression by absolute segregation, where *no* native-born workers would be employed in brown-collar occupations, and thus natives would be completely buffered from pay penalties in those fields. Unfortunately, this is a possible scenario, particularly in the current political climate. (Indeed, if Los Angeles provides a window on the future, it moved towards greater [but not absolute] segregation from 1980-90 [Catanzarite 2000], and by 1990, whites no longer experienced any pay penalty in brown-collar occupations [Catanzarite 1998].)

References

Altonji, Joseph G. and David Card. 1991. "The Effects of Immigration on the Labor Market Outcomes of Less-Skilled Natives." Pp. 201-234 in *Immigration, Trade and the Labor Market*, edited by John Abowd and Richard Freeman. Chicago, University of Chicago Press.

Bonacich, Edna. 1972. "A Theory of Ethnic Antagonism: The Split Labor Market." *American Sociological Review* 37: 547-59.

Borjas, George J. 1999. *Heaven's Door: Immigration Policy and the American Economy*. Princeton, New Jersey: Princeton University Press.

Bryk, Anthony S. and Stephen W. Raudenbush. 1992. *Hierarchical Linear Models*. Newbury Park, California: Sage Publications.

Butcher, Kristin F. 1998. "An Investigation of the Effect of Immigration on the Labor-Market Outcomes of African Americans." Pp. 149-181 in *Help or Hindrance? The Economic Implications of Immigration for African Americans*, edited by Daniel S. Hamermesh and Frank D. Bean. New York: Russell Sage.

Catanzarite, Lisa. 2003b. "Wage Penalties in *Brown-Collar* Occupations Across Metropolitan Labor Markets." Paper presented at the Annual Meeting of the American Sociological Association, August 2003. Revised September 2003.

_____. 2003a. "Race-Gender Composition and Occupational Pay Degradation." *Social Problems* 50, 1 (February): 14-37.

_____. 2002. "The Dynamics of Segregation and Earnings in *Brown-Collar* Occupations." *Work and Occupations* 29, 3 (August): 300-45.

_____. 2000. "Brown-Collar Jobs: Occupational Segregation and the Earnings of Recent-Immigrant Latinos." *Sociological Perspectives* 43, 1 (March): 45-75.

_____. 1998. "Immigrant Latino Representation and Earnings Penalties in Occupations." *Research in Social Stratification and Mobility* 16: 147-79.

Catanzarite, Lisa and Michael B. Aguilera. 2002. "Working with Co-Ethnics: Earnings Penalties for Latino Immigrants at Latino Jobsites." *Social Forces* 49, 1 (February): 101-27.

Charles, Maria and David Grusky. 1995. "Models for Describing the Underlying Structure of Sex Segregation." *American Journal of Sociology* 100 (4): 931-71.

Cohen, Philip N. and Matt L. Huffman. 2003. "Racial Wage Inequality: Job Segregation and Devaluation across U.S. Labor Markets." Unpublished manuscript. University of California, Irvine.

Cohn, Samuel. 1985. *The Process of Occupational Sex-Typing: The Feminization of Clerical Labor in Great Britain*. Philadelphia: Temple University Press.

Duncan, Otis Dudley and Beverly Duncan. 1955. "A Methodological Analysis of Segregation Indexes." *American Sociological Review* 20: 210-217.

England, Paula, Melissa S. Herbert, Barbara Stanek Kilbourne, Lori L. Reid, and Lori McCreary Megdal. 1994. "The Gendered Valuation of Occupations and Skills: Earnings in 1980 Census Occupations." *Social Forces* 73 (1): 65-99.

Grossman, Jean Baldwin. 1982. "The Substitutability of Natives and Immigrants in Production." *Review of Economics and Statistics* 64 (4): 596-603.

Hodge, Robert W. and Patricia Hodge. 1965. "Occupational Assimilation as a Competitive Process." *American Journal of Sociology* 61 (3): 249-64.

Howell, David R. and Elizabeth J. Mueller. 2000. "Immigration and Native-Born Male Earnings: A Jobs-Level Analysis of the New York City Metropolitan Area Labour Market, 1980-90." *Journal of Ethnic and Migration Studies* 26 (3): 469-93.

Johnson, George E. 1998. "The Impact of Immigration on Income Distribution Among Minorities." Pp. 17-50 in *Help or Hindrance? The Economic Implications of Immigration for African Americans*, edited by Daniel S. Hamermesh and Frank D. Bean. New York: Russell Sage.

Kmec, Julie A. 2003. "Minority Job Concentration and Wages." *Social Problems* 50, 1 (February): 38-59.

Milkman, Ruth, Ellen Reese, and Bonita Roth. 1998. "The Macrosociology of Paid Domestic Labor." *Work and Occupations* 25 (4): 483-510.

Ong, Paul and Abel Valenzuela Jr. 1996. The Labor Market: Immigrant Effects and Racial Disparities." In *Ethnic Los Angeles*, edited by Roger Waldinger and Mehdi Bozorgmehr. New York: Russell Sage.

Oppenheimer, Valerie Kincade. 1985. "The Sex-Labeling of Jobs." *Industrial Relations* 7 (May): 21934.

Ortiz, Vilma 1996. "The Mexican-Origin Population: Permanent Working Class or Emerging Middle Class?" In *Ethnic Los Angeles*, edited by Roger Waldinger and Mehdi Bozorgmehr. New York: Russell Sage.

Parcel, Toby. 1989. "Comparable Worth, Occupational Labor Markets, and Occupational Earnings: Results from the 1980 Census." In *Pay Equity: Empirical Issues*, edited by Robert T. Michael, Heidi I. Hartmann, and Brigid O'Farrell. Washington, D.C.: National Academy Press.

Piore, Michael. 1979. *Birds of Passage: Migrant Labor and Industrial Societies*. Cambridge: Cambridge University Press.

Reid, Lori. 1998. "Devaluing Women and Minorities: The Effects of Race/Ethnic and Sex Composition of Occupations on Wage Levels." *Work and Occupations* 25, 4 (November): 511-36.

Reimers, Cordelia W. 1998. "Unskilled Immigration and Changes in the Wage Distributions of Black, Mexican American, and Non-Hispanic White Male Dropouts." Pp. 107-148 in *Help or Hindrance? The Economic Implications of Immigration for African Americans*, edited by Daniel S. Hamermesh and Frank D. Bean. New York: Russell Sage.

Rosenfeld, Michael J. and Marta Tienda. 1999. "Mexican Immigration, Occupational Niches, and Labor-Market Competition: Evidence from Los Angeles, Chicago, and Atlanta, 1970 to 1990." Pp. 64-105 in *Immigration and Opportunity: Race, Ethnicity, and Employment in the United States*, edited by Frank D. Bean and Stephanie Bell-Rose. New York: Russell Sage.

Smith, James P. and Barry Edmonston, eds. 1997. *The New Americans: Economic, Demographic, and Fiscal Effects of Immigration*. Washington, D.C.: National Academy Press.

Sorenson, Elaine. 1989. "Measuring the Effect of Occupational Sex and Race Composition on Earnings." In *Pay Equity: Empirical Issues*, edited by Robert T. Michael, Heidi I. Hartmann, and Brigid O'Farrell. Washington, D.C.: National Academy Press.

Tienda, Marta. 1998. "Immigration and Native Minority Workers: Is There Bad News After All?" Pp. 345-52 in *Help or Hindrance? The Economic Implications of Immigration for African Americans*, edited by Daniel S. Hamermesh and Frank D. Bean. New York: Russell Sage.

Tomaskovic-Devey, Donald. 1993. *Gender and Racial Inequality at Work: The Sources and Consequences of Job Segregation*. Ithaca: ILR Press.

Waldinger, Roger. 1999. "Network, Bureaucracy, and Exclusion: Recruitment and Selection in an Immigrant Metropolis." Pp. 228-59 in *Immigration and Opportunity: Race, Ethnicity, and Employment in the United States*, edited by Frank D. Bean and Stephanie Bell-Rose. New York: Russell Sage.

Waters, Mary C. 1999. "West Indians and African Americans at Work: Structural Differences and Cultural Stereotypes." Pp. 194-227 in *Immigration and Opportunity: Race, Ethnicity, and Employment in the United States*, edited by Frank D. Bean and Stephanie Bell-Rose. New York: Russell Sage.

Wilson, Franklin D. 1999. "Ethnic Concentrations and Labor Market Opportunities." Pp. 106-40 in *Immigration and Opportunity: Race, Ethnicity, and Employment in the United States*, edited by Frank D. Bean and Stephanie Bell-Rose. New York: Russell Sage.

Wong, George Y. and William M. Mason. 1991. "Contextually Specific Effects and Other Generalizations of the Hierarchical Linear Model for Comparative Analysis." In *Journal of the American Statistical Association* 86, 414 (June): 487-503.

Appendix A

Ethnically Heterogeneous, Immigrant-Receiving Metropolitan Areas

Anaheim-Santa Ana

Austin-San Marcos

Chicago

Dallas

Houston

Los Angeles-Long Beach

Miami

Nassau-Suffolk

New York City

Oakland

Phoenix-Mesa

Riverside-San Bernardino

San Antonio

San Diego

San Francisco

San Jose

Tampa-St.Petersberg-Clearwater

Washington (DC)

Appendix B

Top 15 Brown-Collar Occupations-in-Metropolitan Areas (Ranked by Over-Representation of Recent-Immigrant Latino Men)

Occupation-	by-MA	% Recent-Immigrant Latino Men
Waiters' assistants	Ananeim - Sta. Ana	29.3
Gardeners & groundskeepers	Ananeim - Sta. Ana	29.2
Cooks	Ananeim - Sta. Ana	23.8
Roofers, brick,tile,concrete, paving,drilling,extracting	Miami	22.5
Construction Laborers	Los Angeles - Long Beach	20.7
Misc. handlers,helpers, equip cleaners,garage, vehicle washers	Ananeim - Sta. Ana	19.3
Construction Laborers	Ananeim - Sta. Ana	19.1
Farmworkers & other farming, forestry,fishing	Ananeim - Sta. Ana	18.7
Waiters' assistants	Los Angeles - Long Beach	18.2
Painters, construction & maintenance	Los Angeles - Long Beach	17.9
Roofers, brick,tile,concrete, paving,drilling,extracting	Ananeim - Sta. Ana	17.6
Waiters' assistants	New York City	16.7
Gardeners & groundskeepers	San Diego	16.6
Gardeners & groundskeepers	Los Angeles - Long Beach	16.1
Waiters' assistants	Chicago	15.6

4

Immigration and the Employment of African American Workers

Hannes Johannsson and Steven Shulman

Introduction

It is now generally accepted that immigration has negative economic consequences for low-wage workers in general and for African Americans in particular. In contrast to an earlier generation of studies that found few effects of immigration on native workers, more recent evidence shows that sustained, large-scale immigration concentrated in the low-wage sector of the labor market has reduced earnings and employment for the workers who most directly compete with immigrants. George Borjas, for example, used to believe that economic impact of immigration on African American earnings was negligible (Borjas 1990: 87); more recently he has concluded that immigration lowers the aggregate annual earnings of African Americans by between $2.4 billion and $12.3 billion, depending upon the assumptions used in the calculation (Borjas 1998: 65). While some scholars believe that figures such as these demonstrate that the effects of immigration on African Americans are "small" (Bean and Stevens, 2003: 212), others, such as Borjas, are less sanguine about the size of the impact and its regressive effects on ethnic inequality.

The judgment about the effects of immigration on African Americans is complicated by a variety of measurement issues, including the use of decennial census data that tends to mask the short-term effects of immigration, the out-migration of native workers from the cities most impacted by immigration, and labor supply adjustments by native workers. All of these considerations reduce the measured impact of immigration (Johannsson, Weiler, and Shulman 2003). The judgment about immigration is also complicated by the fact that immigration creates benefits as well as costs that accrue to different groups of natives. Immigration increases the earnings of employers and high-wage workers while it lowers the earnings of low-wage workers. Immigration thus has increased income inequality, by some estimates quite substantially (Borjas, Freeman, and Katz 1997; Johannsson and Weiler 2005); but since there are winners as well as losers, the net effect of immigration on native earnings can be positive even though its impact on particular groups is negative. Finally, the judgment about immigration is complicated by political and moral issues that inevitably affect the interpretation of research results. Those who believe that "a nation of immigrants" can only restrict immigration if it is willing to live in hypocrisy and to "blame the victim" for problems that arise elsewhere tend to minimize the negative effects of immigration on native workers. Those who believe that the centrality of the African American experience speaks against the identification of the United States as a "nation of immigrants," and that our primary ethical obligation is to our fellow citizens who are still suffering the effects of historical racism, tend to emphasize the negative effects of immigration on native workers.Accordingly, it comes as no surprise that there is little consensus about the consequences of immigration or the desired direction for immigration reform.

This chapter addresses both the more narrow empirical issues and the broader interpretative issues about immigration. We focus on one possible response to immigration by native workers, labor force withdrawal. Labor force withdrawal is important in its own right since it directly reflects an economic loss and it weakens the attachment of low-wage native workers to the labor market. But it is also important because it affects the measurement of the economic consequences of immigration. When native workers respond to immigration by dropping out of the labor force, they reduce its measured impact for two reasons. First, dropouts are subtracted out from both the numerator and the denominator of the unemployment rate. Since the reduction in the numerator is proportionately greater than the reduction in the denominator, labor force withdrawals perversely tend to lower the unemployment rate. Second, the workers who withdraw are the lowest-wage native workers who most directly compete with immigrants. Consequently, the average wage of the native workers who remain in the labor force is increased by sample selection effects. Labor force withdrawal as a response to immigration thus provides another reason for the underestimation of the negative consequences of immigration in previous studies.

This chapter presents econometric evidence showing that immigration reduces the labor force participation of both African American and European American workers. Our findings indicate that the participation responses to immigration are much larger than previously believed, which we speculate is due to the accumulated effect of sustained, large immigrant inflows. We also show generally insignificant effects of immigration on unemployment, which supports the contention that participation effects tend to conceal the true impact of immigration on employment. We then explain the results and discuss their implications for immigration policy. We show that the arguments that immigration has little effect on native workers are misplaced because they ignore its size, its skill and geographic concentrations, and the interconnected nature of labor markets that creates generalized effects from ethnic niches. We argue in favor of both targeted programs for workers who are adversely affected by immigration as well as for greater restrictions on immigration. Our perspective, justified in the concluding section of the chapter, is that immigration policy should be evaluated like other public policies, that is, in terms of America's historical obligation to reduce ethnic inequality and improve the life circumstances of African Americans.

Data and Model

To examine the impact of immigration on African American employment, we use data from the CPS Basic Monthly Survey, pooled over 1998-2002 to maximize sample size. The logistic equations are of the following form:

$$\text{EMP} = \alpha_1 + \alpha_2(\text{HK}) + \alpha_3(\text{REG}_i) + \alpha_4(\text{TIME}) + \alpha_5(\text{IMFR}_i) + \varepsilon$$

where EMP is a binary variable indicating either labor force status or unemployment status at the time of the survey; HK is a vector of human capital variables, including sex, marital status, age, and education; REG is a vector of regional dummies; TIME is a vector of time dummies; IMFR is the fraction of immigrants in the labor force, where immigrants are defined as persons who entered the United States after 1986 to allow for assimilation; and : is the error term (see Table 1 for variable definitions). This is a fairly typical specification in the econometric literature on immigration (e.g., Borjas, Freeman, and Katz 1997). Units of observation are individuals except for TIME, REG, and IMFR. The i subscript on REG and IMFR refers to metropolitan statistical areas, tagged to each individual's MSA of residence and aggregated up from the CPS data on individuals. Observations are restricted to the 41,018 European Americans and 7,585 African American individuals who live in the seventy MSAs with the largest population share of immigrants. The hypothesis that immigration lowers labor force participation and increases unemployment for native workers is supported if α_5 is negative and significant in the participation equations, and positive and significant in the unemployment equations.

Separate equations are run for African Americans and European Americans to explore ethnic differences in the impact of immigration. The regional dummies provide a general control for regionally specific factors that affect employment (e.g., industrial mix), and the time dummies provide a general control for factors that affect employment propensities that vary over time. The human capital variables control for the individual characteristics that affect employment propensities. Consequently, the results on the IMFR focus variable are

Table 1
Variable Definitions

IMFR	Fraction of MSA population consisting of foreign-born persons who arrived in the United States after 1986.
AGE	Age of individual (sample restricted to persons between 16 and 64 years old)
AGESQ	AGE*AGE
MARRIED	1 if individual has ever been married, 0 otherwise
FEMALE	1 if individual is female, 0 otherwise
HSGRAD	1 if individual is a high school graduate, 0 otherwise
SOMECOL	1 if individual has completed some college, 0 otherwise
COLGRAD	1 if individual has a bachelors degree or more, 0 otherwise
NORTHEAST	1 if Northeast, 0 otherwise
MIDWEST	1 if Midwest, 0 otherwise
SOUTH	1 if South, 0 otherwise
1998	1 if data year is 1998, 0 otherwise
1999	1 if data year is 1999, 0 otherwise
2000	1 if data year is 2000, 0 otherwise
2001	1 if data year is 2001, 0 otherwise

Notes
1. "High school dropout" is the omitted education dummy.
2. "West" is the omitted regional dummy.
3. "2002" is the omitted time dummy.

net of a wide range of factors that can affect labor force participation and unemployment. Results are presented in Tables 2 and 3.

Results

IMFR is the focus variable. Its coefficient is significant and negative in the labor force participation equations for both African Americans and European Americans. However, the IMFR coefficient is insignificant in the unemployment equations. The major employment effect of immigration is to reduce labor force participation. The effect on unemployment is weaker, a finding consistent with that of Bean, Van Hook, and Fossett (1999). This relationship is not only a matter of simple arithmetic. The workers who are most likely to drop out of the labor force are the ones who are least attached to it in the first place. Their skills are the weakest, and their ability to find a new job is corre-

Table 2
Logistic Regression Results
Dependent Variable: Labor Force Participation

Independent Variable	African American		European American	
	Coefficient	Standard Error	Coefficient	Standard Error
IMFR	-1.120497[b]	.4441693	-1.159072[a]	.2140178
AGE	.2101389[a]	.0139201	.2168647[a]	.0073648
AGESQ	-.002869[a]	.0001808	-.0028844[a]	.0000912
MARRIED	.3853639[a]	.0809674	-.142155[a]	.0358158
FEMALE	-.201963[a]	.0626726	-.6539334[a]	.0302673
HSGRAD	1.047987[a]	.0805518	.8947948[a]	.0471507
SOMECOL	1.172306[a]	.0905758	.9283649[a]	.0494687
COLGRAD	1.832645[a]	.1079398	1.491754[a]	.0509036
1998	-.0289389	.0932629	-.0301719	.0458567
1999	.0626204	.0953067	-.0311681	.0470204
2000	.1242172	.0965235	-.0000194	.047176
2001	.1549825[c]	.091318	-.051453	.0433299
NORTHEAST	-.0590793	.1024976	-.1996233[a]	.0379674
MIDWEST	.0425224	.1130499	.0683453	.0446936
SOUTH	.3975787[a]	.0996123	-.0632482	.0403476
CONSTANT	-3.568364[a]	.2575642	-2.546249[a]	.1230399

Notes
1. Superscript a = significant within 1%.
2. Superscript b = significant within 5%.
3. Superscript c = significant within 10%.

spondingly the lowest. If they remained in the labor force, they would be unemployed longer than other workers. Consequently, they would boost measured unemployment. The fact that they instead drop out of the labor force lowers measured unemployment, but this illustrates rather than contradicts the negative impact of immigration on the employment of native workers.

The size of the participation effect can be shown by re-calculating the results as elasticities, shown in Table 4. A 10 percent increase in the share of immigrants in the population decreases the labor force participation of European Americans by 2.35 percent and decreases the labor force participation of African Americans by 3.59 percent. These figures are approximately ten times as large as those found in an earlier generation of studies (Borjas 1990: 92; Bean and Stevens 2003: 207), suggesting that continued large immigrant inflows are having a cumulated effect. If the impact of immigration on employment and earnings rises as IMFR rises, studies that use more recent data would show larger effects. In addition, our data covers a five-year period while some of the earlier studies compared decennial census data for a ten-year interval. The employment effects of immigration will be greater in the short-run since it will take time for native workers to adjust to their effects.

Table 3
Logistic Regression Results
Dependent Variable: Unemployment

Independent Variable	African American		European American	
	Coefficient	Standard Error	Coefficient	Standard Error
IMFR	-.5010445	.7644283	.1822022	.4737928
AGE	.1010505[a]	.0291344	.052911[a]	.0172451
AGESQ	-.0017988[a]	.0004104	-.0007921[a]	.0002268
MARRIED	-.4846296[a]	.155976	-.7710831[a]	.0827934
FEMALE	-.1697042	.106865	-.066849	.0658467
HSGRAD	.0560855	.1553136	-.0578091	.1073092
SOMECOL	-.2507315	.1708864	-.3703241[a]	.1093058
COLGRAD	-.6584838[a]	.2161858	-.5699068[a]	.1170867
1998	-.1955579	.1655028	-.3222921[a]	.0957658
1999	-.0960661	.1664526	-.3283424[a]	.1033116
2000	-.3174969[c]	.1714094	-.4589002[a]	.1039842
2001	-.1590138	.1567036	-.4068969[a]	.0932164
NORTHEAST	.0768266	.1784559	-.1871533[b]	.081965
MIDWEST	-.1367623	.2001565	-.2093303[b]	.0961862
SOUTH	-.1651588	.1777593	-.2761663[a]	.089525
CONSTANT	-3.138603[a]	.4913356	-3.122911[a]	.271789

Notes
1. Superscript a = significant within 1%.
2. Superscript b = significant within 5%.
3. Superscript c = significant within 10%.

The participation elasticities represent a sizeable impact of immigration on labor supply, particularly since they cover the entire population. If they were restricted to low-skill workers, they would certainly be higher (Johannson, Weiler, and Shulman 2003). If we only examined the most immigrant-dense cities, they would also be expected to be larger (ibid.). In addition, the employment impact of immigration in immigrant-dense cities is depressed by the significant out-migration of native workers who face the most job competition from immigrants (Frey and Liaw 1998). It is also worth noting that the absolute value of the IMFR elasticity is larger than the elasticity of any of the other variables except for COLGRAD in the European American equation and SOMECOL and COLGRAD in the African American equations. In other words, reducing immigration would have a bigger impact on the employment of high school dropouts than increasing their high school completion or their likelihood of marriage. Even economic growth can have a relatively small employment elasticity, as the recent "jobless recovery" attests. Our interpretation is that immigration causes a relatively large drop in the labor force participation

Table 4
Selected Labor Force Participation Elasticities

	African American	European American
IMFR	-.3587854	-.2351559
AGE	.0672869	.0439981
MARRIED	.1233943	-.0288408
FEMALE	-.0646689	-.1326719
HSGRAD	.3355673	.1815385
SOMECOL	.3753745	.1883493
COLGRAD	.5868165	.3026513

Note: 1. All variables are within conventional significance levels. See Table 2.

of native workers, particularly low-skill native workers. Because African American workers are concentrated in the low-wage sector of the labor market, the impact of immigration on them is especially acute, as illustrated by the relative size of their IMFR elasticity (over 50 percent higher for African Americans than for European Americans). Our findings show that persistent, large-scale immigration has damaged the employment prospects of urban workers along with other labor market shifts, such as technological change, the suburbanization of job growth, import competition, and capital flight.

Aside from its intrinsic importance, the finding that immigration depresses the employment prospects of both African American and European American workers provides another explanation for the weak results found by some studies of the impact of immigration on earnings (Borjas 1990: 87). Immigration results in labor supply adjustments as the workers most directly affected by it withdraw from the labor force, search for new jobs, or move. Because these workers are most likely to have low earnings, their movement out of the pool of employed persons raises the measured average earnings of those workers who remain (Johannson, Weiler, and Shulman 2003). This is akin to the argument made thirty years ago by James Heckman and Richard Butler (1977) that the earnings of minority workers were artificially inflated when welfare payments induced the lowest wage workers to drop out of the labor force. Immigration similarly causes an upward bias in the measured earnings of native workers who remain employed by creating incentives for low-wage native workers to leave the labor force. Thus, the employment effects of immigration both directly depress economic outcomes for native workers and indirectly conceal their own effects. The surprise is not that some studies have found weak effects, but that so many other studies have found strong effects.

The results on the control variables are generally as expected. Age raises unemployment and labor force participation for both African Americans and European Americans, though it does so at a decreasing rate. As individuals age, they are less likely to be in school, and more likely to be in the labor force. Older workers experience longer durations of unemployment than younger workers. These results are therefore as expected. However, the results on the marriage variable are not entirely as predicted. We expected marriage to re-duce unemployment and increase participation since, net of gender, it strength-ens labor force attachment. Marriage does significantly reduce unemployment for both African Americans and European Americans; however, it significantly raises participation among African Americans and lowers participation among European Americans. The contrast may reflect the higher incomes of married European Americans, who are more able to have one spouse work full-time in the home, while married African Americans are more likely to have both spouses in the labor force. Since African Americans are much less likely than European Americans to be married, ethnic differences in marriage contribute to ethnic differences in employment. The gender control shows the expected results: no significant impact on unemployment, but a negative impact on participation. Finally, and somewhat surprisingly, education does not show a significant impact on African American unemployment except for college graduation. Among European Americans, SOMECOL as well as COLGRAD significantly reduce unemployment, but high school graduation does not have a significant impact. These findings deserve further exploration since unadjusted unem-ployment rates consistently decline as educational attainment rises (though the change becomes very small at higher levels of educational attainment, which may explain the findings here). Finally, educational attainment signifi-cantly increases labor force participation for both African Americans and Eu-ropean Americans as expected.

Since the model includes human capital and structural controls, the results on the immigration variable are independent of a variety of factors that can affect employment. For this reason the results are quite striking. The question is how to interpret them.

Explaining the Negative Impact of Immigration

The sheer size of immigrant inflows combined with their concentration in a few states and urban areas and their concentration in the low-wage sector of the labor market means that immigration has to have a large impact on local labor markets. It is implausible to think that its effects on native workers are negligible. Nonetheless, a number of studies have expressed exactly that point of view. In this section we attempt to explain what is wrong with their reasoning.

The reasons why immigration would reduce employment opportunities are comparatively simple. To the extent that immigrants are substitutes for native workers, they compete for the same jobs. George Borjas (1990: 88-92) once believed that immigrants have "practically no impact" on the employment and earnings of native workers. He explained this finding in terms of weak substitutability between immigrants and native workers, and in terms of the small size of immigrant inflows into the labor force relative to other sources of labor supply such as women and the baby boom generation. These trends, however, have reversed, and immigration is now a much more significant factor driving labor force growth. Ethnographic evidence shows that immigrants have displaced low-skill and African American workers (e.g., Waters 1999), and econometric evidence provides little support for the view that immigrant workers are weak substitutes for native workers, at least as measured by their willingness to take jobs that American workers allegedly do not want (Hammermesh 1998). Since African Americans are especially likely to be low-wage workers for whom immigrants are potential substitutes, they are especially likely to be adversely affected by immigration.

Although immigrants may be potential substitutes for low-wage native workers, their adverse effect on the employment prospects of these workers may be mitigated by a variety of factors, such as the characteristics of cities that facilitate or inhibit job competition as well as the impact of immigration on economic growth. The negative effects of immigration are lower when growth is stronger and when immigrants and native workers are more spatially and structurally separated (Bean, Van Hook, and Fossett 1999). Over time, however, it is likely that immigrants will become more spatially and structurally integrated into the urban areas in which they reside, suggesting that substitutability will increase. Furthermore, the negative impact of immigration may be lower during boom periods, but by the same token it will increase when the boom inevitably comes to an end. Sustained, low unemployment would reduce the negative consequences of immigration for African Americans; unfortunately, that circumstance has rarely been observed, particularly among African Americans with low levels of educational attainment who live in the urban cores. Though the impact of immigration on native workers is not constant, its patterns suggest that its negative effects are likely to cumulate and accelerate over time.

African American workers are especially likely to be found in the low-wage sector of the labor market, which is most affected by immigration. The impact of immigration upon them, however, has a distinct ethnic component because of the interaction of immigration and job discrimination. Immigration reduces the costs of discrimination by giving employers a readily available alternative to hiring African Americans. Immigrants are perceived to be hardworking and uncomplaining, especially in comparison to African Americans, who are perceived to be difficult, untrustworthy, and unreliable (Kirschenman and Neckerman 1991). This is not necessarily racial: employers seem to prefer black immigrants over black natives, and the immigrants themselves often express the same stereotypes about black natives as the employers (Waters 1999). Immigrants certainly are not the cause of job discrimination against African Americans, but they inadvertently facilitate it (Zhou 2001: 222). Again, the result is a drop in employment opportunities for African Americans.

Finally, it has been argued that immigrant workers concentrate in labor market niches that are separated from native workers; consequently, their impact on the employment prospects of native workers is negligible. In this view, immigrants may be potential substitutes for low-wage native workers, but their reliance on social networks for employment separates them from the native labor force and mitigates their impact upon it. For example, Franklin D. Wilson (1999: 133-134) finds evidence that immigrants and native workers are in distinct employment niches, but his results also "clearly suggest that a high immigrant share in 1980 is associated with the odds of being jobless for African Americans and Hispanics and lower occupational status and wages for all groups. Changes in immigrant shares between 1980 and 1990 are associated with greater joblessness for African Americans and lower joblessness for Hispanics, with lower occupational attainment for blacks and Hispanics, and with lower hourly wages for members of all groups." This suggests that labor markets are a cohesive entity: even if workers are in distinct ethnic niches, their wages and employment prospects are linked to one another. The existence of employment niches thus does not necessarily mitigate the adverse employment effect of immigration on native workers; indeed, the opposite may be the case. The networks and niches established by immigrants often are exclusionary, and to the extent that they influence labor market dynamics the result will be a drop in employment opportunities for African Americans who typically have weaker familial and social networks (Waldinger 1999). Immigration thus can both directly create "fierce economic competition" for African Americans, and indirectly exclude them from growing sectors of the labor market (Zhou 2001: 222).

Additional evidence that ethnic niches in employment can be consistent with job displacement is provided by Nelson Lim (2001). He shows that immigrants entered the niches in which African Americans were concentrated in 1970; two decades later they dominated these job clusters while African American had moved out of them and established new employment niches. Lim acknowledges that this pattern appears to be consistent with job displacement effects, but he argues against this interpretation on the grounds that the same pattern is observed in cities with low and high immigrant densities. His view is that other factors must be causing the employment shift among African Americans, and of course it is true that African American employment patterns are affected by many factors aside from immigration, e.g., changes in human capital acquisition, government policies, residential distribution, European American prejudices, employment growth, etc. But his argument against immigration as a cause of African American job displacement is unconvincing. Immigration is one factor among many that cause employment shifts. It may be the precipitating factor in cities with a high immigrant density, and a contributing factor in cities with a lower immigrant density, but there is no reason to deny that it systematically plays a significant role. Furthermore, that role increases in importance among African American workers without a high school degree (Lim correctly notes that this is a decreasing portion of the African American population, but it is still one that poses significant policy challenges as we discuss below). Although many African American workers have shifted into a better employment niche, many others have been left behind; and even among the more fortunate, job displacement can still represent a significant financial and utility loss until the adjustment process works itself out. The most simple and direct interpretation of Lim's findings is that they are consistent with the literature on job niches that has demonstrated the displacement effects of immigration.

Although there is little doubt that immigration reduces employment opportunities for low-wage workers, it also raises the demand for professional services (e.g., teachers, social workers, etc.) and increases the demand for high-skill workers in firms that can expand as they utilize immigrants to meet their low-skill needs. Immigration thus has a mixed set of employment effects, benefiting high-skill workers (and employers) at the same time that it hurts low-skill workers. In this sense immigration is a regressive policy that has increased income inequality. As Michael Rosenfeld and Marta Tienda (1999: 97) conclude, "there is support for both views of immigration: that immigrants take low-skill jobs formerly held by natives and that immigrants also help push natives upward in the occupational stratification system." Even Thomas Muller (1993: 143), a vigorous proponent of immigration, acknowledges that "the net effect of immigration has been to *redistribute* the jobs available for native workers away from manufacturing and lower-skill services toward the white-collar sector, particularly in management and the professions [emphasis in the original]." African American workers are especially likely to experience a net loss from immigration because they are especially likely to be low-wage workers, because they are especially unlikely to be employers, and because the availability of immigrant labor reduces the cost of discrimination to employers. The regressive distributional effect of immigration raises normative issues about immigration policy that we discuss below.

Conclusions

Our results show that immigration significantly and substantially reduces the labor force participation of both African American and European American workers, and that the impact is greater among African Americans. Labor supply reductions are likely to be concentrated among the native workers with the weakest attachment to the labor market, so immigration contributes to their long-term employment problems. The participation adjustments to immigration also tend to reduce the measured impact of immigration on their unemployment and earnings. Although immigration can have positive as well as negative effects on the employment opportunities of natives, the negative effects dominate among the most vulnerable groups of workers. Their greater impact on African American workers suggests that immigration is one of the forces sustaining ethnic inequality.

Immigration benefits some groups and hurts others. We believe that the groups that it hurts—low-wage workers in general, and African American workers in particular—should be the major concern of policymakers. The well being of low-wage workers has dropped sharply over the past three decades, at least as measured by the decline in their real wages. The well being of African American workers has correspondingly been harmed, and many analysts believe that is the major reason that African American progress slowed after the mid-1970s (e.g., Smith 2001). Immigration is not the only cause of these trends, but its impact is significant and it is more within the control of policymakers than other factors, such as technological change, capital flight, import competition, and the suburbanization of job growth. But the obvious response—reducing immigration—raises ethical and political issues that arouse an understandable discomfort among those who want to avoid the appearance of "blaming immigrants" for the problems faced by low-wage native workers.

Immigration undoubtedly benefits current immigrants (even if it increases job competition for previous immigrants), so restricting immigration would reduce the well being of those who would otherwise have chosen to emigrate to the United States. Unfortunately for the advocates of a "Rainbow Coalition" (Shulman and Smith 2004), the well being of immigrants and the well being of African American workers are not necessarily consistent. If immigration harms the well being of low-wage and African American workers, then a choice must be made about which group deserves our primary concern.

We sympathize with the impulse to avoid this unpleasant choice. One possible alternative would be to allow high levels of immigration but to pursue policies that mitigate its effects on African Americans. For example, Frank D. Bean and Stephanie Bell-Rose (1999: 25) suggest that "a slowing of black economic progress as a result of immigration may intensify the need for special programs." Although Bean and Bell-Rose do not elaborate, they presumably are referring to targeted economic development programs in immigrant-dense cities as well as an expansion of special assistance programs like affirmative action.

Unfortunately, persistently high levels of immigration make it unlikely that the contradiction between the interests of immigrants and low-wage native workers will be resolved in this fashion. The Los Angeles riots of a dozen years ago brought the conflict between African Americans and Korean immigrants into the national spotlight, but the ensuing rhetoric about economic development was not matched by any meaningful concrete action. Nor is strengthening affirmative action likely to have much effect since few low-wage African American workers benefit from it. Although we support the use of economic development programs to help low-wage African American workers in the inner cities, we are not optimistic that they will be sufficient to offset the consequences of immigration. As a practical matter it is hard to see what the alternative to a more restrictive immigration policy would be.

The question of the best level for immigration cannot be avoided. A variety of studies, including ours, show that immigration has negative effects on the earnings and employment of low-wage native workers that are substantial enough to be a source of concern. In addition, immigration increases the competition for scarce public resources, particularly education. Studies by Julian R. Betts (1998) and Carolyn M. Hoxby (1998) show that African American high school graduation and college attendance rates go down as the immigrant share of students goes up. This is a very worrisome finding for anyone concerned with the long-run well being of African Americans. Immigration also adds to the fiscal burdens faced by many cities, and spreads public resources (health care, police and fire protection, sanitation services, environmental protection, etc.) more and more thinly. It is hard to see how compensatory programs could offset these effects, or why that approach would be superior to simply reducing immigration.

Immigration does positive things as well, but even these benefits are not unambiguous. Immigration cheapens consumer goods, but it also drives up the cost of housing. Immigration adds to economic growth and urban revitalization, but it also increases job competition and drives down the earnings and employment of low-wage native workers. Immigration adds to ethnic diversity, but it also adds to ethnic conflict. Immigration may increase the public awareness of diversity issues, but it also may dilute the special obligation that many Americans feel to offset the effects of historical racism on African Americans. Immigration represents an addition to labor resources, but it also is the major force driving population growth and its by-products, such as congestion, sprawl, resource depletion, and pollution. It is hard to see how the benefits of immigration exceed the cost when everything is added up.

Most immigrants are hard-working people escaping poverty and searching for the American dream. Americans are sympathetic, but most recognize that their major obligation is to their fellow citizens, especially the most vulnerable. We believe that the well being of African Americans should be at the center of the debate over immigration policy. If immigration reduces economic opportunities for low-wage and African American workers, and if compensatory programs are unable to offset its effects, then immigration should be reduced. The debate should be not over whether to do this, but how.

References

Bean, Frank D. and Stephanie Bell-Rose. 1999. "Introduction: Immigration and Its Relation to Race and Ethnicity in the United States." In *Immigration and Opportunity: Race, Ethnicity, and Employment in the United States*, edited by F. Bean and S. Bell-Rose. New York: Russell Sage Foundation.

Bean, Frank D., Jennifer Van Hook, and Mark A. Fossett. 1999. "Immigration, Spatial and Economic Change, and African American Employment. In *Immigration and*

Opportunity: Race, Ethnicity, and Employment in the United States, edited by F. Bean and S. Bell-Rose. New York: Russell Sage Foundation.

Betts, Julian R. 1998. "Educational Crowding Out: Do Immigrants Affect the Educational Attainment of American Minorities?" In *Help or Hindrance: The Economic Implications of Immigration for African Americans*, edited by D. Hamermesh and F. Bean. New York: Russell Sage Foundation.

Borjas, George J. 1990. *Friends or Strangers: The Impact of Immigrants on the U.S. Economy*. New York: Basic Books.

_____. 1998. "Do Blacks Gain or Lose from Immigration?" In *Help or Hindrance: The Economic Implications of Immigration for African Americans*, edited by D. Hamermesh and F. Bean. New York: Russell Sage Foundation.

Borjas, George J., Richard B. Freeman, and Lawrence F. Katz. 1997. "How Much Do Immigration and Trade Affect Labor Market Outcomes?" *Brookings Papers on Economic Activity* 1.

Briggs, Vernon M. 1992. *Immigration and the National Interest*. New York: M.E. Sharpe.

Butler, Richard and James J. Heckman. 1977. "The Government's Impact on the Labor Market Status of Black Americans: A Critical Review." In *Equal Rights and Industrial Relations*, edited by L. Hausman et al. Madison, WI: Industrial Relations Research Association.

Frey, William H. and Kao-Lee Liaw. 1998. "The Impact of Recent Immigration on Population Redistribution within the United States." In *The Immigration Debate: Studies on the Economic, Demographic, and Fiscal Effects of Immigration*, edited by J. Smith and B. Edmonston. Washington, D.C.: National Academy Press.

Hamermesh, Daniel S. 1998. "Immigration and the Quality of Jobs." In *Help or Hindrance: The Economic Implications of Immigration for African Americans*, edited by D. Hamermesh and F. Bean. New York: Russell Sage Foundation.

Hoxby, Caroline M. 1999. "Do Immigrants Crowd Disadvantaged American Natives Out of Higher Education? In *Help or Hindrance: The Economic Implications of Immigration for African Americans*, edited by D. Hamermesh and F. Bean. New York: Russell Sage Foundation.

Johannsson, Hannes, Stephan Weiler, and Steven Shulman. 2003. "Immigration and the Labor Force Participation of Low-Skill Native Workers." *Research in Labor Economics* 22 (*Worker Well-Being and Public Policy*).

Johannsson, Hannes and Stephan Weiler. Forthcoming in 2005. "Immigration and Income Inequality in the 1990s: Panel Evidence from the Current Population Survey." *Social Science Journal* 42, 3.

Kirschenman, Joleen and Kathryn M. Neckerman. 1991. "'We'd Love to Hire Them But...' The Meaning of Race for Employers." In *The Urban Underclass*, edited by Christopher Jencks and Paul E. Peterson. Washington, D.C.: The Brookings Institution.

Lim, Nelson. 2001. "On the Backs of Blacks? Immigrants and the Fortunes of African Americans." In *Strangers at the Gates: New Immigrants in Urban America*, edited by Roger Waldinger. Los Angeles: University of California Press.

Muller, Thomas. 1993. *Immigrants and the American City*. New York: New York University Press.

National Research Council. 1997. *The New Americans: Economic, Demographic, and Fiscal Effects of Immigration*. Washington, D.C.: National Academy Press.

Rosenfeld, Michael and Marta Tienda. 1999. "Mexican Immigration, Occupational Niches, and Labor Market Competition: Evidence from Los Angeles, Chicago and Atlanta, 1970 to 1990." In *Immigration and Opportunity: Race, Ethnicity, and Employment in the United States*, edited by F. Bean and S. Bell-Rose. New York: Russell Sage Foundation.

Shulman, Steven and Robert C. Smith. 2004. "Immigration, African Americans, and the 'Rainbow Coalition.'" In *African Americans in the American Economy*, edited by Cecilia Conrad, John Whitehead, Patrick Mason, and James Stewart. NY: Rowman and Littlefield Publishers, Inc.

Smith, James P. 2001. "Race and Ethnicity in the Labor Market: Trends Over the Short and Long Term." In *America Becoming: Racial Trends and Their Consequences*, volume II, edited by Neil J. Smelser, William Julius Wilson, and Faith Mitchell. Washington, D.C.: National Academy Press.

Waldinger, Roger. 1999. "Network, Bureaucracy, and Exclusion: Recruitment and Selection in an Immigrant Metropolis." In *Immigration and Opportunity: Race, Ethnicity, and Employment in the United States*, edited by F. Bean and S. Bell-Rose. New York: Russell Sage Foundation.

Waters, Mary C. 1999. "West Indians and African Americans at Work: Structural Differences and Cultural Stereotypes." In *Immigration and Opportunity: Race, Ethnicity, and Employment in the United States*, edited by F. Bean and S. Bell-Rose. New York: Russell Sage Foundation.

Wilson, Franklin D. 1999. "Ethnic Concentrations and Labor Market Opportunities." In *Immigration and Opportunity: Race, Ethnicity, and Employment in the United States*, edited by F. Bean and S. Bell-Rose. New York: Russell Sage Foundation.

Zhou, Min. 2001. "Contemporary Immigration and the Dynamics of Race and Ethnicity." In *America Becoming: Racial Trends and Their Consequences*, volume II, edited by Neil J. Smelser, William Julius Wilson, and Faith Mitchell. Washington, D.C.: National Academy Press.

5

Do Blacks Lose When Diversity Replaces Affirmative Action?

Gerald Jaynes and Frederick McKinney

Introduction

What effect is the unprecedented growth of minority populations in contemporary America having on the labor market prospects of native-born African Americans? Since at least the mid-1980s when the enormous influx of immigrants of color emerged as a national political and media issue, commentators have predicted (and in some cases charged) that immigration is harmful to native-born workers and is especially detrimental to African Americans.[1] Applying the economic law of supply and demand to this question in a straightforward fashion suggests the seemingly inescapable prediction that increased immigration causes greater competition for jobs and leads to lower wages and possibly greater joblessness. Focusing the analysis more narrowly to apply the law of supply and demand to the internecine competition among racial and ethnic minorities vying for resources made scarcer by the extra-market constraints and opportunities facing minorities only strengthens this conclusion. Yet despite the commonsense appeal of a straightforward interpretation of the law of supply and demand and despite convincing anecdotal and case study evidence of immigrants' displacement effects on native-born workers in particular markets, meticulous and rigorous statistical analyses of the effects of immigration on the wages and employment of the native-born nationwide have failed to confirm the predictions of doom and gloom (for a discussion of these studies see Jaynes 2000; for specific analyses see Borjas 1987 and Wilson and Jaynes 2000).

On its face, there is a persuasive argument for believing that immigration of minorities harms the employment prospects of native-born African Americans.

Its proponents argue that African Americans made inroads into higher paying jobs because government institutions passed and began enforcing equal opportunity laws beginning in the mid 1960s. Furthermore, employers, pushed on by the antidiscrimination enforcement of government and the political ascendancy of social values proclaiming equal opportunity for black Americans adopted affirmative action policies specifically addressed at increasing the employment of blacks and redressing the harmful legacies of slavery and Jim Crow. However, contemporary immigration of large numbers of peoples classified under civil rights laws as minorities has exacerbated preexisting tensions among minority groups and white women. This tension is said to emanate from each group's attempt to maximize its own benefits in markets where equal opportunity pressures on employers and political institutions create demand for the services of members of protected groups. The employment successes of white women and other minority groups, the argument continues, were detrimental to the employment of blacks seeking higher status occupations and diminished the overall progress of blacks.

The civil rights movement led by black Americans and the evolution of American political and economic institutions during recent American history are directly tied. This interaction between African American activism and American institutions is manifested in important court cases such as Brown v. Board of Education and path-breaking legislation such as the Civil Rights Act of 1964 and the Voting Rights Act of 1965, each an important bedrock in the development of current economic opportunities enjoyed by formerly excluded groups. The benefits of these laws and the civil rights movement's establishment of methods of struggle for recognition of equal rights had carryover to groups such as gays and lesbians, women, Hispanics, Native Americans, Asian Americans, the old, and the sick. And although it is largely agreed that the struggle for the rights of African Americans had parallels in the women's movement and in continuing mobilizations by other minority groups, there is a commonly held belief in the African American community that blacks paved the way for others to follow in their respective pursuit of equal opportunity and economic inclusion.

In the wake of these parallel movements for equal opportunity among other groups, during the decades since 1980, the argument continues, the gaining of covered minority status by white women and the increasing numbers and political power of Latino and Asian Americans has dispersed the focus of equal opportunity policy across a broad spectrum of separate and competing interest groups and diluted the employment opportunities available to African Americans. It is seen by many students of civil rights history as no surprise that affirmative action (a practical policy focused on the objective of redressing the black American experience of slavery and segregation) has given way to calls for workforce diversity. The thrust of this perspective may be stated simply: since political pressures for affirmative action centering on black economic disadvantage have given way to policies stressing diversity in the workplace, black employment opportunities have diminished because employers reticent to hire blacks to satisfy affirmative action policies are able (under "cover" of diversity goals) to hire white women and other "more acceptable" minorities in place of blacks.

This atmosphere of group competition and increasing population diversity has led to an intensification of comparative ethnic group gains and losses. For example, widely cited statistics indicating that, when compared to other major race/ethnic groups, African Americans bore a disproportionate share of job losses during the 1990-1991 recession seemed to provide strong evidence for the argument that diversity was hurting blacks. The *Wall Street Journal* reported (9/14/93) that during the 1990-91 recession that officially began July 1990, blacks were the only major race/ethnic group to suffer net employment losses while every other group gained jobs. The *Journal* reported the largest corporations shed black employees at the most disproportionate rates. Blacks lost 59,479 jobs, while Asians gained 55,104, Hispanics 60,040, and Whites 71,144 jobs.

The employment picture is somewhat more complicated than perusal of these numbers might indicate. In fact, employment rates for black men and women did fall during the 1990-91 recession. Employment rates also fell for each of the other major race ethnic groups—after all, one of the defining characteristics of a recession is a decreasing employment rate. Employment rates for black men age twenty and higher fell 1.7 percent between 1990 and 1991; the rate for black women of similar age fell more, 2 percent. In comparison, the employment rates of all men and women twenty years old and more fell 2.1 percent and 1 percent respectively. Thus, while black women's employment suffered disproportionately compared to all women, black men's did not when compared to all men. A similar pattern of complexity appears in the employment statistics describing the 2000-2001 recession. While rates of employment recovered and exceeded their pre-1991 values for all groups by 1998, black adults (again ages twenty or greater) did suffer somewhat higher rates of employment loss during the later downswing. Black women's rate of employment fell about nine-tenths of 1 percent compared to about five-tenths of 1 percent for all women and black men's rate dropped 2 percent compared to 1.2 percent for men generally. However, during the same two-year period, employment-to-population rates for people of age sixteen or greater tell a different story. The combined rate for blacks of both genders fell 4.6 percent; the rates for Asian Americans and white Americans fell 2.4 percent and 12 percent respectively, suggesting that white youth suffered the greatest employment losses of any age-race group.

Whatever might explain the unemployment statistics from the 1990-91 recession, black employment seems to have rebounded considerably during the ensuing years. And, available data strongly suggest that black employment in corporate America has been as healthy as for other groups. During 1995, well beyond the bottom of the cycle defined by the 1990-91 recession but before the boom cycle of the late 1990s, The Equal Employment Opportunity Commission's (EEOC) survey of employers found that minority Americans accounted for one-quarter of the total employees of the nation's largest employers. Black Americans accounted for 13.2 percent, Hispanics 8 percent, Asian/Pacific Islanders 3.4 percent, and American Indians and Alaskan Natives .5 percent. At the beginning of the century in 2000 minority employment exceeded 29 percent with Hispanics the largest growing ethnic group making the largest gains from 8 percent to 10.4 percent, while blacks' participation rates reached 14 percent.[2] Women's overall employment participation in the EEOC data increased .5 of 1 percent. Thus, during the sustained economic expansion, precisely the time period during which policies calling for "diversity" became most ascendant in the American business community, black Americans managed to improve their position amid a growing labor market brimming with competition among many surging groups.

The remainder of this chapter presents the results of several tests of the hypothesis that diversity harms the employment opportunities of black Americans through regression analyses of industry level data from the Equal Employment Opportunity Commissions' survey of employers. We caution the reader at the outset that nothing reported here makes any claims about whether white women and minorities on the whole are discriminated against. Our conclusions refer only to the comparative treatment of blacks vis-à-vis the others. The statistical evidence suggests that overall blacks' employment prospects are not affected by the employment of white women or non-black minorities. Moreover, blacks' access to supervisory employment may be enhanced.

Data and Methods

The underlying data for the findings we report come from the U.S. Equal Employment Opportunity Commission (EEOC) report *Job Patterns for Minorities and Women in Private Industry, 2000* (EEOC 2001). The EEOC periodically publishes such reports summarizing data from its Employer Information Report (EEOC-1) surveys. These surveys (which are required of employers with work forces of 100 or more (and in some cases fifty or more) provide a detailed snapshot of the gender and race/ethnic composition of reporting employers' workforces. The data as reported by the EEOC are compilations of individual employers within an industry and thus provide workforce composition numbers by industry. The data also provide composition information about the occupational distribution of race/gender groups for nine broadly classed occupations. The results reported here are based on a random sample of sixty-six industries from the EEOC survey (for descriptive statistics see Table 1).

There are some weaknesses with this data but the primary weakness for purposes of this study is that the EEOC-1 survey does not cover employers with small work forces. Thus, differences in the distribution of firm size by industry have the effect that the proportionate samples across industries are not uniform. Thus, for given industries, the total employment numbers reported by the EEOC can vary considerably from those reported by the U.S. Bureau of Labor Statistics. Using the U.S. Bureau of Labor Statistics employment numbers as a benchmark, reported employment in the EEOC report ranges from a high of 67 percent of the total employment in manufacturing to a low of 13 percent in construction (Table p. 9, EEOC 2001).

Nonetheless, to the extent that we are interested in the employment patterns and workforce compositions of large U.S. employers, and especially corporations, these data are an invaluable source for analysis. In 2000, nearly 40,000 employers employing approximately 53 million workers filed EEO-1 reports, about one-half of all U.S. private payroll employees. Tables 1-2 report summary statistics for the data sample.

Table 1
Summary Statistics

Mean	Standard	Deviation	Minimum	Maximum	N
Average Industry Wage	$597.88	216.3	$177	$1133	61*
Total Employees in Industry	900344	2061802	67477	13465076	66
Women in Industry	472556	1212233	13715	8199969	66
Minority Employees	240315	475719	14061	2389507	66
Black Employees	133843	324323	4792	2180707	66
Officials & Mngrs	93141	201568	4538	1261956	66
White Women Officials & Mngrs	29831	73249	1008	474338	66
Minority Officials & Mngrs	14152	31710	645	198288	66
Black Officials & Mngrs	6447	14613	234	87436	66
Professionals	159183	493266	1358	3654607	66
White Women Professionals	71920	265342	690	1876664	66
Minority Professionals	30538	95902	164	721351	66
Black Professionals	11154	35854	66	266325	66

*We were only able to find wage data for sixty-one of the industries.

Table 2
Summary Statistics—Percentages

Variable	Percentage
Minority Percentage of All Employees	26.7%
Black Percentage of All Employees	14.9%
White Women Percentage of AllEmployees	38.6%
Minority Percentage of Officers and Managers	15.2%
Black Percentage of Officers and Managers	6.9%
White Women Percentage of Officers and Managers	32%
Minority Percentage of Professionals	19.2%
Black Percentage of Professionals	7%
White Women Percentage of Professionals	45.2%

The primary question we examine is whether an increase in the percentage of other minorities and women in an industry's workforce has a negative impact on the percentage of African American employees. We examine this question for three employment categories: all occupations, i.e. the total workforce; professional employees; and those employees classified as officials and managers. In all three cases the basic equation we test is of the form:

$$\%By = \alpha + \beta_1 \cdot \%My + \beta_2 \cdot \%Wy + \beta \bullet x + \mu$$

In the model, "%By" equals the proportion of workers of occupation y who are black, "%My" equals the proportion of workers of occupation y who are minority and not black, "%Wy" equals the proportion of workers of occupation y who are white women, x is a vector of control variables, and μ is an error term. Thus, the dependent variable in all regressions is the industry percentage of African American employees of a given occupation.

Results

The results of the three regressions are reported in Table 3. The second column reports the results from a regression of the percentage of all African American employees on the explanatory variables—the percentage of all non-African American minority employees, the percentage of white women employees, and a set of control variables. The third column reports the results of the regression of the percentage of African American professional employees against the percentage of non-African American minority professionals, the percentage of white women professionals, and control variables. And the fourth

Table 3
Regression Results

Dependent Variables	All Employees	Professional Employees	Officials and Managers
Constant	.198* (4.97)	-.0044 (.193)	-.019 (1.25)
% Non-Black Minority	.059 (.64)	.055 (.784)	.175* (2.36)
% White Women	-.038 (.67)	.037 (1.19)	.0374 (1.81)
Wage	-.00012* (3.8)	2.93E-06 (.165)	1.18E-05 (1.01)
Healthcare	.06* (2.77)	.0103 (.809)	-.00523 (.614)
Location	.110* (5.07)	-.0234 (1.93)	-.0156 (1.79)
Percentage all Employees black		.318* (4.6)	.412* (8.9)
Percentage of Officers and Managers or Professionals		.0295 (1.12)	-.0247 (.491)
Statistics			
n	61	61	61
R Squared	.517	.548	.784
F Statistic	11.78*	9.189*	27.46*

* Indicates significance greater than the alpha .05 level.

The numbers in parentheses are the t-statistics for the relevant estimated parameters.

column reports the results of a regression of the percentage of African American officers and managers against the percentage of non-African American minority officers and managers, the percentage of white women officers and managers, and control variables.

These regressions indicate that with respect to the EEOC survey data, the hypothesis that either white women or other minorities diminish the employment opportunities of blacks must be resoundingly rejected. Systematically, we find that either there is no statistically significant linear relationship between the dependent variables and the hypothesized explanatory variables, or that in the cases where there is a statistically significant relationship that relationship is positive. We can tentatively conclude that diversity is at worse neutral to the employment opportunities of African Americans and, in some higher status occupations, diversity quite possibly has positive effects on the employment prospects of African Americans.

Generally, we find, as many economists might have predicted, that the vast preponderance of the explained variation in the proportion of an industry's workforce that is black is in fact due to various economic control variables other than the hypothesized demographic variables. The control variables we apply are mean weekly wages for each industry's production workers, a location dummy variable that controls for the geographic presence of concentrations of African American population (coded 1 if the industry is concentrated in the South or in urban metropolitan areas), a dummy variable capturing the special effects of the "healthcare industry" (coded 1 if the SIC industry classification is more generally a healthcare field), the proportion of the industry workforce that is female, and finally, the proportion of the industry workforce that is black.

The relationship of these control variables to the employment of blacks varies across the estimated equations, but is generally consistent with the predictions of microeconomic theory. Consistent with the well-known fact that blacks earn lower average wages than the population at large, the regression coefficient on wages is negative for the equation estimating effects on all black employees, suggesting that increases in mean industry wages decrease the employment of blacks. We are cautious in making too much of this result however, because it might not be robust to the addition of data measuring the average education levels of industry workforces. That note of caution concerning possible affects of education is reinforced by the positive (although statistically insignificant coefficients) on the wage variable for black professionals and for officials and managers suggesting that blacks may be attaining these positions in higher paying industries.

Some 13.1 percent of African American employees in the EEOC data work in one of the six healthcare industries included in our sample. Average wages in healthcare industries were $150 per week less than the average for all industries, and the proportion of women employed in healthcare industries averaged (77 percent) approximately twice as high as the average for all other industries (39 percent). Moreover, the healthcare industry's proportion of blacks employed was about 45 percent greater than the other industries and the proportion of black professionals in healthcare averaged 10 percent compared to about 6 percent for all other industries. These last two facts help explain why the proportion of officials and managers in healthcare industries (8.8 percent) was also nearly 50 percent larger than the average proportion for other industries. We felt that the significant employment presence of blacks in healthcare industries warranted special consideration of that industry to ensure that employment conditions for blacks there did not unduly influence the results of our regressions. This hypothesis was confirmed as the estimated coefficient on the healthcare dummy variable proved to be statistically consistent in one of the regressions.

The dummy variable for location was deemed necessary for obvious theoretical reasons. We hypothesized those industries whose firms were located in geographic areas with greater than average black population proportions would be expected to hire greater proportions of blacks. This hypothesis was confirmed by the first regression where the dependent variable is the proportion of all black employees. However, the location variable had negative coefficients in the two remaining equations, although the coefficients were not statistically significant.

The data do not support the hypothesis that hiring either white women or minorities who are not black decreases the employment chances of black workers. As reported above, most of the explained variation in the proportion of an industry's workforce that is black is due to the economic control variables. Slightly more than one-half (.506) of the variance in the proportion of total black employees across industries is explained by the economic control variables, wages, black location, and healthcare industries. Adding the hypothesized explanatory variables proportion of white women employees and proportion of non-black minority employees raises the coefficient of determination by a mere .011, and the coefficients of both of the additional hypothesized explanatory variables are small and quite insignificant (see Table 3).[3] Whatever important variables might explain more of the variation in the black proportions of industry workforces, it does not appear to be the presence of white women or other minority employees.

In the second regression, we add the percentage of total employees that are black to the list of control variables. The explanatory variables, wages, location, healthcare and the percentage of the overall workforce that is black, also explains about one-half of the industry variation in the %black professionals employed. In the reported regression both the coefficients on the percentage of other minorities and the %white women professionals in an industry's workforce are positive, suggesting that if those variables have any affect on the employment opportunities of black professionals it is beneficial, but the coefficients are not statistically significant. This result holds even after controlling for the proportion of the workforce that is professional and the proportion that are women. Similar to the previous model, the hypothesis that the proposed explanatory variables %non-black professionals and %white women professionals will have negative effects on the employment of black professionals must be rejected.

As might be expected, the percentage of all employees in an industry who are black is the most important explanatory variable for the proportion of officials and managers who are black, explaining about 68 percent of the industry variation. However, even after controlling for that important variable, it appears that the proportion of other minorities who are officials and managers positively affects the proportion of officials and managers who are black. In the absence of further analyses and confirmation of the result we refrain from making a strong statement about this finding. We prefer to argue that it simply reinforces the prior findings (at least with respect to large employers) that there is simply no statistical basis for arguing that the employment of white women or minorities who are not black have negative effects on the employment of African Americans.

Increasing population diversity is not likely to decrease opportunities for qualified African Americans. We suggest an alternative hypothesis: increasing diversity actually improves the employment prospects of African Americans by raising employers' demand for all minorities.

Discussion: Does Greater Diversity Negatively Impact Black Employment?

The proposition that increases in the employment rates of non-African American minorities and rising labor market participation of white women reduces employment demand for African Americans requires not only an empirical test, its possibility also requires an explanation. Here we discuss some of the proposed explanations and we also discuss the likely reasons why our statistical tests suggest those hypotheses and their explanations should be rejected. There are several explanations that could explain a negative effect of employment diversity policies on black employment if it were found to be true. Among these are two straightforward mechanisms that could cause a tradeoff between the employment of African Americans and other minority groups. The first mechanism hypothesizes that a significant number of employers harbor a strong distaste against African American employees, and that this distaste for blacks exceeds any corresponding distaste for hiring other minorities. The second mechanism is a variant of the kind of conspiracy theories found among some African Americans who believe that a group of elite decision makers act covertly to prevent black Americans from making significant economic and social advances. Let's try to understand what assumptions and supporting behaviors would be required to make these hypotheses reasonable explanations of current employment patterns among race/ethnic groups.

To deny the mechanisms is not to deny the existence of discrimination in labor markets. However, in our view, both of these mechanisms face insurmountable conceptual difficulties as explanations of contemporary behavior by employers. The conspiracy hypothesis seems particularly unwarranted. It too assumes that high-level decision makers have a preference for non-African American employees. The major difference between the two explanations is that a conspiracy is a much more pernicious form of discrimination. Conspiracy theories have greater credibility when there are a few decision makers, as in the case of markets characterized by oligopoly. But when the number of decision makers increases, and becomes very large as in the case under consideration, the requirements and costs of coordinating and maintaining the conspiracy become very high. This is particularly the case when there are incentives on the part of the conspirators to cheat. Such incentives would clearly exist in a large labor market where qualified blacks that are being discriminated against would face low opportunities relative to other groups and could be expected to be available at comparatively attractive wage and benefit levels. Profit seeking employers would have financial incentives to hire qualified members of the discriminated group.

With respect to the first hypothesis, it is possible to accept the proposition that many employers find blacks an especially disliked group but still recognize that conditions must be conducive for biased decision makers to be able to put their preferences into action. Corporate decision makers, particularly in the area of human resource management would be required to have the ability to carry out their preferences and discriminate against African Americans in favor of other minorities. The source of these preferences could be based on old-fashioned racism or newer models of statistical discrimination. For the purposes of this discussion the origin of the discrimination does not matter. The argument that employers could hire other minorities or white women in preference over qualified blacks makes an implicit and unwarranted assumption. That assumption is that firms can satisfy equal opportunity laws and widespread disapproval of overt discrimination within the society simply by providing a headcount of "minority" employees without any regard for the intra-minority composition of their workforces. But this is not true. Anti-discrimination laws do not simply state that employers cannot discriminate against minorities. Employers are enjoined against discriminating against individuals who are members of specific protected groups. Any employer who systematically discriminates against African Americans will not be in compliance with the law and could not successfully argue in a judicial proceeding that his failure to hire or promote qualified blacks is justified because he hires and promotes other minorities at sufficient levels to substitute for the undercount of qualified blacks.

The implicit and unwarranted assumption that firms can be in compliance with equal opportunity laws by hiring a sufficient number of "minority" and women employees without regard to the applications and qualifications of each of the protected groups (that minorities and women are fungible) is indicative of a fundamental misunderstanding of the legacy of the civil rights movement. Although the pragmatic goal of that movement was to gain equal rights for black Americans, its wider implications for democracy in the United States was to bring the nation's ideology into alignment with its practices by broadening the benefits of equal participation in American society to all Americans. Not surprisingly, four decades ago, neither the immediate practical objective nor the broader conceptual meaning was immediately accepted by all

Americans. In particular, with respect to its hiring and promotion policies, American business's initial reaction to the anti-discrimination legislation emanating from the civil rights movement was slow and sometimes hostile. But eventually greater receptivity to broad based equal opportunity employment policies emerged and today it can be said without equivocation that corporate America in general is more supportive of the goals of affirmative action and diversity than is the federal government or the courts.

This sea change in the attitudes of corporations has hardly been the result of a benevolent change of mind and a decision to do the right thing merely for its own sake. The successes of the civil rights movement set in motion forces that made the current immigration and sometimes tumultuous process of social incorporation of new ethnic populations into the society possible. In particular, since 1960 many groups' civil rights activities have enhanced opportunities for the growing numbers of Hispanics from Mexico, Central and South America, and the Caribbean. Today, corporate America understands that Hispanics are the largest and fastest growing minority and that Asian Americans are the wealthiest minority. This recognition impresses upon corporate policymakers the need to pay greater attention to bilingual proficiency and the need to have the staff with these skills. But more importantly, corporate America understands what the new demographics mean for the reality of the marketplace. Minorities in general are a large, growing, and increasingly important segment of the markets on which corporate profits depend. Madison Avenue executives find it not only profitable but also necessary to a continuing satisfactory bottom line that they pay evermore attention to minority consumers. It is also apparent that corporations vying for the consumption revenues of minorities cannot expect that those same minorities will remain clients of companies that refuse to provide them with equal employment opportunities.

The forces that are driving the current movement toward employment policies espousing the concept of diversity are primarily economic. One of the most profound effects of contemporary immigration and the diversification of the U.S. population is the growing economic clout of minority consumers in major product and service markets throughout the nation. The effects on consumer markets (and thus firm profit potentials) of the presence of growing proportions of minority consumers increases firms' motives to transact with minorities as both customers and employees. Yet, firms especially interested in "the Hispanic market" cannot simply hire Hispanics at higher rates and ignore pools of qualified blacks and Asian Americans. As we demonstrated above, a tradeoff between African American employees and other minority employees and women suggests that management generally and human resource managers specifically have a broad objective that lumps all minority workers into a single category. Firms with such a perspective would view the hiring of a woman employee or an Asian American employee as a substitute for hiring an African American employee. As the avalanche of reverse discrimination lawsuits brought by white Americans against businesses during the 1980s showed, such a policy would prove costly and infeasible, as equal opportunity means protection for all groups.

Notes

1.   The Bush administration's recent proposal to allow heretofore illegal workers to attain legal status on the grounds that they are filling jobs that other Americans do not want is bringing attention to the issues of inter-ethnic competition discussed in this chapter. Because our data pertain only to permanent salaried employees of employers with large workforces, we caution readers however not to jump to conclusions regarding this particular policy based on the findings of this chapter.
2.   Economists typically think of participation rates as measuring the percentage of the relevant population that is either employed or unemployed. The term participation rate here is used by the EEOC to define the fraction of the surveyed labor force that is from a particular ethnic/racial group.
3.   Adding the proportion of women in an industry's workforce as a control variable might lead a careless researcher to conclude that both white women and other minorities have a large negative and statistically significant effect on the employment of blacks. When the %women employees is added to the basic equation as an explanatory variable, the R2 increases substantially to .723 and the respective coefficients on the %white women and %other minority become negative and statistically significant. However, inspection of the model makes it clear that the result is due to extremely high co-linearity between the %women in an industry and the %white women (correlation = .946). These two variables have variation inflation factors equal to 17.08 and 16.07 respectively. Each has a very small characteristic root (.004 and .02 respectively) and correspondingly high condition indexes over 18 and 32. As would be expected, the ill-conditioned correlation matrix produces highly unstable and unreliable coefficient estimates. For example, removing the regressor %white women from the model causes the regressor %other minority to change sign (from -.235 to .086) and become statistically insignificant. Moreover, the variable %women employed in the industry also becomes statistically insignificant.

References

Borjas, George. 1987. "Immigrants, Minorities, and Labor Market Competition." In *Industrial and Labor Relations Review* 40 (3): 382-392.

Jaynes, Gerald D. 2000. *Race and Immigration: New Dilemmas for American Democracy*. New Haven: Yale University Press.

Wilson, Franklin D. and Gerald D. Jaynes. 2000. "International and Domestic Migration and the Employment and Wages of the Native-Born." In *Work and Occupations*.

6

Somewhere Over the Rainbow?
African Americans, Unauthorized Mexican
Immigration, and Coalition Building*

Manuel Pastor, Jr. and Enrico A. Marcelli

Introduction

While evidence from many of the nation's leading immigration scholars suggests that contemporary immigration to the United States has had negligible or small positive social and economic effects in the aggregate during the past two decades (Smith and Edmonston 1997), some analysts stress that unauthorized and lower-skilled immigration may curtail economic outcomes for similarly skilled African-Americans and other minorities. The argument seems sensible enough, particularly given the segmentation of American labor markets and numerous case studies of ethnic succession in industries ranging from janitorial to hospitality (Cranford 2000; Waldinger 1996, 1997, 1999; Waldinger and Lichter 2003). These apparent adverse effects have given rise to a new chorus of restrictionist sentiment, with some moral justification provided by the need to address historic and contemporary racism directed specifically against American blacks.

Why then has immigration not arisen as a central issue for traditional leaders in the African American community? A recent provocative paper suggests that "the most basic explanation is that since the 1970s, and especially since Jesse Jackson's campaigns for the presidency, Black leaders have been seek-

* The authors thank Justin Scoggins of UC Santa Cruz for valuable research assistance, Ricardo Ramirez and Janelle Wong of USC for suggesting key data sources on public opinion, and Steven Shulman of Colorado State University–Fort Collins for helpful comments on an earlier draft.

ing to build a 'rainbow coalition' of 'people of color,' including recent immigrants" (Shulman and Smith 2004). Putting coalition needs first, it is argued, has led to a downplaying of potentially divisive issues, including the economically corrosive impact of immigrants. Vernon Briggs (2003) seems to concur with this view, suggesting that the Congressional Black Caucus has not defended the interests of African Americans vis-à-vis unauthorized immigrant workers, partly to maintain an alliance with the Congressional Hispanic Caucus.

Some black leaders have spoken forcefully on the immigration issue. Barbara Jordan—a highly respected African American politician—endorsed reductions in legal immigration as chair of the U.S. Commission on Immigration Reform, but her untimely death occurred before the commission's mandate was fulfilled in 1997. Congress eventually decided to keep the "front door" of legal immigration open and to attempt to seal the "back door" of unauthorized immigration. Shulman and Smith (2004) suggest that bolder leadership such as Barbara Jordan's might make a difference for identifying, pursing, and realizing black interests in this arena.

What are the economic effects of immigration and is the "rainbow" coalition position of many black leaders—one that, it is argued, leads to muting opposition to immigration restrictions—actually counter to the broad aims of improving the lot of African Americans in the United States? In this chapter, we tackle these questions with a particular focus on what might be termed a true "hotspot" of the debate: undocumented immigration in one of the most rapidly changing states in the Union: California. We briefly review research findings on how immigration in general influences the employment and earnings of African Americans; our discussion in this regard is very short since much of this literature is covered elsewhere. We then turn to our own original work estimating the size and location of the unauthorized Mexican immigrant labor force in California, and consider whether this labor force is in competition with African Americans. The results are mixed: the geographic pattern suggests that there are few displacement effects but an occupational analysis does suggest some competition when there are exceptionally high numbers of undocumented migrants in the same field.

We then turn more directly to politics and policy. We begin this section with a dilemma: public opinion data suggest that blacks, many of whom are lower-skilled and seemingly in direct competition with Latino immigrants, are at least as, and often more, sympathetic toward immigrants than whites. This pattern shows up even in California where there has been well-publicized conflict over immigration issues and where black-Latino competition over economic and political space has often been sharp. A regression analysis of attitudes in Los Angeles suggests one reason for the pattern: African Americans are ambiguous in their views of immigrants as economic competitors but do see them as potential political allies.

To explain this, we eschew notions that African American sympathy is the result of ignorance or false consciousness, and instead discuss how the estimated gains from reducing any immigrant-induced wage penalty should be weighted by the probability that immigration enforcement technology can be effective and by the costs that such a political position might impose on forming coalitions around other issues of interest. Within such a calculus, it is rational for African Americans to be less restrictionist toward immigration than a simple competitive labor-market perspective might suggest, especially because such a restrictionist position would weaken coalitional possibilities on other issues and/or may fan prejudicial attitudes that will diminish political and policy gains later. We conclude by arguing that it may be useful to move away from debates around *immigration* (e.g., enforcement) policy *per se* and focus instead on *immigrant* (e.g., integration) policy that can lift up all communities.

Economic Impacts

Past Research

For several reasons (e.g., an increased demand for goods and services, an influx of capital, complementary skills or work attitudes), there exists no unambiguous theoretical expectation regarding how an increased supply of foreign-born labor will impact native-born labor market outcomes in the aggregate. Particular groups such as teenagers, women, and lower-skilled black men, however, have historically and conventionally been thought to be harmed by an influx of immigrant workers because the latter are often assumed to be lower-skilled and to have little or no capital that may be employed to augment the demand for lower-skilled labor (Bailey 1987; Borjas 1998).

Some recent empirical evidence indicates that the wages of lower-skilled black men in locations with relatively high concentrations of immigrants may be adversely affected (Stoll, Melendez, and Valenzuela 2002). On a national level, however, the most sophisticated research on African American labor market outcomes to date suggests that immigration during the 1980s had "a negative impact, not especially large, but clearly identifiable" on lower-skilled blacks' earnings and employment—or alternatively, "African Americans do not appear to have benefited economically from immigration to the same degree as native whites" (Hammermesh and Bean 1998: 9-13). The production of relatively weak evidence for the competition hypothesis has been attributed to a dearth of longitudinal data that would permit one to estimate whether displacement or replacement better describes black-immigrant occupational succession, increasing skill-complementarity between African Americans and immigrants, employer preferences, and ethno-racial social capital/closure (Waldinger and Lichter 2003).

One route some researchers have taken to determine effects involves turning attention to that group of immigrants that is thought to be especially harmful to lower-skilled Americans: unauthorized, undocumented, or illegal residents. Even then, only small effects have been detected (Bean, Lowell, and Taylor 1988; Bean, Telles, and Lowell 1987; Winegarden and Khor 1991; Marcelli et al. 1999). However, much of this work is based on the influx of the undocumented prior to 1990; it is quite possible that the changing structure of the economy and continuing increases in the size of the undocumented population could have led to larger effects in recent years.

Below we offer the first estimates from the 2000 Census on the geographic and labor market relationships of unauthorized Mexican immigrants and African Americans in California, a state that has experienced a continued inflow of relatively lower-skilled unauthorized Mexican immigrants over the past decade. The results are quite preliminary—we offer some descriptive measures here and leave the more detailed econometric work to a future piece—but they do set up our consideration of the public opinion and political dynamics that are at the heart of this paper.

Labor Market Impact Analysis: Data and Methods

As a first step in our analysis of how unauthorized Mexican immigrant workers may have affected African American male earnings and employment outcomes—and following Marcelli and Heer (1997) and Marcelli, Pastor, and Joassart (1999)—we develop two unauthorized immigrant residency status prediction equations from two surveys of Mexican immigrants in Los Angeles County. The 1994 Los Angeles County Mexican Immigrant Residency Status Survey (LAC-MIRSS) is a randomized foreign-born Mexican household survey that collected information on residency status and various other demographic and economic characteristics for 661 Mexican immigrants residing in 271 households (Marcelli and Heer 1997). The logistic regression equation [1] developed from these data predicted residency status (RS) accurately approximately 85 percent of the time using only four variables—AGE, SEX, educational attainment (EDUC), and time in the United States (YEARS).

$$RS = \alpha + \beta_1 Age, \beta_2 Sex, \beta_3 Educ, \beta_4 Years \qquad [1]$$

The second survey, the 2001 LAC-MIRSS, is also a randomized foreign-born Mexican household survey that collected similar data for 829 Mexican immigrants from 456 households. Employing these data in equation [1] again accurately predicted RS about 82 percent of the time. Marcelli and Cornelius (2004) provide an overview of the 2001 LAC-MIRSS data.

A second step in our analysis takes the parameters generated from the 1994 and 2001 LAC-MIRSS data (β_1 through β_4) and applies these to the foreign-born Mexican adult populations enumerated in the 5% 1990 and 2000 Public Use Microdata Samples (PUMS) to generate a probability of having been unauthorized to reside in the United States, and then to assign unauthorized residency status to those with relatively high estimates.[1] Past research has shown that this survey-based residency status estimation methodology produces estimated numbers of unauthorized Mexican (and other Latino) immigrants that are remarkably consistent with those interpolated from estimates produced using the more traditional residual methodology (Heer and Passel 1987; Marcelli 1999). Furthermore, recent work by Marcelli and Lowell (2004) using the 2001 LAC-MIRSS reports only a slightly higher number of Mexican immigrants in Los Angeles County than either the 2001 Current Population Survey or the 2000 PUMS, and it is noteworthy that the U.S. Immigration and Naturalization Service (2003) employed census under-coverage rates estimated from the 2001 LAC-MIRSS (Marcelli and Ong 2002) to adjust their national estimate of the number of unauthorized immigrants residing in the United States. The LAC-MIRSS thus appears to offer credible estimates of the number of legal and unauthorized Mexican immigrants that, when combined with census data, can be used to investigate how these populations impact the economic outcomes of other ethno-racial groups.

A third step in our labor market analysis draws our sample. We select only individuals aged sixteen to sixty-four who were in the civilian labor force (employed or unemployed) and not enrolled in school because we are initially concerned with labor market competition. California's labor force (as defined above) grew from approximately 12.2 to 13.0 million, or by 6.8 percent, between 1990 and 2000. And although the rise in the female component (9.9 percent) was larger than that of the male (4.5 percent), the latter population represents a significantly higher absolute number of workers (7.2 versus 5.7 million in 2000). For this reason, as well as the fact that male labor force participation is less likely to be influenced by informal household responsibilities, we focus the rest of the paper on males only. With this focus, we examine what happened to the employment and earnings of African American male workers in three different labor market segments characterized by high, medium, and low levels of unauthorized Mexican immigrants throughout the state during the same decade.

We also extend the estimation procedure to show the geography of the undocumented Mexican labor force in California and use that to determine whether changes in the locational distribution of unauthorized Mexican immigrant between 1990 and 2000 led to geographic displacement and mobility of African American labor force participants over the same period. For this latter task, we chose the 2000 PUMAs as the relevant geographic level. A PUMA is a Public Use Microdata Area; it is the lowest geographic area in which full individual responses from the Census (given in the Public Use Microdata Samples or PUMS discussed above) are tagged. They are much larger than Census tracts since attaching the tract location to a person might make it possible to identify the individual; the Census Bureau tries to balance respondent confidentiality and geographic characterization by locating the residence in a broader unit labeled a PUMA. There are two levels of PUMAs, with the larger (in terms of geographic area) coming from the 1 percent PUMS and the smaller from the 5 percent PUMAs.

In our analysis, we use the 1% PUMA shapes from 2000. We use the larger shapes primarily because we need to cross-walk the 1990 data into the 2000 shapes to do the geographic comparisons, and this is more easily and reliably done with the larger shapes. However, we use the 5% PUMA data from both 1990 and 2000 (with each observation retagged into the 1% PUMA boundaries) since that maximizes the numbers of observations and hence accuracy in our estimates. A glance at the 2000 PUMA shapes will suggest that they are very much like localized labor markets in California and hence seem to be an appropriate level for this sort of analysis.

Labor Market Impact: Empirical Results

We start our analysis with the geographic overview. As can be seen in Figures 1 and 2, the geographic distribution of unauthorized Mexican immigrant male workers during the 1990s has become more dispersed. In 1990 this population was primarily concentrated in Los Angeles County, the central valley and central coast areas; by 2000, their residential concentration (that is, their share of the male labor force in the relevant PUMA) had surpassed 10 percent outside of Los Angeles County in Monterey, Fresno and Imperial County, and Northern California had also experienced an increase. In short, the population of unauthorized Mexican immigrant workers became more numerous and more dispersed throughout California during the previous decade, even as concentration continued in certain locations (see below).

A closer look at two metropolitan areas within California—the San Francisco Bay Area and Los Angeles—provides a bit more insight on the changes and also suggests potential residential competition with African Americans. Figure 3 shows that unauthorized Mexican males have not only become more concentrated in the San Jose-Santa Cruz region, an area with very few blacks, but also in the more traditionally African American areas of Oakland and Richmond. Figure 4 indicates where the move-in has actually been the most dramatic—Los Angeles and Orange Counties, with significant increases in the South L.A. area, among others. Figure 5 rounds out the geographic picture by showing the top ten PUMAs in California with regard to the percent of undocumented Mexican male immigrants as a percent of the male workforce; aside from the rural areas pictured in the pop-up, we see that the main areas where unauthorized immigrants reside are to the east of the industrial corridor

Figure 1

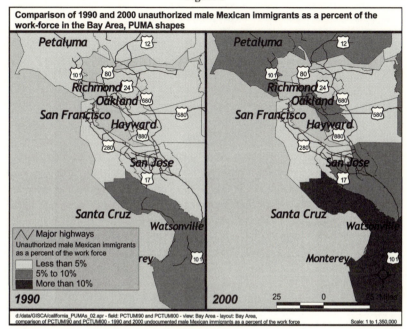

Comparison of 1990 and 2000 unauthorized male Mexican immigrants as a percent of the work-force in the Bay Area, PUMA shapes

Figure 2

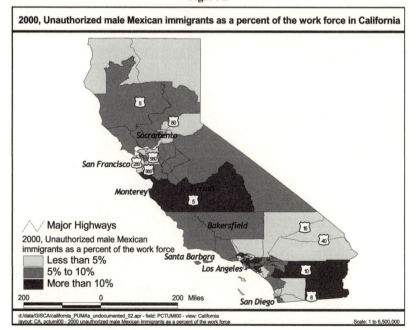

2000, Unauthorized male Mexican immigrants as a percent of the work force in California

Figure 3

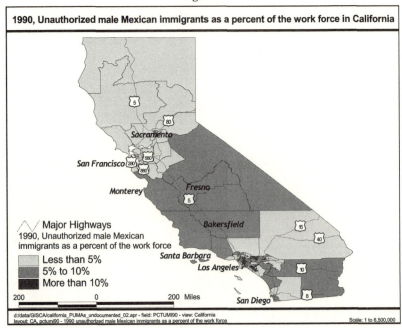

1990, Unauthorized male Mexican immigrants as a percent of the work force in California

Figure 4

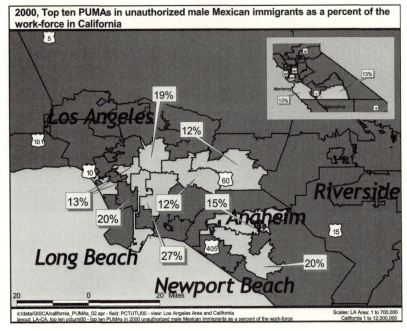

2000, Top ten PUMAs in unauthorized male Mexican immigrants as a percent of the work-force in California

Figure 5

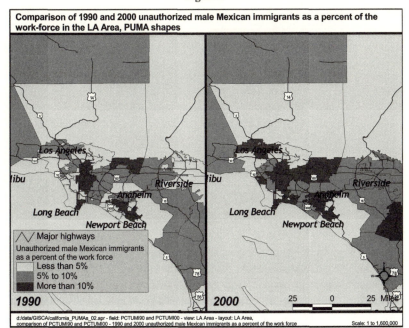

Comparison of 1990 and 2000 unauthorized male Mexican immigrants as a percent of the work-force in the LA Area, PUMA shapes

in Los Angeles, along the San Gabriel Valley, and in the Anaheim-Santa Ana area.

If significant displacement is going on in the workforce, we would expect that areas that experienced an increase in undocumented Mexican workers would have also experienced a decrease in, or at least a less rapid growth of, African American workers. Figure 6 tries to look at this question with a scatterplot of growth for both groups, with each growth rate calculated against the size of the overall 1990 workforce; this normalization avoids a problem with small base years (small numerical gains on a small initial starting point will yield large growth rates even when the population has grown insubstantially) and also sidesteps the obvious fact that a larger share of one portion of the workforce in 2000 is likely to mean a smaller share of the other. As it turns out, unauthorized Mexican immigrant and black male labor force participants appear to have been moving into and out of the same areas in California between 1990 and 2000, perhaps because of job creation and loss in those areas, with this trend indicated by the scatterplot in general and the fitted regression line in particular.[2]

Geographic mobility patterns, while providing some evidence that the two populations of concern here are not competing with one another economically—or if they are, that it is not resulting in geographic displacement—are insufficient for answering the question of whether one lower-skilled immi-

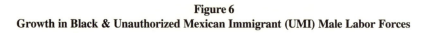

Figure 6
Growth in Black & Unauthorized Mexican Immigrant (UMI) Male Labor Forces

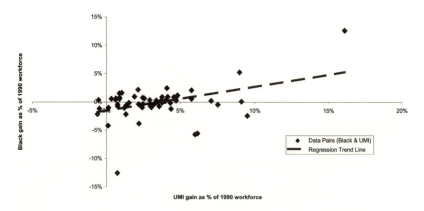

grant group is impacting the fortunes of another U.S.-born minority group. Additional evidence may come from considering how the earnings and employment patterns of African American male workers were affected in occupations with different levels of unauthorized Mexican immigrants. In general, we should expect black earnings and/or employment to have fallen (or to have fallen more) in occupations with higher levels of unauthorized Mexicans between 1990 and 2000 if the two groups are competing with one another.

Although we do not attempt to formally model African American male employment or hourly wage outcomes here econometrically, descriptive statistics presented below suggest that the influx of unauthorized Mexican male workers may have had both negative and positive effects. It will be helpful to first define what is meant by low, medium, and high levels of unauthorized Mexican immigrant male occupational representation. Following past practice (Marcelli, Pastor, and Joassart 1999), we created three labor market segments distinguished by the proportion of unauthorized Mexican male workers. Based on the estimated occupational representation of unauthorized Mexican immigrant male workers in thirty-three categories defined for the 2000 Census (Figure 7) and analysis of relatively large "breaks" in this distribution, our occupational segment characterized by a low level of representation includes fifteen categories with less than 2.5 percent unauthorized Mexicans (e.g., air transportation, firefighter, architect). Our medium level or segment of occupations includes eleven occupations (e.g., healthcare support, motor vehicle driver) with less than 12 percent unauthorized Mexicans, and our high level or segment of occupations includes seven occupations with more than this threshold (e.g., material moving, food services).

Because the Bureau of the Census defined various occupation categories differently in 2000 than it did in 1990, it is impossible to compare changes in

Figure 7
Proportion of Male Unauthorized Mexican Immigrant Workers by Occupation, California, 2000

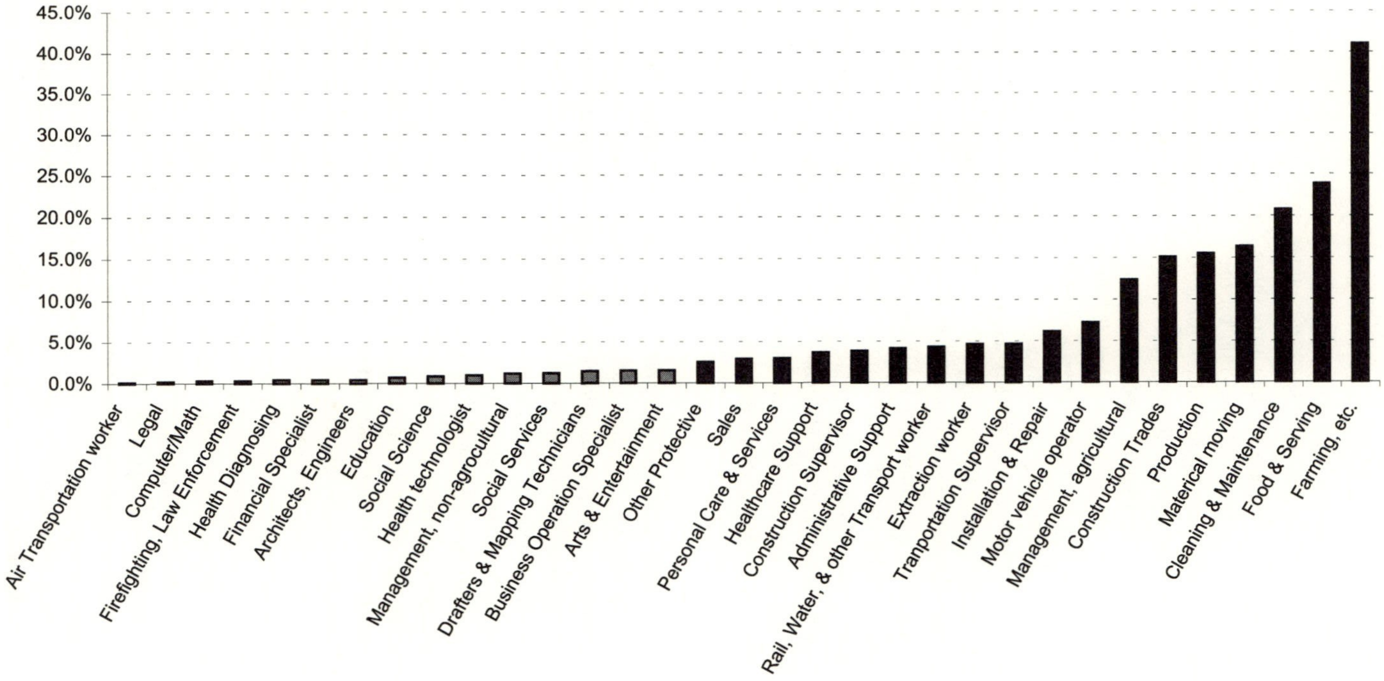

employment or wages by occupation directly. To analyze these for particular ethno-racial groups during the previous decade requires use of the Census Bureau's occupational "cross walk" tables. In general, the Bureau estimated employment changes in the thirty-three occupational categories shown in Figure 7 between 1990 and 2000 for the total U.S. labor force and has made available the conversion tables for linking the thirteen major occupational categories in 1990 to the thirty-three 2000 categories. The only method of estimating employment changes for individual groups thus requires application of the conversion algorithm developed for the entire U.S. labor force.

Table 1 reports employment and hourly wages estimates for unauthorized Mexican immigrant and African American males in 1990 and 2000 by California's three labor market segments as defined above. Although the number of black male workers aged sixteen to sixty-four employed in the occupational segments with low and medium levels of unauthorized Mexican immigrants rose between 1990 and 2000 (ΔBLK), it declined by approximately 38,000 or 30 percent in those occupations with relatively high proportions. And although black male wages (W_{blk90}, W_{blk2k}) were higher than the wages of unauthorized Mexican workers (W_{umi90}, W_{umi2k}) in all three labor market segments throughout the 1990s and rose in the low and medium segments, they fell by $1.82 or 10 percent even as those of Mexican workers rose by $1.53 in the segment with the highest proportion of unauthorized Mexican workers.

One may infer a labor market competition story from Table 1. However, it may also be the case that some black males moved from occupations with higher proportions of unauthorized Mexican workers to those with lower proportions, partly because of the effects of complementary migrant labor; this would be consistent with the sharp decline in African American workers in the high-UMI sector and the increases in the other segments, and would also square with the wage enhancement effects of immigrants on African Americans found by Ong and Valenzuela (1996) for a Los Angeles sample. Moreover, the negative association detected between an influx of unauthorized Mexican workers, on the one hand, and the employment and hourly earnings of blacks, on the other, may disappear once individual characteristics and other factors are controlled for in an econometric model; tied together with the possibility of African American occupational mobility, this may suggest that those left behind were those with the lowest human capital. We intend to investigate these complexities in future econometric work.

Still, while the geographic picture presents little evidence of displacement and the wage effects lack the proper controls, the data do suggest why some have been worried about the impacts on job loss and income. Historically, lower employment and lower wages in occupations filled by lower-skilled immigrant groups have helped to generate restrictionist immigrant sentiment in the United States. What have been the attitudes and political strategies of African Americans

Table 1
Unauthorized Mexican Immigrant and U.S.-Born Black
Labor Market Outcomes from 1990 to 2000 by Level of Unauthorized
Mexican Immigrant Male Workers in 2000, California

Occupations with Low, Medium, and High Levels of Unauthorized
Mexican Immigrant Male Workers

	Low	Medium	High
ΔUMI	10,035	-1,032	204,949
ΔBLK	4,066	9,589	-38,126
%ΔUMI	84.0%	-1.0%	87.3%
%ΔBLK	4.6%	6.8%	-30.2%
Wumi90	$13.34	$9.36	$9.54
Wblk90	$26.82	$17.12	$18.16
Wumi2k	$17.18	$14.22	$11.07
Wblk2k	$31.14	$18.13	$16.34
ΔWumi	$3.84	$4.86	$1.53
ΔWblk	$4.32	$1.01	-$1.82
%ΔWblk	16.1%	5.9%	-10.0%

in the wake of these patterns, particularly in California, a state so affected by international migration of both the documented and the undocumented?

Public Opinion and Politics

The Public Opinion Dilemma

We began the chapter by noting that some authors wonder why a position in favor of immigration restrictions has not gained more ground among black civil rights leaders. In our view, the economic evidence is ambiguous and this explains part of the picture. But those who would suggest the relative silence on immigration is partly the result of black elites being out of touch with working-class constituents are missing an important fact: grassroots African Americans have also often been more sympathetic toward immigrants than their white counterparts.

For example, a recent Gallup poll (June 2003) indicates that 49 percent of whites say that immigration should be decreased while only 11 percent suggest that it should be increased; in contrast, 44 percent of blacks are in favor of a decrease in immigration while a full 20 percent would support an increase. The same poll finds income is a significant predictor of a more sympathetic attitude towards immigration, with 75 percent of those with incomes exceeding $75,000 agreeing that immigration is good for the country with the comparable figure being 46 percent for those with incomes below $30,000; given the skew toward the bottom end of the income distribution in the African American community, this makes the black support for increasing immigration all the more surprising.[3]

In California, one of the states most deeply affected by immigration and one where Latinos are clearly in demographic ascendancy, sometimes to the seeming detriment of black political power, public opinion polls suggest that the state's African Americans, while not as sympathetic to immigrants as California's Latinos, are far more sympathetic than whites. For example, when asked to rank immigrants as a benefit or a burden, 53 percent of whites chose burden with 47 percent selecting benefit; blacks are a nearly polar opposite with 55 percent choosing benefit and 45 percent selecting burden (Hajnal and Baldarassare 2001: 10). The pattern is striking since whites are, according to most theory and empirics, far better positioned to benefit from the generalized economic gains from immigration.

As for the more vexing problem of undocumented immigration, the voting on Proposition 187, the controversial 1994 effort to restrict access of undocumented immigrants and their children to key public services, including education and health facilities, also showed a racial divide: while whites voted for the measure 63 percent to 37 percent, African Americans rejected it by the same proportions as did Asian Americans with only 47 percent voting yes and 53 percent voting no (Latinos, despite some early polls showing sympathy, rejected the measure 77 percent to 23 percent; *Los Angeles Times* exit poll, 1994). While the significant anti-187 vote by blacks was partly due to the nature of the proposition itself—by the time the election came, the measure was seen not as a dispassionate approach to stemming the local costs of immigration but rather a broader and racialized attack on Latinos—the voting differential is still significant and important, particularly given the likelihood that Latino immigrants and blacks were in the most direct competition for the health and education services to be restricted.

The pattern of black tolerance is even apparent in Los Angeles County, the acknowledged heart of undocumented immigration in the state (recall Figure 5) and a place where multiple instances of ethnic succession in neighborhoods, including throughout South Los Angeles and adjoining inner-ring suburbs (like Compton), have made for inter-ethnic conflict. Making use of the Los Angeles Survey of Urban Inequality, we ran a crosstabs of race with attitude on the impacts of immigrants on one's ethnic group; the results are depicted in Figures 8 and 9.[4] African Americans do believe that continued immigration will diminish economic opportunity for their group at a rate higher than whites and seemingly feel more strongly about it than whites; at the same time, it is striking that a much higher percentage of blacks than whites also believe that continued immigration will, in fact, improve economic opportunity for blacks.

As for political attitudes, while a plurality of blacks believes that immigration will diminish black political strength, African Americans are also actually far more optimistic that immigration will improve their political prospects. It should be stressed that this survey was conducted around the time of the L.A. civil unrest when the area economy was also mired in its worst postwar recession and when ethnic tensions were at an all-time high, particularly with blacks and Latinos squabbling over monies for rebuilding and blacks and Koreans struggling over the reconstruction of liquors store in South Central Los Angeles (see Pastor 1995); that the attitudes are this positive is impressive.

Disentangling Public Opinion

Of course, one possibility is that immigration preferences do not reflect economic realities at all. Citrin et al. (1997), for example, makes use of the 1992 and 1994 National Election Surveys and finds that attitudes about immigration policy are largely shaped by deeper values than by current economic position and costs. Kessler (2001), however, has redone the work with the five of the NES surveys (1992 to 2000) and deployed a more sophisticated econometric procedure.[5] He attempts to control for both economic status and political positions (conservative versus liberal, Republican versus Democrat) and degree of prejudice (with the hypothesis being that those who are more prejudiced might be more predisposed to favor restrictions on immigration). He finds that prejudice is strongly and consistently related to restrictionist sentiment but also the economic variables do matter and in ways that would be predicted by the assumed economic effects: lower-skilled workers are more likely to wish for restrictions while higher-skill workers are less likely to favor reductions in immigration.

What about the particular attitudes of blacks? Kessler finds a positive disposition toward restriction but the effect is statistically insignificant. Does this contradict the favorable attitudes we describe above? Not really. The construction of Kessler's prejudice measure is almost entirely focused on the African American experience, with fifteen of the seventeen components of the composite prejudice measure focused on views of the legacy of slavery, the work ethic of blacks, and whether blacks have gotten more or less than is "deserved"; the two components that do not specifically refer to blacks are concerned with Affirmative Action and are asked in the context of another question on aid to blacks. It is highly unlikely that blacks score highly on this sort of prejudice measure—and that they are the only group for whom this test is unreliable suggests that it may not be a good test of general unease toward the "other." This leaves the black dummy variable to absorb the statistical effects of any black prejudice towards other groups—something that case studies of black-Korean and black-Latino conflict suggest may be present—and, even under these circumstances, no significant results can be found.

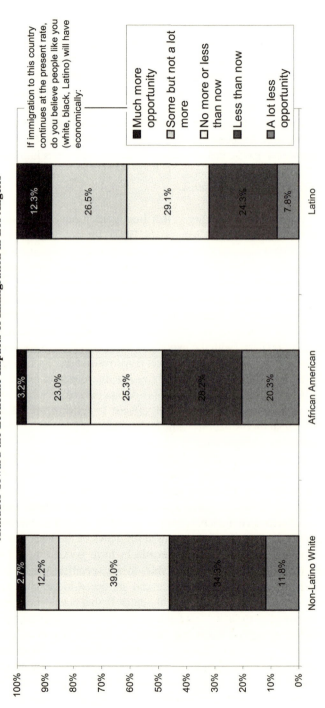

Figure 8
Attitudes Toward the Economic Impacts of Immigration in Los Angeles

If immigration to this country continues at the present rate, do you believe people like you (white, black, Latino) will have economically:

- Much more opportunity
- Some but not a lot more
- No more or less than now
- Less than now
- A lot less opportunity

Non-Latino White
- 2.7%
- 12.2%
- 39.0%
- 34.3%
- 11.8%

African American
- 3.2%
- 23.0%
- 25.3%
- 28.2%
- 20.3%

Latino
- 12.3%
- 26.5%
- 29.1%
- 24.3%
- 7.8%

Figure 9
Attitudes Toward the Political Impacts of Immigration in Los Angeles

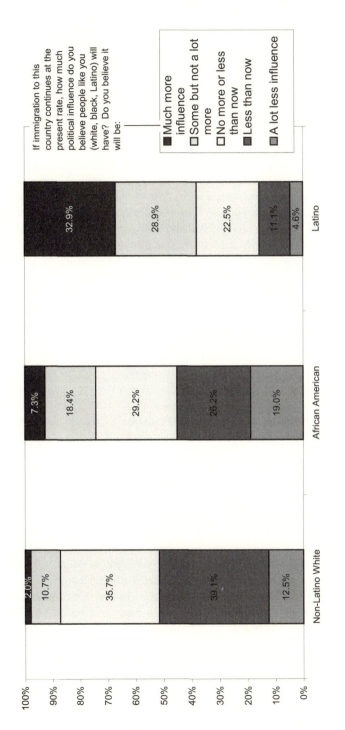

To get at the issue more clearly, we decided to implement a Kessler-style model using data on attitudes from the Los Angeles Survey of Urban Inequality (LASUI), the broad results for which were recorded above. We focus on the two questions on immigration reviewed earlier, both of which asked respondents whether they felt that their particular ethnic group would be hurt or helped, and to what degree, if the current levels of immigration into the U.S. continued. Again, we wish to emphasize that the survey was conducted in the wake of the Los Angeles civil unrest, a time in which ethnic tensions were severe and the area economy was in its worst recession in the postwar period.

Following Kessler's (2001) strategy, we employ an ordered logit regression, structuring the dependent attitudinal variables such that a positive coefficient reflects a respondent belief that the effects on one's own group are more positive. The independent variables are all listed in Table 2, with the race, age, and gender variables being self-evident. *Degree of Education* is a categorical variable where respondents are broken into three groups: those with less than a high school degree, those with a high school degree, and those with a college degree or higher. The results we report are robust to other categorizations of education or to a variable that is a straightforward measure of years of schooling.

We also employ two variables reflecting attitudes toward race. As noted above, we were displeased with Kessler's approach since it empirically limited racism to only anti-black attitudes. Moreover, we are not sure that attitudes toward policy measures like Affirmative Action are strictly expressions of the degree of racism (just as restrictionist attitudes toward immigration are not necessarily signals of nativist impulses). We thus look at two variables that seem more rooted in prejudice *per se*: *Racist Comment* and *Belief in Innate Inferiority*.

Racist Comment is a dummy variable that takes the value of one when the respondent used a derogatory racial term somewhere in the interview process (these were multi-hour interviews in which interviewers were asked to record respondent attitudes as well as answers), and *Belief in Innate Inferiority* is a categorical variable recording to what degree the respondent agreed that worse economic and social outcomes for blacks or Latinos were due to an in-born inability to learn (half the group was asked about blacks and the other half was asked about Latinos, with individuals selected into the question pattern at random). The advantage of both these variables over Kessler's is that it allows us to capture black prejudice against others to the extent that it might exist.

Table 2 shows the results; over all the specifications reported, the number of observations is approximately 4,000 with the observations weighted in accordance with the instructions of the survey designers (for more details on weighting this dataset, see Pastor and Marcelli 2000). We should stress that all the results here are robust across modestly different specifications of the variables and attempts to enter the variables in various combinations than those

Table 2
Attitudes in Los Angeles County on the Impacts of Immigration

Degree to which economic prospects for your group will improve if immigration continues at current levels:

Variables	Coefficients	T-stat Sig.	Coefficients	T-stat Sig.	Coefficients	T-stat Sig.
African American	0.074	0.88	0.077	0.92	0.058	0.69
Latino	0.761	7.46 ***	0.767	7.52 ***	0.727	7.06 ***
Asian	1.394	13.40 ***	1.389	13.36 ***	1.387	13.08 ***
Degree of Education	0.181	6.03 ***	0.181	6.03 ***	0.168	5.42 ***
Age	-0.011	-5.50 ***	-0.011	-5.50 ***	-0.013	-6.50 ***
U.S.-born	-0.378	-4.67 ***	-0.38	-4.69 ***	-0.392	-4.78 ***
Male	0.08	1.38 #	0.079	1.36 #	0.094	1.62 #
Racist Comment			-0.235	-1.57 #	-0.22	-1.46 #
Belief in Innate Inferiority					-0.01	-0.28
Psuedo R-squared	0.163		0.163		0.165	
Chi-Square for Model	669.1		670.2 ***		662.3 ***	

Degree to which political prospects for your group will improve if immigration continues at current levels:

Variables	Coefficients	T-stat Sig.	Coefficients	T-stat Sig.	Coefficients	T-stat Sig.
African American	0.257	3.06 ***	0.263	3.13 ***	0.256	3.01 ***
Latino	1.813	17.10 ***	1.828	17.25 ***	1.802	16.84 ***
Asian	1.821	17.18 ***	1.817	17.14 ***	1.831	16.95 ***
Degree of Education	-0.01	-0.33	-0.012	-0.40	-0.035	-1.13
Age	-0.01	-5.00 ***	-0.01	-5.00 ***	-0.011	-5.50 ***
U.S.-born	-0.539	-6.57 ***	-0.54	-6.59 ***	-0.518	-6.24 ***
Male	-0.096	-1.66 *	-0.097	-1.67 *	-0.076	-1.29
Racist Comment			-0.382	-2.55 **	-0.422	-2.79 **
Belief in Innate Inferiority					-0.068	-1.89 *
Psuedo R-squared	0.271		0.272		0.277	
Chi-Square for Model	1191.7	***	1195.3	***	1192.7	***

*** indicates significance at the .01 level
** indicates significance at the .05 level
* indicates significance at the .10 level
Source: Los Angeles Survey of Urban Inequality

shown, including runs with just the race variables; we offer the limited columns of results simply to conserve space.

Let us focus first on the race variables. Recalling that the omitted group is whites, we can see that Latinos and Asians are enthusiastic about both the economic and political impacts of immigrants, with political impacts enjoying larger coefficients. African Americans are actually slightly more optimistic than whites about the economic impacts but the result is not statistically significant; however, they are far more optimistic about the political impacts and that result is significant at the .01 level.

Degree of education is positively and significantly associated with believing that immigration will bring economic gains, a result which squares with economic theory that suggests those with higher levels of human capital have more to gain from complementary labor. There is a negative association of education with a sense that immigrants will contribute to political gains—suggesting that working class residents might feel more positive about political impacts—but the result is not significant. Older and U.S.-born workers are more pessimistic about both the economic impacts of immigration; males are more optimistic about economic impacts but only at the .20 level while there is a statistically significant concern about political impacts.

On the straight attitudinal variables, *Racist Comment* has a statistically significant negative association with views about the political benefits of immigration and a marginally negative association with economic benefits. Interestingly, a belief in innate inferiority has virtually no effect on views about the economic benefits but has a statistically significant impact on views about political prospects; in short, those who have a dim view of the natural skills of "the other" do not tend to see them as economic competition but worry about the political strength that might be gained by pure numbers.

The key result here for the purposes of this chapter is that African Americans are no more pessimistic than whites about the economic impacts of immigration despite the belief of many economists that they are the true losers. As for politics, blacks are more optimistic that immigration will bring gains. These are the makings of a "rainbow coalition," although it is one that will very clearly need to address the desires for economic advancement by African Americans if it is to remain solid.

Thinking Through the Policy Game

Of course, one potential explanation for the relatively sympathetic position of African Americans is that they are simply failing to express their own interests, perhaps motivated by core values around civil rights or perhaps driven by a form of "false consciousness." Some might argue that whites are afflicted by the same challenge of accurately perceiving self-interest, since the expressed opinions and voting patterns evidenced by whites suggest a hostility toward immigrants that is inconsistent with the benefits received. By this measure, of course, Latinos would then seem to be the most deluded, since there is a remarkable empathy for immigrants despite the fact that many are most directly in line for competition in crowded and segmented urban labor markets (Marcelli and Heer 1997).

Economists, however, are usually bothered by explanations that rely on the irrationality of the actors in either economics or politics. White racism, for example, is not seen as an error by workers failing to perceive their class interest; it is instead seen as a rational individual response to a system of disproportionate benefits, and one only likely to change when the apparent gains from race are more clearly offset by the losses due to weakened class power. By the same token, we prefer an explanation of black attitudes toward immigration based on a notion of rational actors: African American empathies, we would argue, are actually in line with longer-run interests around exactly the "rainbow coalition" some have questioned. To develop this perspective requires understanding both the nature of tradeoffs and the off-stage dynamics of demographic change, factors we sketch out below.

To understand our perspective, consider the following political economy game. Let the world consist of three groups: native whites, native blacks, and a group of Latinos who are a mix of native and immigrant, with some share of the immigrant sub-group naturalized and enjoying full enfranchisement as citizens. Assume that wealth assets are disproportionately concentrated in the hands of whites, a fact well-documented by many authors (Oliver and Shapiro 1995; Wolff 2000), and that skill distributions, given racial disparities in access to educational opportunities, are such that human capital levels are significantly higher in the white community as well.

Let increased immigration of Latinos—under the assumption that such immigrants are relatively low-skilled or will, due to linguistic and documentation challenges, settle for wages below a usual award to human capital—raise the return to financial capital and highly-skilled labor but depress the overall wage. This is a "set-up" for black-immigrant competition à la Borjas (1998) as relative benefits will accrue to higher-skill and asset-rich whites, and the costs from the overall pressure on the wage will fall more strongly on lower-skill and asset-poor native blacks. The exact size of the "wage penalty" will depend on the initial distribution of financial and human capital, the size of the influx, and other factors, such as the state of the macroeconomy.[6]

Under what circumstances would it make sense for native blacks to take a lead in opposing increased immigration? This would depend on the gains that could be had by shrinking the wage penalty versus the gains to be gotten from an alternative strategy, say, a tax on financial assets which, because of the current disproportionately low level of assets held by blacks, would yield a higher than average reward for African Americans, or an increase in the minimum wage which would also have disproportionately positive impacts for blacks. Importantly, the calculus of relative gains also depends on the relative certainty about each outcome, that is, the likelihood of obtaining necessary allies (political feasibility), and the available technology to enforce the desired course of action (that is, policy efficacy).

For the tax strategy, the technology of applying a new tax is well known and the assets are already in-country; the uncertainty here stems from whether a coalition can hold and also whether an excessively high tax might trigger a capital strike or flight. As for political feasibility, assuming generalized white resistance to a wealth tax (because of the racialized distribution of assets), the only feasible coalition for the new tax policy would be an alliance with Latinos and with asset-short whites—that is, a rainbow coalition. As for the minimum wage, enforcement seems to be largely effective, reinforced by social norms as well as government officials; indeed, even informal labor markets seem to have their floors set by the government-mandated minimum. Again, the coalition here is rainbow in nature: low-income workers of any race can benefit.

The immigrant restriction strategy, on the other hand, faces numerous problems. First, as indicated by the continuing debate, there are still some elements of uncertainty with regard to the size of the wage penalty and hence the potential gains (versus the clearer sense with regard to the minimum wage). The first source of uncertainty here is the ambiguity of the cross-effects of migrants on blacks, particularly as they vary by sector and degree of human capital. A second source of uncertainty stems from the macroeconomic effects that might wash out some of the cross-sectional losses, that is, the gains to the overall economy from immigration could have positive spillovers for African American communities and this has to be weighed against micro effects. A third source of uncertainty lies in whether any identified effects one might observe are actually coming from sources other than the immigrant competition *per se*, such as long-term declines in the quality of employment.

However, the real problem here may lie in the arenas of coalition building and policy efficacy. First, whites tend to gain less from restrictions and Latinos are not generally allies in these efforts. In fact, white attitudes, as noted above, seem to have more to do with cultural values than economics—whites are worried about losing cultural dominance while Latinos welcome the mix for this and other reasons explored below (especially a potential enhancement of political power). Seeking allies without resorting to the cultural arguments that appeal to some whites is a challenge.

Second, immigration "technology" seems to be quite problematic: It is, after all, unclear whether improved border control, employer sanctions, and related measures can actually do the restrictionist trick. Border enforcement has been enhanced in recent years but this has mostly resulted in a shift in the migration paths toward less safe strategies, including dangerous border crossing through the Arizona desert and a higher rate of fatalities for Mexican migrants (Cornelius 2000). The flow itself does not seem to have been diminished greatly, in part because labor demand for migrants has become "embedded" into the very structure of economies like California's (Cornelius 1998) and partly because extended social networks have resulted in a circular chain of migration in which the usual push and pull factors have been supplemented by the assumption of the transnational movement of labor (see Marcelli and Cornelius 2001 and Massey 1998). What has been altered by enforcement is the decision to return: migrants are now rationally recognizing that return costs are higher and are therefore pursuing longer stays in the United States (Massey 2003).

What about employer sanctions or a system of national identification cards? Employer sanctions are in effect but have not been effective; they have, however, helped to produce higher screening of Latino workers, raising concerns about discrimination. National identification systems may enjoy a resurgence in the wake of the September 11 attacks on New York and Washington but they have been fiercely opposed by civil libertarians on the right and the left. In short, we do not see either effectiveness or political viability for these policies and the very fact that there is such a significant presence of undocumented residents in our own frontline state of California suggests the difficulty of identification and removal. All this makes immigration restriction a less appealing strategy simply because it may be less feasible in the enforcement realm than, say, the aforementioned increase in asset taxes (for which there are escapes but also more viable technologies of detections) or an increase in the minimum wage (which, as noted, tends to be reinforced by social norms as well as government officials).[7]

We also believe that a restrictionist approach could cause political problems for blacks themselves. Strategies today must be considered in the context of a repeated policy game. Suppose, as is realistic, that white and black birth rates are lower than those of Latinos. Suppose further that the mix of immigrant to citizen in the Latino population is to some degree a choice; after all, for years, Mexican immigrants, often dreaming of returning to Mexico after their migration sojourn, were the least likely to become naturalized U.S. citizens, but they are now going through the citizenship process in great numbers. This would suggest that whatever political calculus is conducted now about immigration policy will also have to consider what happens in light of a repeated game in which the share of Latinos is growing, citizenship and voting can be quite elastic, and memory matters.

This was an insight forgotten by California's former Republican governor, Pete Wilson, when he coupled his run for reelection with the fate of Proposition 187. The perception grew that the proposition was not simply about taming illegal immigration but was also aimed at taking political advantage of racial anxieties about the growing Latinization of the state. The result was a defensive burst in Latino naturalization, registration and voting, and by 2002, not a single statewide office was held by a Republican. The hemorrhaging of the Republican Party—a party whose attachment to traditional family values could have some appeal to Latino and immigrant constituents—was only arrested in 2003 by running a socially moderate movie star, Arnold Schwarzenegger, in the unusual terrain of a recall election.

Indeed, the projected growth of Latinos helps explain why this group has (beyond cultural reasons) concrete interests in enhanced immigration even though it seems to experience the most negative economic impacts from recently arrived immigrants (Catanzarite 2003): immigration raises their voting numbers into the future as new immigrants naturalize or give birth to U.S. citizens. Whites and blacks obviously have little interest in this and indeed might have a long-term interest in restricting the growth of this group. However, African Americans should be (and, in fact, are) concerned that restrictionist legislation could fuel other forms of prejudice, much as Proposition 187 in California became a precursor for Proposition 209, which banned Affirmative Action. The whole scenario implies that whatever gains might be made now through restriction may be undone later by anti-black backlash (perhaps by Latinos and perhaps by whites) on issues of central import.

Indeed, if we return to Kessler's complex econometric model of immigration policy preferences, we can identify one key political dilemma for black leadership: if, as seems to be the case, both economics and prejudice drive pro-restrictionist sentiment, then it is a challenge to initiate a policy that would use concern about immigrants to drive black economic improvement without fanning flames of prejudice that could crackle back on black political leadership and the African American community itself.

Conclusion

Coalitions evolve when groups are able to put multiple issues on the table, in the process finding areas of common concern and also areas where there are possible tradeoffs between competing priorities. African Americans and immigrants share multiple economic goals, including higher levels of employment, better mechanisms for accessing financial wealth, the need for higher wages and other standards at the bottom of the labor market, and the central role of education and job training to lift levels of human capital. There are also obvious conflicts around issues such as access to state resources and employment, funds for language accommodations, and, of course, immigration levels themselves. The art of coalition building involves judging which of these conflicts is important enough to test the limits of a broader political consensus, and around which one a group should strive to find reasonable tradeoffs in the spirit of mutual support.

The issue—one on which people may quite rationally disagree—is how immigration policy fits into this rubric. Our main point here is that it is important that African Americans determine a position that does not unnecessarily align with the nativist impulses that emerge more from prejudice than economic rationality.[8] Those impulses, after all, could erode coalitional possibilities even as they lead to other policies that will undercut black economic and political gains, making a victory on holding back competitive immigrants only a temporary lull in a long economic storm.[9]

We actually believe that this is an issue ripe for compromise, and the relatively positive view of immigration amongst many African Americans reflected in the polling data above suggests a wellspring of sympathy and understanding on which to build such a compromise. We know, for example, that Latino demands for a "fair share" of public employment in some urban areas tend to directly challenge blacks for whom public sector jobs have been critical for economic advancement to the middle class (as were such jobs for many European immigrants). New immigrants are more rooted in the private sector; for them and for Latinos as a whole, avoiding the possible discriminatory impacts of employer sanctions may be a far more important issue. Can we hope to see African American leaders agree to resist restrictionist immigration policies in return for, say, more understanding by new immigrants and others of the unique role of public employment for the African American community?

In crafting their side of rainbow compromises, immigrants need to be far more conscious of what Zhou (2001: 221) terms the "shrunken territory of Blacks" and how this has given rise to a new sort of defensive politics. This shrinkage is partly a result of shared urban space: as Ethington, Frey, and Myers (2001) point out in the case of Los Angeles, even as African Americans remained relatively segregated from whites, blacks saw the probability of having a Latino neighbor rise from 11 percent in 1970 to 41 percent in 2000. But the shrinkage is also the result of a political system seeking to once again bypass African Americans and their interests. The sense of exclusion this induces is exacerbated by the fact that Latinos have now become America's largest minority group and by the celebratory tone in which the media assesses new immigrant drive and disparages persistent poverty in black urban neighborhoods.

In this light, Latinos must recognize that immigration is indeed a legitimate topic for discussion and that some restrictions may be feasible or desirable. After all, few wish for open borders; fewer still think that such openness is a politically realistic position. The policy issue is whether to reduce, maintain, or increase current levels of legal migration and whether to leave in the shadows those who are currently unauthorized within the country. Our view is that an orderly legalization is appropriate and we would also argue that a modest increase in legal immigration would actually be beneficial and would allow for better management of a flow that is only occasionally and quite imperfectly bottled up now. Aside from this area of sharp disagreement, we actually have much in common with Shulman and Smith (2004) who, while supportive of restrictions, are also explicit about the need to better incorporate, and raise the living standards for, immigrants who are already here, a strategy we and others have labeled *immigrant* versus *immigration* policy (Blackwell, Kwoh, and Pastor 2002; U.S. Commission on Immigration Reform 1997).

In fact, we think that there is actually a deeper commitment that we share: the advance of a progressive agenda in general and of black economic and political empowerment in particular. While we acknowledge that many of our own political projects and policy preferences are more in sync with those of immigrant advocates, we would suggest that all of us should be particularly concerned with the fate of African Americans in the contemporary economy. This is partly for reasons of historic redress and fairness but also because of the central role African Americans have played in the history of progressive change in the United States, including around the liberalization of immigration legislation itself. We are thus concerned that those suggesting that African American leaders take a more active stance on immigration policy—or better put, adopt a restrictionist position that is too easily painted as anti-immigrant—will both shipwreck needed alliances for years to come and in the process diminish rather than enhance black political power.

Notes

1. Specifically, we sort all foreign-born Mexican adults by their estimated probability of having been unauthorized in descending order and then assign unauthorized residency status to a number (counting from top to bottom) close to the sum of all the probabilities.
2. Since we were concerned about the potential for the outliers to distort the regression line, we eliminated two of the most extreme observations; the fitted line still sloped upward, albeit with a far lesser slope. At the best then, there is *prima facie* no relationship. The upward slope (which is consistent with the "no displacement" hypothesis) is stronger when one considers the changes in the levels of all undocumented Latino immigrants; in this chapter, we focus on the undocumented Mexicans since our estimates are a better fit for that group.
3. In an earlier poll in the mid-1990s reported by *Newsweek*, 66 percent of whites and only 46 percent of blacks indicated that there should be decreases in the levels of immigration to the United States (see Johnson et al. 1997). While the polls are not comparable, this does suggest a decline in black receptivity to immigrants.
4. We used the appropriate adjusted weights; unweighted results look very similar. Johnson et al. (1997) report a slightly different set of results, showing that more than half of blacks and a similar percent of whites believe that continued immigration will lead to a less or a lot less political influence for their group, with over 55 percent of blacks and over 45 percent of whites indicating that continued immigration would yield lower levels of economic opportunity for their group. This, however, is a somewhat selective reporting of the results (we report the range of responses) and those results, published relatively early in research use of the Survey of Urban Inequality also seem to not take account of sample weights, an approach which was increasingly clarified and standardized as use of the Survey increased over time.
5. A further advantage of the Kessler approach is the use of five surveys covering a range of macroeconomic conditions. There is a tendency for restrictionist sentiment to rise in a recession and observations for the early 1980s and the mid-1990s are somewhat anomalous.

6. We understand that the debate is about more than labor market effects and includes concerns about fiscal shortfalls, service delivery problems, and other matters; we are trying to simplify the analysis here and would suggest that it could easily be applied to those other areas. For one attempt to estimate the wage penalty from a higher presence of recent Latino immigrants, see Catanzarite (2003); interestingly, after stressing the wage penalty in her analysis, Catanzarite does not support immigration restrictions as a primary strategy but rather argues for improving the social state of immigrants.

7. This questioning of border control or employer sanctions does not rule out other strategies such as enforcement of wage laws such that immigrant workers are less able to undercut natives. The latter might be easier to enforce and is one of the approaches recommended by Shulman and Smith (2004); we return to this point in our conclusion.

8. A restrictionist immigration policy stance, of course, does not automatically imply prejudice and may derive from perceived or actual economic competition with immigrants. Our point here is that in the absence of such evidence a restrictionist position may do more harm than good for both African Americans and immigrants.

9. Briggs (2001) well understands the coalition game and cogently argues that this is not a good fit around immigration issues. Again, reasonable people may disagree on this issue of fit within coalitions.

References

Bailey, Thomas. 1987. *Immigrant and Native Workers: Contrasts and Competition.* Boulder, CO: Westview Press.

Bean, Frank D., B. Lindsay Lowell, and Lowell J. Taylor. 1988. "Undocumented Mexican Immigrants and the Earnings of Other Workers in the United States." *Demography* 25 (1): 35-49.

Bean, Frank D., Edward E. Telles, and B. Lindsay Lowell. 1987. "Undocumented Migration to the United States: Perceptions and Evidence." *Population and Development Review* 13 (4): 671-690.

Blackwell, Angela Glover, Stewart Kwoh, and Manuel Pastor. 2002. *Searching for the Uncommon Common Ground: New Dimensions on Race in America.* New York: W.W. Norton Press.

Borjas, George J. 1998. "Do Blacks Gain or Lose from Immigration?" Pp. 51-74 in *Help or Hindrance: The Economic Implications for African Americans*, edited by Daniel S. Hammermesh and Frank D. Bean. New York: Russell Sage Foundation.

Briggs, Vernon. 2003. "The Economic Well-Being of Black Americans: The Overarching Influence of U.S. Immigration Policies."

————. 2001. Remarks at a Panel on Immigration and American Labor, Washington, DC, National Press Club, sponsored by the Center for Immigration Studies. www.cis.org/articles/2001/unionpanel.html.

Catanzarite, Lisa. 2003. "Wage Penalties in Brown-Collar Occupations." Latino Policy & Issue Brief, no. 8, September. Los Angeles: UCLA Chicano Studies Research Center.

Citrin, Jack, Donald P. Green, Christopher Muste, and Cara Wong. 1997. "Public Opinion Toward Immigration Reform: The Role of Economic Motivations." *The Journal of Politics* 59 (August): 858-881.

Cornelius, Wayne. 2000. "Death at the Border: The Efficacy and 'Unintended' Consequences of U.S. Immigration Control Policy, 1993-2000." Working Paper No. 27. San Diego, CA: The Center for Comparative Immigration Studies, UC San Diego.

Cornelius, Wayne A. 1998 "The Structural Embeddedness of Demand for Mexican Immigrant Labor: New Evidence from California." In *Crossings: Mexican Immigration in*

Interdisciplinary Perspectives, edited by Marcel M. Suarez-Orozco. Cambridge, MA: Harvard University Press.

Cranford, Cynthia. 2000. "Economic Restructuring, Immigration and the New Labor Movement: Latina/o Janitors in Los Angeles." Working Paper No. 9. San Diego, CA: The Center for Comparative Immigration Studies, UC San Diego.

Ethington, Philip J., William H. Frey, and Dowell Myers. 2001. *The Racial Resegregation of Los Angeles County*. University of Southern California Race Contours Project, Public Research Report 2001-04.

Hammermesh, Daniel S. and Frank D. Bean, eds. 1998. *Help or Hindrance: The Economic Implications for African Americans*. New York: Russell Sage Foundation.

Hanjal, Zoltan and Mark Baldessaere. 2001. *Finding Common Ground: Racial and Ethnic Attitudes in California*. San Francisco, CA: Public Policy Institute of California.

Heer, David M. and Jeffrey S. Passel. 1987. "Comparison of Two Methods for Computing the Number of Undocumented Mexican Adults in Los Angeles County." *International Migration Review* 21: 1446-1474.

Johnson, James H. Jr., Walter C. Farrell Jr., and Chandra Guinn. 1997. "Immigration Reform and the Browning of America: Tensions, Conflicts, and Community Instability in Metropolitan Los Angeles." *International Migration Review* 31, 4.

Kessler, Alan. 2001. "Immigration, Economic Insecurity, and the 'Ambivalent' American Public." Working Paper No. 41. San Diego, CA: The Center for Comparative Immigration Studies, UC San Diego.

Marcelli, Enrico A. 1999. "Undocumented Latino Immigrant Workers: The L.A. Experience." Pp. 193-231 in *Illegal Immigration in America: A Reference Handbook*, edited by D. W. Haines and K. E. Rosemblum. Westport: Conn., Greenwood Press.

Marcelli, Enrico A. and Wayne A. Cornelius. 2001. "The Changing Profile of Mexican Migrants to the United States: New Evidence from Southern California." *Latin American Research Review* 36 (3): 105-131.

Marcelli, Enrico A. and David M. Heer. 1997. "Unauthorized Mexican Workers in the 1990 Los Angeles County Labour Force." *International Migration* 35 (1): 59-83.

Marcelli, Enrico A. and B. Lindsay Lowell. 2004. "Transnational Twist: Pecuniary Remittances and the Incorporation of Mexican Immigrants in Los Angeles County." *International Migration Review*, forthcoming.

Marcelli, Enrico A. and Paul M. Ong. 2002. "2000 Census Coverage of Foreign-born Mexicans in Los Angeles County: Implications for Demographic Analysis." Paper presented at the 2002 Population Association of America meetings, Atlanta, GA.

Marcelli, Enrico A., Manuel Pastor, Jr., and Pascale M. Joassart. 1999. "Estimating the Effects of Informal Economic Activity: Evidence from Los Angeles County." *Journal of Economic Issues* 33 (3): 579-607.

Massey, Douglas. 2003. "Closed-Door Policy." *The American Prospect* 14, 7 (July/August).

_____. 1998. "March of Folly: U.S. Immigration Policy After NAFTA." *The American Prospect* 9, 37 (March 1-April 1).

Oliver, Melvin L. and Thomas M. Shapiro. 1995. *Black Wealth, White Wealth: A New Perspective on Racial Inequality*. New York, NY: Routledge.

Ong, Paul and Abel Valenzuela, Jr. 1996. "The Labor Market: Immigrant Effects and Racial Disparities." In *Ethnic Los Angeles*, edited by Roger Waldinger and Mehdi Bozorgmehr. New York: Russell Sage.

Pastor, Manuel. 1995. "Economic Inequality, Latino Poverty and the Civil Unrest in Los Angeles." *Economic Development Quarterly* 9, 3.

Pastor, Manuel and Enrico Marcelli. 2000. "Men N the Hood: Spatial, Skill, and Social Mismatch for Male Workers in Los Angeles." *Urban Geography* 21, 6.

Shulman, Steven and Robert C. Smith. 2004. "Immigration, African Americans, and the 'Rainbow Coalition.'" In *African Americans in the American Economy*, edited by Cecilia Conrad, John Whitehead, Patrick Mason, and James Stewart. NY: Rowman and Littlefield Publishers, Inc.

Smith, James P. and Barry Edmonston. 1997. *The New Americans: Economic, Demographic, and Fiscal Effects of Immigration*. Washington, D.C.: National Academy Press.

Stoll, Michael A., Edwin Melendez, and Abel Valenzuela. 2002. "Spatial Job Search and Job Competition among Immigrant Native Groups in Los Angeles." *Regional Studies* 36(2): 97-112.

U.S. Commission on Immigration Reform. 1997. *Becoming and American: Immigration and Immigrant Policy*. Washington, D.C.

U.S. Immigration and Naturalization Service. 2003. Estimates of the Unauthorized Immigrant Population Residing in the United States: 1990 to 2000 (http://www.immigration.gov/ graphics/shared/aboutus/statistics/Ill_Report_1211.pdf).

Waldinger, Roger. 1999. "Network, Bureaucracy, and Exclusion: Recruitment and Selection in an Immigrant Metropolis." Pp. 228-259 in *Immigration and Opportunity: Race, Ethnicity, and Employment in the United States*, edited by Frank D. Bean and Stephanie Bell-Rose. New York, NY: Russell Sage Foundation.

_____. 1997. "Black/Immigrant Competition: New Evidence from Los Angeles." *Sociological Perspectives* 40 (2): 365-386.

_____. 1996. *Still the Promised City: African-Americans and New Immigrants in Postindustrial New York*. Cambridge, MA: Harvard University Press.

Waldinger, Roger and Michael I. Lichter. 2003. *How the Other Half Works: Immigration and the Social Organization of Labor*. Berkeley, CA: University of California Press.

Winegarden, C. R. and Lay Boon Khor. 1991. "Undocumented Immigration and Unemployment of US Youth and Minority Workers: Econometric Evidence." *Review of Economics and Statistics* 73 (1): 105-112.

Wolff, Edward N. 2000. "Recent Trends in Wealth Ownership, 1983-1998." Working Paper No. 300. The Jerome Levy Economics Institute, Bard College.

Zhou, Min. 2001. "Contemporary Immigration and the Dynamics of Race and Ethnicity." In *America Becoming: Racial Trends and Their Consequences*, Volume 1, National Research Council Commission on Behavioral and Social Sciences and Education, edited by Neil Smelser, William Julius Wilson, and Faith Mitchell. Washington, DC: National Academy Press.

7

Immigration and Race: What We Think We Know

Robert Cherry

Since the 1965 changes in immigration laws, there have been widely differing views on the value of the new wave of immigration. Some think immigration has very large economic and social benefits while others believe that immigration has substantial social and economic costs. The debate intensified as the annual number of immigrants increased dramatically over the last three decades, leading the National Academy of Science (NAS) to provide a comprehensive assessment of its financial impact. Its 1997 report, however, chose not to assess directly immigration's impact on native-born blacks but simply stated that "none of the available evidence suggests that [blacks] have been particularly hard-hit at the national level.[1]" After its publication, many books have assessed this impact and their findings will comprise the core of this chapter.

General Overview

Before detailing the specific evidence provided, this section will present the general perspectives of the authors of six recent books. The most strident criticism of current immigration policies is presented by Vernon Briggs. *In Immigration and American Unioni*sm, Briggs contends that the share of workers who are unionized has always been sensitive to the scale of immigration. He claims that the rise of union share during the 1930s was at least partially the result of the cutoff of immigration while the steep decline in union shares in recent years can be partially explained by the 1965 laws. Based on this perceived relationship, Briggs lamented,

> It is hard to see how organized labor can expect to gain from a continuation of mass immigration.… It can seek an expedient course and embrace mass immigration for

political advantage, which it seems to be doing. But if it actually does so, it will have abandoned its traditional role as the advocate for the economic well-being of American workers.[2]

Briggs is unsympathetic to current union claims that supporting immigration increases their ability to organize Hispanic workers.[3] He believes that even if unions are able to organize some additional Hispanic workers, the vast majority of less-skilled immigrants will be in unorganized work environments where they will undermine wages and working conditions. Briggs claims that when the AFL-CIO leadership in 2000 advocated an amnesty for illegal immigrants it was an "act of Judas," eliminating any possibility that they can be considered "a champion of American workers."[4]

George Borjas is also critical of current immigration policies. In *Heaven's Door*, he argues that the welfare, education, and medical costs associated with immigration are substantial due to the low earnings capacity of a growing share of immigrants. In response to these costs, Borjas proposes a point system where age, occupations, and education determine the value of each applicant for immigration. He favors using this point system to choose immigrants even though "my family would have been unable to 'pass the test' implicit in the skills-oriented immigration policy that I think would best serve the interests of the United States."[5]

In *Immigration and Race: New Challenges for American Democracy*, Gerald Jaynes contends that economic success among Caribbean, Cuban, and Korean immigrants primarily reflects the large proportion of highly educated individuals in these groups.[6] This contention parallels a similar claim made by Borjas. In the 1980s, grandchildren of European immigrants had higher earnings and educational attainment than blacks. Borjas points out that at the beginning of the twentieth century, immigrants were more disadvantaged than blacks; 87 percent of immigrants but only 68 percent of blacks were literate and immigrants earned 27 percent more than blacks. Borjas estimates that if immigrants in 1910 had the same black earnings and literacy disadvantages as African Americans, the grandchildren of these immigrants in 1985 would have very similar wages and education to that of African Americans. Thus, both authors discount completely cultural explanations for the relative economic success of some immigrant groups.[7]

Jaynes is, however, much more concerned with the social rather than economic consequences of immigration. He believes that Myrdal's assessment of the American psyche is still true: "Deeply ingrained in the nation's history and culture has been a profound need to have a population of lower-class blacks assuring whites that their values hold true." Within this context, immigrant success stories validate the American dream of equal opportunity because they imply that "African Americans' perpetual subordinate status…is due to their own inadequacies."[8]

Jaynes believes blacks are victims of a racist society and are not responsible for the unwillingness of their natural allies—immigrants and other people of color—to support them in struggles against the white power structure. While he believes that racist attitudes of immigrants are an important source of disunity, he contends that African Americans are selfless: even though 80 percent believe immigrants take away their jobs, blacks are more favorable to immigration and bilingual education than whites.

Three books Frank Bean coauthored suggest the problem is not losses but lack of African American gains. In *Immigration and Opportunity*, Bean and Stephanie Bell-Rose claim that economic and financial circumstances "prevent blacks to a considerable extent from deriving the same degree of economic gain from immigration that accrues to majority whites."[9] In *Help or Hindrance? The Economic Implications of Immigration for African Americans*, Hamermesh and Bean claim: "[Various research projects] add up to more compelling documentation that the positive economic effects emphasized by the National Research Council are substantially less likely to extend to African Americans."[10] In *America's Newcomers and the Dynamics of Diversity*, Bean and Gillian Stevens claim: "The racial and ethnic diversification…brought about by immigration…seems at least at this point in time not to have improved the overall economic status of African Americans."[11]

Impact on Native-Born Black Workers

Though the NAS report did not explicitly assess immigration's impact on native-born blacks directly, it did have findings that have clear implications. For example, a widely accepted result of the NAS study is their finding that those with high levels of financial and human capital benefited from immigration while those with low levels of financial and human capital were harmed by recent immigration. Native-born blacks are underrepresented among the beneficiaries and overrepresented among those harmed. Extrapolating from these findings, Borjas estimated that native-born blacks gain only $3 billion from financial holdings but lose $15 billion as workers, resulting in a per capita loss of about $300 annually. Most studies, however, focus attention on less educated workers who are disproportionately black and Hispanic.

Focusing on its impact on less educated workers makes sense given the increasing share of immigrants with limited education. In both the 1980 and 1990 census, 37 percent of immigrants were high school dropouts. In contrast, the share of natives who were dropouts declined from 23 percent in 1980 to 15 percent in 1990. As a result, between 1980 and 1990 the immigrant share of the U.S. labor force with less than a high school degree rose; among males, from 16 to 30 percent while, among females, it rose from 17 to 28 percent.[12]

During the 1990s, there was a further increase in the proportion of immigrants who were less educated. Friedberg and Hunt estimated that 43 percent of early 1990s immigrants did not possess the equivalent of a high school degree.[13] As a result, by 1998, the newest immigrants were almost four times more likely to be high school dropouts.[14] Moreover, these findings do not fully account for the increased immigrant supply of less skilled workers because they substantially ignore the growing number of undocumented workers. In particular, Bean and Stevens conservatively estimate that the number of Mexican illegals who reside in the United States has increased from 1.3 million in 1980 to 2.7 million in 1990 to 3.6 million in 2000.[15]

Not surprisingly, the NAS report found that "almost one-half of the decline in real wages for native-born high school dropouts from 1980 to 1994 could be attributed to the adverse impact of unskilled foreign workers."[16] David Jaeger estimated that immigration accounted for 15 to 25 percent of the increase in the high school-college wage gap during the 1980s.[17] These statistical studies complement historical studies that document examples of immigrant workers displacing native-born workers. For example, Briggs notes,

> Black janitors had their union broken in the 1980s by nonunion Hispanic workers. Management in the hotel industry in Los Angeles…was able to lower its wage rates and benefits by switching from a Teamsters local union made up mostly of black workers to a Seafarers' local whose members were mostly recent immigrants. In a 1982 strike at a Los Angeles tortilla factory, native-born workers were replaced by illegal immigrants…and wages were cut by 40 percent for those workers who returned.[18]

Christian Zlolniski documents similar dynamics in Silicon Valley where the employment of janitors grew even faster than the employment of computer engineers. She found that "janitorial work devolved from a stable, well-paid entry-level occupation for minority and established immigrants, to an unstable, low-wage, dead-end job for recent, mostly undocumented immigrants who arrived in the region in the 1980s."[19]

Further support is presented by Thomas Espenshade who found Puerto Ricans migration during the 1970s had adverse consequences on the earnings of native black males in New Jersey. Since Puerto Rican migrants had many of the characteristics of subsequent Hispanic immigrants, his study does foreshadow subsequent evidence that less-skilled Hispanic immigrants displaced African American men.

Using data from 205 local area labor markets, Cordelia Reimers assessed the impact of the 1980s immigration of high school dropouts. The wages of native-born black male dropouts were more adversely affected by a growth of the immigrant share of dropouts in local labor markets in those cities where the immigration high school dropouts were already substantial. These adverse consequences were most noticeable for those native-born black dropouts who had the highest wages. In particular, a one percentage-point increase in immigration would have no statistically significant predicted effect on the wages of the poorest paid native-born black male dropouts but a statistically significant effect on those earning above the median, reaching a 4.7 percent reduction on the highest paid. By contrast, above median paid native-born Mexican American dropouts benefited from increased immigration of unskilled workers.[20]

Reimers study also highlights how important it is to specify precisely the population investigated and the economic measures used. While she found that native-born Hispanic dropouts who have incomes above the group median benefited from immigration, Bean and Stevens noted that new immigrants "consistently exert negative effects on the wages of *other immigrants.*"[21]

More generally, Kristin Butcher found that estimates of immigration effects are sensitive to the measurement of immigration used. In particular, adverse impacts were more pronounced when the measure of immigrants included only those with low education rather than all immigrants. She also found that immigration has a much more significant adverse impact on the black-white earnings gap than on the black-white employment gap.[22]

Reimers' finding of a statistically insignificant *wage* effect for native-born black dropouts earning the lowest wages was interpreted by Hamermesh and Bean to indicate that immigration had a less severe impact on these dropouts than those who were better paid. This interpretation may be faulty. Other studies suggest that for the poorest paid dropouts, immigration has a significant adverse effect on their labor force participation rates.

George Johnson attempted to simulate the effect of the 10 million increase in the immigrant population during the 1980s on the wages and labor supply of unskilled black workers. For his preferred parameters, wages of unskilled black workers declined by about 3 percent if there was a general unskilled labor market. If, however, blacks and Hispanics were completely segmented from other (white) members of the unskilled workforce, Johnson estimated that immigration would reduce the supplies of unskilled black workers by 16.5 percent.[23]

In a more recent study, Hannes Johannsson, Stephan Weiler, and Steven Shulman focused on the labor supply response of native-born dropouts to an influx of immigrant workers.[24] Using data from 1995-99, they divided their sample into two groups: twenty-eight cities where immigrants comprise more than 25 percent of the dropout workforce; and forty cities where they comprise less than 25 percent. Using both static and fixed-effects models, they found that a rise in the immigrant share of the local dropout workforce had adverse impacts on the labor force participation rate of native-born dropouts, especially in the more immigrant-dense cities. In their fixed-effects model, if the immigrant share increased by 10 percent, the labor force participation rate of native-born dropouts would decline by an average of 2.7 percent in the twenty-eight immigrant-dense cities and by an average of 0.3 percent in the other forty cities.

Using Census and CPS data from 1960 through 2001, George Borjas estimated the impact of immigration on national wages after adjusting for both age and experience. Not surprisingly, he finds that wages of native-born workers are most sensitive to an influx of immigrants with the same level of education and work experience. In particular, he estimated that immigration during the 1980-2000 time period was responsible for an 8.9 percent wage decline for native-born high school dropouts. Consistent with Riemers' results, he finds that for the highest paid high school dropouts—those with eleven to twenty years experience—the wage decline was over 13 percent. Borjas also found that the adverse wage impact was quite significant among college graduates, averaging 4.9 percent across experienced groups. By contrast, the adverse wage impact was no higher than 3.5 percent for any of the experienced groups of native-born high school graduates.[25]

Finally, a recent Canadian study also found that immigration had adverse wage effects on Canadian-born workers. Using the long form from the 1981, 1991, and 2001 national data, Marc Frenette used a fixed effects model to determine the impact of recent immigrants on the wages of Canadian-born workers adjusting for occupational groupings. He estimated that a 10 percentage-point supply increase would lower the wages of Canadian-born workers by about 3 percent. This adverse effect was overwhelmingly concentrated in the blue collar manual occupations, especially during the 1990s. In particular, he estimated that during this time period, a 10 percentage-point supply increase was responsible for an 8.2 percent wage decrease in this occupational grouping but had no adverse consequences for workers in non-professional white collar occupations. Using an alternative occupational classification scheme, he estimated that in the lowest skill category a 10 percentage-point supply increase would lower wages by 10.2 percent.[26]

Alternative Explanations for Adverse Effects

Many researchers do not believe that these studies justify restricting the entry of less skilled immigrants. They contend that the weakening position of less educated native-born workers is significantly the result of structural factors rather than immigration. One structural explanation centers on the movement of industrial jobs out of the central city to suburban industrial parks combined with the continued racial housing segregation that Douglas Massey documents.[27] Between 1975 and 1989, the share of young black men in manufacturing in the Midwest fell from 40 percent to 12 percent. By contrast, the share of young white men fell by only 10 percentage points as presumably they had more mobility to follow manufacturing jobs to their new suburban locations. Thus, John Bound and Richard Freeman suspected that "an important part of this differential change [was] the closing of older plants in the central cities of the Midwest."[28]

Similarly, the *Wall Street Journal* analyzed data from 35,000 companies that are required to file reports with the federal Equal Employment Opportunity Commission (EEOC). These companies reported that from 1990 through

1991, their total employment increased by 126,000 while blacks lost 60,000 jobs in their companies. The companies claimed structural factors rather than racism explained these differences. For example, General Electric cited the closing of older plants in Maryland and Illinois in which blacks had been employed disproportionately. Sears cited the relocation of two distribution centers from inner cities to suburbs, to which blacks without cars could not commute.[29]

Marta Tienda pointed out a weakness in this structural explanation. She found that in Chicago, the relocation of manufacturing firms cannot explain the employment success of Mexican immigrants. These immigrants faced the housing segregation that also trapped them in the central city and yet were able to raise their labor force participation rates and have unemployment rates that were less than one-half those of blacks. Tienda concluded that discrimination among employers who prefer Hispanic workers and not structural factors was the most important reason for the weakening labor market position of black workers.[30]

Others have stressed the more general issue of globalization. They contend that manufacturing jobs that blacks disproportionately held were shifted to low-wages service jobs that only immigrants were willing to take. In this case, the growth of immigrant employment is due to sectoral employment shifts rather than discrimination. William Frey contends that this may explain the outmigration of whites from cities with large immigrant populations between 1970 and 1985 when the decline in manufacturing was very high. He does not believe, however, that this restructuring can explain the more recent outmigration of native-born blacks.[31]

Borjas also rejects globalization as an important reason for the growing wage gap between less skilled and more skilled workers. He estimated that almost one-half of the growth in the wage differential between high school dropouts and non-dropouts during the period 1979 to 1995 can be explained by the growing supply of immigrants with less than a high school education. By contrast, only 10 percent of this increased gap can be explained by globalization of trade.

The sectoral shift argument assumes that there is complementarity where immigrants take jobs that native-born workers are unwilling to take.[32] Hamermesh tested this hypothesis by looking at the relative amenities of the jobs held by immigrants compared to native-born workers. He found no evidence that immigrants take jobs with adverse amenities; they may work for less but do not take otherwise undesirable jobs.[33] Interestingly, it was black workers who seem to have the most undesirable jobs as measured by night shift work and injury rates. This further weakens the possibility that the shift from manufacturing to service jobs can explain the declining employment position of less educated native-born black workers.

Bean and Stevens focused on other possible ways in which immigrants and native-born blacks do not compete for jobs. They point out that if there is a rapid growth of high-level services, the immigrant-black relationship is complementary. This perspective builds on two previous studies in which Bean was a participant.

Bean, Jennifer Van Hook, and Mark Fosset analyzed data from the 187 metropolitan areas that had at least 500 black men in the labor force. Using a fixed-effects model, they found that variations in immigration across these metropolitan areas during the 1980s had no statistically significant effect on either changes in the black labor force participation or unemployment rates. However, the socioeconomic status (SES) of job occupations was a statistically significant variable. In particular, cities with a rising SES tended to have greater increases in black labor force participation rates and greater decreases in the black unemployment rate than cities with a declining SES. This suggests that in cities where there was a relative growth of "better" jobs, as black workers rose up the occupational ladder, immigrants replaced them at the bottom-rung jobs.[34]

Bean, Fossett, and Kyung Tae Park found that complementarity is dependent on local labor market conditions. They found no direct correlation between the growth of the immigrant population and changes in black unemployment rates across metropolitan areas (SMSAs). There was, however, a statistically significant relationship once the SMSAs were disaggregated according to the white unemployment rate. In SMSAs with high white unemployment rates, there was a positive correlation between the growth of the immigrant population and changes in black unemployment; in SMSAs with low white unemployment rates, there was a negative correlation. Thus, when labor markets are tight, as measured by the white unemployment rate, immigrant and native-born black men are complementary so that black workers benefit from increased immigration. By contrast, when there are excess labor supplies, immigrants are substitutes who displace black workers.[35]

Richard Freeman believes that many studies overstate the adverse impact of immigration because they do not take into account international trade dynamics. This is similar to Thomas Muller's views. Muller suggests that since immigration lowers the production cost of many goods, it allows more production to remain in the domestic economy. In the absence of low-wage immigrants, there would be less domestic production and more imports of low-waged goods.[36] Freeman concluded, "Since immigration has only modest effects on income distribution and GDP...the primary beneficiaries from immigration are immigrants and their descendents."[37]

Competition for Niche Employment

Rather than looking at broad citywide measures, some researchers instead assessed specific employment niches to determine the impact of immigration, particularly from the Caribbean and Latin America. These researchers reasoned that, to the extent employers prefer immigrants from these regions, black displacement should be observed within occupations and industries. In addition, displacement should be more apparent in specific settings where informal hiring practices put a premium on employment networks that are thought to be more prevalent in these immigrant communities.

Mary Waters assessed employment dynamics of New York City cafeteria workers in a major financial corporation. She found an almost complete turn-over from African American to Caribbean American workers between 1980 and 1996. This displacement was at least partially due to the shift from using help-wanted advertisements to relying completely on recommendations from current employees. The corporation, however, would stop taking recommendations from those current employees whose previous referrals proved to be unsatis-factory. Since African American referrals didn't pan out as much, employment networking became dominated by Caribbean employees.

Roger Waldinger contends that since blacks do well in situations without networks, they do not build up employment networks in the same way that the hiring process reinforces immigrant networks.[38] He believes that these net-works are important even in settings, like hospitals and hotels, where employ-ers use formal hiring practices for most job openings but continue to use employment networks to fill their low-end jobs.

Besides superior employment networks, Waldinger cites additional rea-sons why black niches have not been sustained. Echoing the traditional Marx-ian divide-and-conquer theory, he contends that employers might seek Hispanic workers because they fear the potential bargaining power of an all-black workforce. In addition, black niches are weakened in industries that serve a diverse clientele. For example, black niches in hospitals are weakened as more users are non-English speaking. Black employment is further limited when having limited Spanish linguistic skills makes it more difficult for them to communicate in the workplace and gain aid from experienced Hispanic work-ers.

Waters also believed that this shift was accelerated by stereotypic attitudes. Both Caribbeans and white workers perceived native-born black workers as being lazy and more willing to shift to welfare than Caribbeans. Consistent with these stereotypes, Waters pointed out that Caribbeans have much higher labor force participation rates than African Americans, even when controlling for family structure. As Table 1 illustrates, these differences are also reflected in consistently higher employment rates for foreign-born than native-born blacks.

Caribbean Americans and African Americans have different histories and longstanding geographical separation so that they are perceived to have en-tirely different cultural norms. As a result, the employment differences are perceived to be deeply rooted in distinct cultural differences. The problem with this cultural explanation becomes clear when we look at the Hispanic labor force. The employment gaps between foreign-born and native-born His-

Table 1
Employment Rates for Out-of-School Males, 16-24 Years Old
by Race and Ethnicity, Three-Year Averages 1994-1996 and 1999-2001*

	United States		Central Cities		New York City	
	94-96	99-01	94-96	99-01	94-96	99-01
NH White						
Native	80.4	81.6	81.5	82.0	72.2	73.9
Foreign	76.2	78.8	77.3	76.6	65.6	68.5
NH Black						
Native	55.8	57.3	53.0	53.8	41.8	40.2
Foreign	64.6	69.7	60.0	66.0	46.9	58.4
Hispanic						
Native	68.7	72.8	66.2	68.4	45.2	52.2
Foreign	81.0	85.1	81.9	85.9	64.6	82.3

*Puerto Ricans are native-born. NH denotes non-Hispanic.

Source: Bureau of Labor Statistics, *Current Population Survey*, March files. Compiled by Mark Levitan, Community Service Society of New York.

panics (Table 1) are just as large.[39] It is, however, hard to argue that native-born and foreign-born Hispanics are very culturally diverse and have distinct *cultural* norms that would affect employment behavior. Thus, these employment and labor force participation gaps are likely to be the result of selective immigration rather than representative of distinct cultural norms.

David Howell and Elizabeth Mueller looked more broadly at New York City employment niches. They identified sixteen occupation-industry cells in which 1980 male employment was disproportionately native-born black. In these niches, they found (Table 2) that over the next decade, total employment grew by 5.3 percent while immigrant employment grew by 50.6 percent.[40]

In contrast to Waters, Howell and Mueller did not find that this displacement significantly adversely affected total black employment. In these niches, native-born white and native-born Hispanic men were displaced. The ability of native-born black men to sustain total employment in their niches was due to two factors: (1) nine of the niches had significant public-sector employment where black men were insulated from informal network hirings; and (2) black men were able to maintain employment shares in their two fastest growing niches—security guards and heavy trucking.

Howell and Mueller did find, however, that immigration adversely affected the wages of native-born black men. Across the 621 job classifications, an increase in the immigrant share had an adverse effect on the earnings of white and black native-born workers, but little or no overall effect on Hispanic

Table 2
Changes in the Composition of NY Metro Male Employment of Native-Born
and Immigrant Populations, 1980-90

	All Jobs (621)			Native-Born Black Niche Jobs (16)		
	1980 (000)	1990 (000)	Chg. (%)	1980 (000)	1990 (000)	Chg. (%)
Total Employment	2148.5	2222.4	+3.5	241.5	254.4	+5.3
N-B. White	1213.4 (56.5%)	1059.6 (47.7%)	-12.7	108.7 (45%)	82.6 (32.5%)	-24.0
N-B. Black	285.7 (13.3%)	267.1 (12%)	-6.5	62.2 (25.8%)	60.1 (23.6%)	-3.4
N-B. Hispanics	166.2 (7.7%)	128.5 (5.8%)	-22.7	23.4 (9.7%)	18.8 (7.4%)	-19.6
Recent Immigrants	297.0 (13.8%)	405.9 (18.3%)	+36.6	29.5 (12.2%)	44.4 (17.5%)	+50.6

Source: Howell and Mueller, "Immigration and Native-Born Male Earnings," Table 1.

Puerto Ricans are native-born.   N-B denotes native born.

workers. Consistent with previous studies, downward wage effects were particularly strong in low-wage blue collar and low-wage service jobs.[41]

Michael Rosenfeld and Marta Tienda analyzed ten varied occupations in three cities to judge the impact of immigration on niche employment. Consistent with Table 1 data, Mexicans in these cities had higher labor force participation rates and lower unemployment rates than native-born blacks in both the 1980 and 1990 census. Rosenfeld and Tienda believe that a core explanation for these disparities is the superior effectiveness of Mexican employment networking, whether due to stronger communal ties or preferences of employers who promote these networks as a means of avoiding hiring less desirable (black) workers.

Rosenfeld and Tienda found that black workers who were squeezed out of low-employment occupations were those with the lowest wages, so that they were not likely to move up the job ladder. In all three cities, black maids at the lowest pay levels were displaced so that the average wage of the remaining black maids rose substantially. Similarly for machine operator jobs, native-born blacks were displaced at the lowest paying jobs so that the decline in the number of native-born blacks in LA and Chicago was associated with a substantial real wage rise while the growing employment of Mexicans lowered the average wage paid to Mexican workers. Rosenfeld and Tienda concluded,

"We have shown that black workers who remain behind in the low-skill jobs confront fewer job opportunities and sharply increased rates of unemployment."[42]

Some researchers have assessed changing job niches at the national level. Desirable niches reflect disproportional employment in occupational-industry cells that pay well relative to the education levels of their workforce. Undesirable niches reflect disproportionate employment in occupational-industry cells that pay poorly relative to the education levels of their workforce. Mary King found that during the 1980s, the employment of younger black workers shifted from their relatively desirable niches to their relatively undesirable niches.[43] Franklin Wilson assessed whether or not immigration can explain this deterioration in job niche employment. Using a somewhat different set of industry-occupation cells, Wilson found that immigrant flows in the 1980s weakened niche employment of black men and lowered their occupational attainment.[44]

Welfare Use and Taxpayer Burden

Over the past thirty years, immigrant households have moved from having lower rates of welfare receipt to having higher rates than native-born households. Between 1996 and 1998, the immigrant use rate averaged 10 percent while the native-born rate averaged 7 percent. Welfare reform and a strong labor market dropped immigrant use rates disproportionately so that by 1999 the gap was only 1.7 percentage points. When all types of public assistance are included, however, Borjas (Table 6.3) estimated that immigrant households had use rates 7.0 percentage points above native-born households.

Bean and Stevens note that the disproportionately high use rate is found only among two groups: Asian refugees and labor migrant countries (Mexico, Guatemala, and El Salvador). They state,

> Together, the refugee and labor migrant groups make up over 30 percent and are not representative of the broader class of people who are admitted under U.S. immigration law. When refugee and most labor migrants are separated out, gross welfare receipt levels among the remaining immigrants are actually lower than those of native households.[45]

Bean and Stevens suggest that high use rates among immigrants from Mexico and Central America do not support claims that welfare programs are a magnet. In 1999, the use rate among poor immigrants from these countries was only 13.5 percent whereas it was 18.6 percent among native households who were poor. Bean and Stevens also note that immigrants receive very little noncash benefits apart from school lunch programs. Somewhat contradicting their viewpoint, however, they documented the disproportionately high welfare rate of elderly households from these countries: 23.1 percent compared to 5.6 percent for native-born elderly. They believe that this high welfare use rate is related to the inability of those who migrated after the age of fifty-five to qualify for social security. One might infer that these older migrants might have migrated in anticipation of these welfare benefits.[46]

Bean and Stevens did note that 34.6 percent of immigrants who arrived after the age of fifty-five received social security income. They neglected to mention, however, that the vast majority of these older immigrants received social security benefits in excess of their social security contributions. More generally, Alan Gustman and Thomas Steinmeier documented the social security subsidy received by the typical immigrant worker: immigrants receive a greater proportion of contributions in benefits than native-born workers. The subsidy is greatest for immigrants who earned at least $10,000 annually and worked in the United States for between ten and twenty years. These immigrants would receive social security benefits of between 70 and 80 percent of those paid to native-born workers with comparable wages who were employed for their full work life.[47]

Borjas generally believes that many immigrants are well aware of the relatively generous government welfare programs. He noted that there are publications available that explain to prospective and recent immigrants how to access the various welfare programs. He presented data that suggested that welfare programs also are likely to discourage immigrants who fail from returning to their home country.

Borjas also contends that the decision made by many immigrants to choose California reflected welfare considerations. In 1980, California residents comprised 9.7 percent of households nationally who did not receive cash benefits and 11.2 percent of those who did. Among immigrants who had arrived in the previous five years, 30.1 percent of those who did not receive cash benefits but 36.9 percent of those who did resided in California. During the 1980s, California's welfare system became more generous relative to other states. This had little effect on the residential decision of native-born households but seemed to have a significant effect on recent immigrants. During the decade, while the share of Mexican immigrants residing in the United States grew by 53 percent, those residing in California grew by 67 percent.[48] This shift to California was disproportionately among those who gained cash assistance. By 1990, 28.9 percent of recent immigrants who did not receive cash benefits but 45.4 percent of those who did resided in California.[49] A more recent study of the impact of the 1996 welfare reform act, however, indicated that changing benefits had no effect on immigrant decisions on where to reside.[50]

Borjas also pointed out a fundamental problem with the Bean-Stevens approach. Suppose they are correct that poor immigrants do not use welfare to a greater degree than poor native-born households and that most of the increase in welfare usage by the immigrant elderly is not the result of immigration of those past their prime working years. It would still be the case that by allowing a disproportionate share of immigrants to be less educated and past their prime working years to immigrate, the United States is accepting substantial welfare burdens.

Another way to look at the fiscal cost of immigration is to estimate the net effect for each immigrant admitted. In the short run, there are substantial payments by government: welfare, food stamps, schooling, and additional infrastructure requirements. For California and New Jersey, the NAS study estimated these costs net of taxes collected. As already noted, in the long run, immigrants tend to be less government-assistance dependent and pay more taxes as their earnings rise. In addition, immigrant children enter the workforce and also become net taxpayers. Thus, it is possible that during their lifetime, immigrants and their descendants pay more in taxes than the cost of government services provided to them.

In order to judge the long-term fiscal impact of immigration, the NAS study estimated the cumulative fiscal impact over the three hundred years following the entry of a representative immigrant into the country in 1994. Initially, immigration creates annual burdens on taxpayers. Beginning in 2016, however, there begins to be annual benefits. Adding up the present value of the benefits over the next 278 years, they concluded that each immigrant provides a net benefit of $80,000.

Borjas points out that this result is extremely sensitive to assumptions made. If the time frame were limited to fifty years, the net benefits would decline to $11,000; and if a reasonable alternative federal tax policy is substituted, there is a net *loss* of $15,000. In addition, the net benefits are only at the federal level since immigrants and their children are not expected to pay substantial state taxes but will be paying substantial federal payroll taxes. Finally, Borjas noted, "The economic benefits that might begin to show up after the year 2016 provide little comfort to the households that lived in California in the 1990s; they had to pay an additional $1,200 a year in taxes because of immigration."[51]

Native-Immigrant Competition *within* Minority Communities

There is a great deal of evidence that the Clinton-era economic expansion was particularly beneficial to young (sixteen- to twenty-four-year-old) out-of-school black men. Their employment rate rose from 56.6 to 61.4 percent between 1994 and 1999; and for those working fulltime, it rose from 43.8 to 53.4 percent. This employment growth was most apparent in cities that experience relatively low unemployment rates.[52]

While these aggregate statistics were quite hopeful, a significant group of young black men did not benefit from the expansion. In 1999, 19 percent were neither in school nor at work—a higher percentage than at the peak of the previous economic expansion. In addition, young black men in school continued to have dramatically lower employment rates than young white men in school: 28.6 percent of black students but 50.7 percent of white students were employed.[53]

Recent evidence seems to suggest that even the positive aggregate employment statistics are problematic. Table 1 indicates that increases in the employment rates of young out-of-school black men over the economic expansion were almost entirely among the foreign-born. Indeed, in New York City's relatively weak labor market, the employment rate of young out-of-school *native-born* black men actually declined from 41.8 to 40.2 percent.

Some studies have found that immigration may have an impact on native-born students in the educational sector. In particular, Julian Betts explored the effect of immigration on high school graduation rates of native-born black and Hispanic students.[54] He posited two competing effects.

On the one hand, immigration has a crowding-out effect: Immigrants obtain educational-support funding that reduces the educational resources received by disadvantaged native-born students. During the 1980s, the share of children living in poverty grew by 70 and 123 percent within the Hispanic and Asian populations, respectively, but by only 14 and 22 percent within the black and white populations, respectively. Michael Fix and Wendy Zimmerman analyzed the impact of these poor immigrant populations on Chapter 1 funding, the largest single grant program for K-12 schools. Though the increased utilization of Chapter 1-funded services by immigrant populations did not reduce the number of black children served, it was generally associated with a substantial drop in expenditures per pupil.[55] Building on this evidence, Betts stated:

> If it is more expensive to teach a given set of skills and knowledge to immigrant students than to native-born students, and if, as appears to be the case, government funding has not risen to reflect fully these additional costs, it is likely that native-born students' rate of learning at school will fall. Once immigrant students arrive in school, native-born students would either have to exert more independent effort or stay in school longer in order to acquire a given amount of human capital. The induced rise in the marginal costs of school suggests that American-born students will on average reduce the amount of education they acquire.[56]

On the other hand, Betts noted that immigration increases the wage gap between high school dropouts and those with a high school education. An increased wage gap provides an increased economic incentive to stay in school. Betts' study found, however, that the crowding-out effect dominated so that educational attainments decreased. Specifically, for a 10 percent increase in the immigrant to population ratio, "the predicted drops in graduation probabilities ... are 4.7 percent for blacks and 8.8 percent for [native-born] Hispanics."[57] Extrapolating from these results, Betts estimated that immigration in the 1980s lowered the high school graduation rate of blacks and native-born Hispanics by one and three percentage-points, respectively.

Caroline Hoxby explored the possible ways in which immigrant crowding out might occur at colleges.[58] Data from 1989-93 indicated that at less selective schools, 29 percent of students who took remedial reading classes were foreign born. At the opposite end of the spectrum, in the most selective schools—colleges with students who average a combined SAT score of at least 1100—29.5 and 17.3 percent of all Hispanic and black students, respectively, were foreign-born; 12.4 and 17.0 percent, respectively, were foreign-born noncitizens.

Hoxby posited a number of mechanisms by which immigrants crowd out native born: (1) displacement and reshaping of EOP programs that offer academic and financial support to "educationally and economically disadvantaged" populations; (2) displacement in selective schools of natives by black and Hispanic students from elite Caribbean and Latin American families; and (3) monopolizing and reshaping academic and financial counseling services. Hoxby found that at the most selective colleges, approximately thirty-seven native-born blacks students are displaced for every 100 black foreign-born students admitted; approximately thirty-nine native-born Hispanics for every 100 Hispanic foreign-born admitted. Indeed, there was a one-for-one displacement if the foreign-born are nonresident aliens.

Hoxby also estimated the impact that immigrant students had on the share of economically disadvantaged native students. She found that the share of native-born students from low-income families or parents with limited educational attainment was adversely affected in the middle range of colleges—those whose student body had an average combined SAT score of between 900 and 1100. In support of Hoxie's findings, Linda Datcher Loury noted that "there is anecdotal evidence that a large percentage of attendees at some elite colleges are the children of West Indian immigrants. While this is not crowding out in the usual sense, since these individuals are natives, there is a potentially large effect on the children of native-born blacks from the children of immigrants."[59]

One particular area where there is some concern that foreign students are displacing native-born students is in graduate science and engineering programs. Jessica Gurcak et al. noted that while "students with temporary visas earned 5.4 percent of science and engineering bachelor's degrees [in 1990], compared to 27.0 percent of master's degrees and 32.4 percent of Ph.D.s." As this trend has undoubtedly increased since 1990, it is feared that these foreign students might fulfill university diversity goals and, hence, displace native-born minority students.

Gurcak and her colleagues did not believe that this displacement is occurring. They found that in graduate programs, both acceptance and enrollment rates are higher for minority applicants than for non-U.S. citizens. In particular, they found "no evidence that affirmative action policies were benefiting foreign-born scientists and engineers, and no displacement of minority graduate school applicants."[60]

All seem to agree that the lack of native-born black (and Hispanic) representation in science and engineering graduate programs is primarily due to a lack of these students in undergraduate programs and their weak K-12 science and math training. Some researchers, however, believe that if there were not a ready supply of foreign students in these graduate programs, the shortage would force the entire U.S. educational system to take more seriously student math and science learning. Both David North, and Leon Bouvier and John Martin believe that minority representation in science and engineering would increase once the nation made a commitment to increasing the supply of domestically-trained personnel.[61]

George Borjas recent work looks at the possibility of foreign-born students crowding out native-born students in graduate schools. As to enrollment and degrees awarded, Borjas finds that the only group that is systematically displaced by foreign enrollment is white students, especially white male students. He finds that there is no evidence to suggest that the number of doctorates awarded to foreign students in a particular group has an adverse effect on the number awarded to natives in the same group. In particular, he finds that an increase of ten black foreign students in a doctoral program is associated with an increase of six black natives earning doctorates. Thus, it appears that a commitment to affirmative action results in an increase in both native and foreign black doctorates.[62]

Business Ownership and Ethnic Conflict

Since President Richard Nixon's support for "black capitalism," there have been a number of government policies to stimulate black ownership.[63] Despite these efforts, Table 3 points to the continued deficiency of black businesses. Though the Hispanic community had a smaller number of adults than the black community in 1997, it owned 43 percent more firms. Even this comparison overstates black enterprise since the gap is larger if we only include "meaningful" businesses—those with sales and receipts of at least $25,000 annually. Indeed, Hispanic businesses had almost three times the sales and receipts of black businesses. More troubling, the gap increased during the 1990s, as the growth of black businesses was less than the growth of either Hispanic or Asian businesses.

Alejandro Portes and Min Zhou analyzed the factors that contribute to self-employment within specific ethnic groups.[64] They found that for immigrant groups but not for native-born blacks, being married and having children is positively correlated with self-employment. This places native-born blacks at a disadvantage and may be one explanation for their lower self-employment rates.[65]

Limited self-employment has meant that in many black communities the vast majority of businesses are immigrant owned. This has created tensions, sometimes spilling over into confrontations. Reflecting Jaynes' framework, Claire Jeanne Kim presents an overly sympathetic assessment of the motives and actions of the black community during the 1990 boycott of a Korean

Table 3
Comparison of Minority-Owned Firms: 1997 and 1992

	Black	Hispanic	Asian
All Firms (thousands)			
1997	780	1121	785
1992	620	862	603
Growth Rate	25.7%	30.0%	30.2%
Meaningful Firms* (thousands)			
1997	230	451	506
1992	142	246	265
Growth Rate	62.0%	83.3%	90.2%
Sales and Receipts (millions)			
1997	42.7	114.3	161.1
1992	32.2	76.8	95.7
Growth Rate	32.5%	48.9%	68.4%

*Firms with annual sales of at least $25,000

Sources: Dept of Commerce, *Minority-Owned Business Enterprises*, 1997 and 1992.

grocery store in Brooklyn. Kim states, "Every black person whom I interviewed recounted that he or she or a friend or family member had been mistreated by a Korean merchant on at least one occasion."[66] She contends, however, that the boycott organizers transformed the legitimate rage Haitian and Caribbean immigrants felt into a general mobilization of blacks against broader grievances.

Kim should have been a bit more critical of claims that Korean anti-black attitudes were so pervasive and at least specified examples of the alleged mistreatment. Her bias is even more pronounced in her treatment of the leaders of the boycott, the December 12th Movement. She presents them as "the city's most radical African American and Caribbean activists" who were subjected to "COINTELPRO-style investigations."[67] However, Kim neglected to mention their deeply held anti-Semitic views, which led them to consistently scapegoat Jews for the desperate plight of native-born blacks.

Kim is also problematic in her treatment of Edna Bonacich's middleman minority theory. Bonacich's theory focuses on the use of middleman to control and exploit those who are socio-economically below them. Though she criticized the theory, Kim neglected to mention that the December 12th Movement and its supporters used this middleman minority theory during the 1969 school boycott to characterize the role of Jewish school teachers (and social workers) as controllers of poor black families. These leaders emphasized replacing Jewish teachers with black teachers while they demanded replacing Korean merchants with black merchants during the 1990 boycott. Thus, the December 12th Movement consistently promoted the interests of black professionals and entrepreneurs, which are not necessarily consistent with the interests of black workers. Unfortunately, Kim did not explore this potential intra-group conflict.[68]

At a more comprehensive level, Robert Fairlie and Bruce Meyer examined the relationship between changes in immigration and changes in black self-employment across ninety-four large metropolitan areas over the 1980-90 decade. Under reasonable assumptions, the upper limit on the displacement of native-owned businesses by immigrant entrepreneurs is quite small: at most, only one native-owned business is displaced for every ten immigrant businesses. Since the displacement effect is felt broadly even in the worst case scenario, they concluded, "[T]he potential black losses are small."[69]

To further support this assessment, they estimated the relationship of the share of immigrants in the local population to the black ownership rate there. They found a positive correlation: the higher the immigrant share of the population, the higher the black ownership rate. Fairlie and Meyer noted that this may reflect a statistical bias: immigrants are more likely to live in cities that are more favorable to small business entrepreneurship, including black ownership. When they estimated the relationship between *changes* in the immigrant population and *changes* in the black ownership rate, Fairlie and Meyer did obtain the expected negative relationship. It was, however, quite small—one black owner is displaced for every thirty-three immigrant businesses—and was not statistically significant.

Portes and Zhou also assessed the impact of immigrant entrepreneurship on the rate and success of black self-employment. They rejected the view that immigrant enterprises displace native-born black self-employment. Instead, Portes and Zhou argued,

> Immigrant enterprises can spin off new kinds of economic opportunities, with direct consequences for the entire working population of the area. The presence of successful small immigrant firms can also provide an incentive for others to try their hand at the same lines of businesses and multiple examples of how to do this. Accordingly, cities where immigrant economies are prominent should also have higher rates of African American entrepreneurship and higher economic returns for those choosing this career path.[70]

In support of this thesis, Portes and Zhou found that black self-employment rates were above the national average in New York, Los Angeles, and Miami, three cities that have a high concentration of immigrants. Moreover, they estimated that black entrepreneurs had substantially higher earnings in these three cities, even after controlling for other factors that influence earnings. When they extended their analysis to the sixty-two largest metropolitan areas, Portes and Zhou found no support for claims that immigrant businesses harm black entrepreneurship.

Concluding Remarks

This survey provides some consistent findings: (1) less educated native-born workers have been harmed by immigration—lower wages and lower employment rates—especially in areas that have a high and growing concentration of immigrants and in areas that have a weak overall economy; (2) government social welfare expenditures in high immigrant areas are substantial and long-lasting due to the large proportion of less educated and older immigrants; (3) there is substantial displacement of native-born blacks, especially from private-sector job niches; (4) immigrants deplete compensatory educational services and modestly displace native-born minorities from educational affirmative action programs; and (4) native-born black entrepreneurship is not adversely affected by immigration.

Unfortunately, most of the research reviewed reflected studies using 1990 or earlier data. Since the 1990s had a stronger economic performance than the earlier period, this suggests that less educated native-born black workers would not be as adversely affected. The data in Table 1, however, found that less educated native-born blacks continued to be displaced by immigrants, as did the study by Johannsson, Weiler, and Shulman. In addition, the slowdown in growth of government employment during the 1990s was likely to reduce desirable job niches for black workers. Finally, the educational support service problems that Fix and Zimmerman documented continued in the 1990s, exemplified by the growth in the number of limited-English proficient children in the nation's schools outpacing the growth of federal spending on bilingual education.[71]

Displacement effects do not necessarily justify immigration restrictions. In theory at least, this problem could be ameliorated by more government educational-support spending and government jobs programs. Moreover, it is important to heed Richard Freeman's position that there will be adverse production consequences from immigration restrictions. For example, the trade union movement recently has called for restrictions on the number and use of computer-related workers in the United States on H-1B visas.[72] While H1-B workers may be replacing native-born workers and moderating the wages of computer and engineering personnel, restricting their numbers is likely to accelerate the outsourcing of these jobs. Siddharth Srivastava reports,

> The U.S. government's move to slash H1-B visa entrants into the United States appears likely to blow up in the faces of those who sought the October 1 cut from 195,000 skilled workers to 65,000. While nobody is sure exactly how the dynamics are going to play out, many analysts believe that cutting the numbers of skilled information-technology (IT) workers into the United States will result in U.S. companies sending the jobs overseas to much cheaper countries.[73]

Finally, do the research findings offer compelling reasons to rethink immigration policy? I do not believe that job displacement effects alone are sufficient to justify a shift to a Canadian point system. If instead of less educated immigrants, policies shifted to more educated immigrants, adverse wage and employment effects would just shift to a different set of occupations. Indeed, if more educated immigrants in professional fields block the advancement of native-born workers there, this will have a "crowding-out effect." More native workers must seek employment in less-desirable labor markets, depressing wages in these markets. For example, Borjas estimated that a 10 percentage-point increase in the supply of college graduates lowers the wage of non-college graduates by 3 percentage points. By contrast, he found no adverse impact of an increased supply of high school dropouts on the wages of workers with more education.[74]

I do think, however, that the social welfare burden does warrant a rethinking of immigration policies along the lines Borjas suggests. In evaluating the Canadian situation, Lucia Lo et al. stated,

> The economic immigrants have the highest ability to pay income tax. This is especially true of the independent immigrants whose language and jobs skills are subject to full assessment at time of application under the point system. This proves that the point system has been working well for the economic well-being of Canada.[75]

Since U.S. immigration policies should be based at least partially on economic grounds, allocating a substantial portion of immigration slots on an economic basis seems appropriate.

Notes

1. James Smith and Barry Edmonston, eds., *The New Americans: Economic, Demographic, and Fiscal Effects of Immigration*, S-5 (National Academy Press, 1977).
2. Vernon M. Briggs, *Immigration and American Unionism* (Cornell University Press, 2001), p. 168.
3. Ruth Milkman [*Organizing Immigrants: The Challenge for Unions in Contemporary California* (Cornell University Press, 2000)] believes organizing immigrants is a key to revitalizing the union movement.
4. Ibid., 181.
5. George J. Borjas, *Heaven's Door: Immigration Policy and the American Economy* (Princeton University Press, 1999), p. xiv. This is similar to proposals made by Barry Chiswick, "Immigration Policy: The Case for Radical Reform," *Milken Institute* (Summer 1994), pp. 25-27.
6. Gerald D. Jaynes, ed., *Immigration and Race: New Challenges for American Democracy* (Russell Sage Foundation, 2000).
7. For a rejection of cultural explanations for the relative economic success of Jewish immigrants, see Stephen Steinberg, *The Ethnic Myth* (Antheum, 1981) and Robert Cherry, *Discrimination: Its Economic Impact on Blacks, Women, and Jews* (Lexington Books, 1989), chapter 10.
8. Jaynes, op. cit., p. 7.
9. Frank D. Bean and Stephanie Bell-Rose, eds., *Immigration and Opportunity: Race, Ethnicity, and Employment in the United States* (Russell Sage, 1999), p. 1.
10. Daniel S. Hamermesh and Frank D. Bean, eds., *Help or Hindrance? The Economic Implications of Immigration for African Americans* (Russell Sage, 1998), p. 12.
11. Frank D. Bean and Gillian Stevens, *America's Newcomers and the Dynamics of Diversity* (Russell Sage, 2003), p. 223. Bean and Stevens's pro-immigration sympathies become most transparent when they favorably present immigration recommen-

dation by Massey, Durand, and Nolan as a "set of thoughtful and far-sighted proposals to address Mexican migration" (p. 12), while dismissing those made by Borjas, even though his proposals are patterned after current Canadian policies.

12. David Jaeger, "Skill Differences and the Effect of Immigrants on the Wages of Natives," Working Paper 273, U.S. Bureau of Labor Statistics (Dec. 1995).

13. Rachel Friedberg and Jennifer Hunt, "The Impact of Immigrants on Host Country Wages, Employment and Growth," *Journal of Economic Perspectives* 9 (Spring 1995), pp. 23-44.

14. Borjas, op. cit., p. 27.

15. Bean and Stevens note that the discrepancy between 2000 Census population estimates and projections made from demographic analyses suggests that the number of Mexican illegals was somewhat higher than 3.9 million.

16. Quoted in Briggs, op. cit., p. 153. Jaeger estimated that immigration was responsible for about one-third of the wage decline experienced by native-born high school dropouts.

17. Also see Borjas, Richard Freeman, and Lawrence Katz, "How Much Do Immigration and Trade Affect Labor Market Outcomes," *Brookings Papers on Economic Activity*, pp. 1-67.

18. Briggs, op. cit., p. 175.

19. Christian Zlolniski, "Unskilled Immigrants in High-Tech Companies: The Case of Mexican Janitors in Silicon Valley," *The International Migration of the Highly Skilled*, edited by Wayne Cornelius, Thomas Espenshade, and Idean Salehyan (Center for Comparative Immigration Studies, 2001), p. 270.

20. Cordelia Reimers, "Unskilled Immigration and Changes in the Wage Distributions of Black, Mexican American, and Non-Hispanic White Male Dropouts." In Hamermesh and Bean, op. cit., pp. 107-148.

21. Bean and Stevens, op. cit., p. 222.

22. Kristin Butcher, "An Investigation of the Effect of Immigration on the Labor-Market Outcomes of African Americans." In Hamermesh and Bean, op. cit., pp. 149-182.

23. George Johnson, "The Impact of Immigration on Income Distribution of Minorities." In ibid., pp. 17-50.

24. Hannes Johannsson, Stephan Weiler, and Steven Shulman, "The Impact of Immigration on the Labor Supply of Low-Skilled Workers," *Research in Labor Economics*, Vol 22, edited by Solomon Polachek (Elsevier Science Ltd., 1992).

25. George J. Borjas, "The Labor Demand *is* Downward Sloping: Reexamining the Impact of Immigration on the Labor Market," *Quarterly Journal of Economics* 118 (Nov 2003), pp. 1335-1376.

26. Marc Frenette, "Immigrant Occupational Concentration and Native-Born Earnings," Statistics Canada, Analytical Studies Research Paper Series, forthcoming. For other studies that assess the impact of immigration on Canadian wages see James Ted McDonald and Christopher Worswick, "The Earnings of Immigrant Men in Canada: Job Tenure, Cohort, and Macroeconomic Conditions," *Industrial and Labor Relations Review* 51 (Apr. 1998) and Marc Frenette and Rene Morissette, "Will They Ever Converge? Earnings of Immigrants and Canadian-born Workers Over the Last Two Decades," Statistics Canada (October 8, 2003). Website: http://www.statcan.ca/english/IPS/Data/11F0019MIE2003215.htm

27. Douglas Massey, "The Residential Segregation of Blacks, Hispanics, and Asians, 1970-1990." In Jaynes, op. cit., pp. 44-73. Jeffrey Zax ["Immigration, Race, and Space." In Hamermesh and Bean, op. cit., pp. 222-52.] found that during the 1980s, cities that had more immigration tended to have less minority segregation.

28. John Bound and Richard Freeman, "What Went Wrong? The Erosion of the Relative Earnings of Young Black Men during the 1980s," *Quarterly Journal of Economics* (Feb 1992), 215n.

29. Marc Breslow, "The Racial Divide Widens," *Dollars & Sense* #197 (Jan./Feb. 95).

30. Marta Tienda, "Immigration and Native Minority Workers: Is There Bad News After All?" In Hamermesh and Bean, op. cit., pp. 345-52.

31. William Frey, "New Black Migration Patterns in the United States: Are They Affected by Recent Immigration?" In Bean and Bell-Rose, op. cit., pp. 311-44.

32. Low-cost immigrant private household workers are one example of complementarity since they allow many U.S. women with children to remain in the labor market. George Vernez ["Surveying Immigrant Communities," *Focus* 18 (Fall 1995), pp. 19-23] estimated that 60 percent of Salvadorean women in Los Angeles were employed as private household workers.

33. Daniel S. Hamermesh, "Immigration and the Quality of Jobs." In Hamermesh and Bean, op. cit., pp. 75-106. Also see Jaeger.

34. Frank D. Bean, Jennifer Van Hook, and Mark Fossett, "Immigration, Spatial and Economic Change, and African American Employment." In Bean and Bell-Rose, op. cit., pp. 31-63.

35. Frank D. Bean, Mark Fossett, and Kyung Tae Park, "Labor Market Dynamics and the Effects of Immigration on African Americans." In Jaynes, op. cit., pp. 143-162.

36. Thomas Muller, *Immigrants and the American City* (New York University Press, 1994).

37. Richard Freeman, "What does Economics Contribute to Debates over Immigration?" In Hamermesh and Bean, op. cit., p. 358.

38. Roger Waldinger, "Network, Bureaucracy, and Exclusion." In Bean and Bell-Rose, op. cit., pp. 228-260.

39. Robert Kaestner and Neeraj Kaushal ["Immigrant and Native Responses to Welfare Reform," *Journal of Population Economics* (forthcoming)] found that welfare reform had a large positive employment effect on recent arrivals. This was particularly true in New York City where the state Home Relief program that primarily served less educated young men was terminated. This helps explain the dramatic jump in the New York City employment rate of foreign-born Hispanics.

40. David Howell and Elizabeth Mueller, "Immigration and Native-Born Male Earnings," *Journal of Ethnic and Migration Studies* 26 (July 2000), pp. 469-493.

41. For similar results for native-born black women, see David Howell and Elizabeth Mueller, "The Effects of Immigrants on African-American Earnings," Jerome Levy Institute Working Paper #210 (November 1997).

42. Michael Rosenfeld and Marta Tienda, "Mexican Immigration, Occupational Niches, and Labor-Market Competition." In Bean and Bell-Rose, op. cit., p. 97.

43. Mary King, "Are African Americans Losing Their Footholds in Better Jobs?" *Journal of Economic Issues* 32 (Sept. 1995), pp. 641-668.

44. Franklin Wilson, "Ethnic Concentrations and Labor Market Opportunities." In Bean and Bell-Rose, op. cit., pp. 106-41.

45. Bean and Stevens, op. cit., p. 72.

46. They do not reach this conclusion. First, they suggest that family unification and not welfare use was the reason for elderly migration. Second, one-half of the increase in elderly use was among those who came when they were young and simply aged into welfare. Bean and Stevens include in recent arrivals only those who were collecting welfare and had lived in the United States less than ten years. This would exclude most of the immigrants who came when they were in their fifties so may be too restrictive a demarcation between recent and longstanding immigrants.

47. Alan Gustman and Thomas Steinmeier, "Social Security Benefits of Immigrants and U.S. Born," NBER Working Paper #6478 (Sept. 1998).
48. Bean and Stevens, op. cit., Table 3.6.
49. Borjas, op. cit., Table 6.4.
50. Neeraj Kaushal, "New Immigrants' Location Choices," *Journal of Labor Economics* (forthcoming).
51. Borjas, op. cit., p. 125.
52. Richard Freeman and William Rodgers, "Area Economic Conditions and the Labor Market Outcomes of Young Men in the 1990s Expansion," *Prosperity for All? The Economic Boom and African Americans*, edited by Robert Cherry and William Rodgers (Russell Sage, 2000).
53. Robert Cherry, *Who Gets the Good Jobs? Combating Race and Gender Disparities* (Rutgers University Press, 2001), chapter 8.
54. Julian Betts, "Educational Crowding Out: Do Immigrants Affect the Educational Attainment of American Minorities?" In Hamermesh and Bean, op. cit., pp. 253-81.
55. Michael Fix and Wendy Zimmerman, "Educating Immigrant Children: Chapter 1 in Changing Cities." In Jaynes, op. cit., pp. 185-221.
56. Betts, op. cit., pp. 255-56.
57. Ibid., p. 265.
58. Caroline Hoxby, "Do Immigrants Crowd Disadvantaged American Natives Out of Higher Education?" In Hamermesh and Bean, op. cit., pp. 282-321.
59. Linda Datcher Loury, "Reflections on Family Issues in Immigration." In Hamermesh and Bean, op. cit., p. 379.
60. Jessica Gurcak, Thomas Espenshade, Aaron Sparrow, and Martha Paskoff, "Immigration of Scientists and Engineers to the United States: Issues and Evidence," *The International Migration of the Highly Skilled*, edited by Wayne Cornelius, Thomas Espenshade, and Idean Salehyan (USMEX Press, 2001), p. 73.
61. Leon Bovier and John Martin, *Foreign-Born Scientists, Engineers, and Mathematicians in the United States* (Center for Immigration Studies, 1995); David North, *Soothing the Establishment: The Impact of Foreign-Born Scientists and Engineers on America* (University Press of America, 1995). For a particularly negative view of U.S. policy see Eric Weinstein, "How and Why Government, Universities and Industry Create Domestic Labor Shortages," http://nber.nber.org/~peat/PapersFolder/Papers/SG/NSF.html
62. George Borjas, "The Impact of Foreign Students on Native Enrollment in Graduate Programs." http://www.ilr.cornell.edu/cheri/ CHERI, Conference, Cornell University (May 20-21, 2003).
63. For one summary and evaluation of these efforts, see Robert Cherry, *Who Gets the Good Jobs?* op. cit., chapter 9.
64. Alejandro Portes and Min Zhou, "Entrepreneurship and Economic Progress in the 1990s." In Hamermesh and Bean, op. cit., pp. 143-171.
65. For a comprehensive assessment of explanations for the low black self-employment rate, see Robert Fairlie and Bruce Meyers, "Ethnic and Racial Self Employment Differences and Possible Explanations," *Journal of Human Resources* 31 (1996), pp. 757-709.
66. Claire Jeanne Kim, "The Politics of Black-Korean Conflict." In Jaynes, op. cit., p. 89.
67. Ibid., p. 93.
68. For an analysis of black-Jewish conflicts in the context of the 1969 NYC school boycott, see Robert Cherry, "Middleman Minority Theories: Their Implications for Black-Jewish Relations," *Journal of Ethnic Studies* 17 (Spring 1990), pp. 117-138;

for a critique of Bonacich's theory see, Robert Cherry "American Jewry and Bonacich's Middleman Minority Theory," *Review of Radical Political Economy* 22 (June 1990), pp. 139-151.

69. Robert Fairlie and Bruce Meyer, "Does Immigration Harm African-American Self-Employment?" In Hamermesh and Bean, op. cit., p. 189.
70. Portes and Zhou, op. cit., p. 160.
71. Thomas Espenshade, "Immigration and Social Policy," *Focus* 18 (Fall 1995), pp. 4-6.
72. See Congressional testimony of Mr. Michael Gildea, Executive Director, Professional Employees Section AFL-CIO (July 29, 2003). http://judiciary.senate.gov/testimony.cfm?id=878&wit_id=2517
73. Siddharth Srivastava, "H1-B Visas: US Gets It Wrong Again." *Asia Times Online* (Oct. 8, 2003). Website: www.atimes.com
74. Borjas, "The Labor Demand Curve *is* Downward Sloping," op. cit. In addition, there is evidence of a correlation between the lag in earnings growth of younger Canadian-born workers with the lag in earnings growth of immigrant workers [James Ted McDonald and Christopher Worswick, "The Earnings of Immigrant Men in Canada: Job Tenure, Cohort, and Macroeconomic Conditions," *Industrial and Labor Relations Review* 51 (Apr. 1998); and Marc Frenette and Rene Morissette, "Will They Ever Converge? Earnings of Immigrants and Canadian-born Workers Over the Last Two Decades," Statistics Canada, Analytical Studies Research Paper Series, No. 215 (2003).
75. Lucia Lo, Valerie Preston, Shuguang Wang, Katherine Reil, Edward Harvey, and Bobby Siu, "Immigrants' Economic Status in Toronto: Rethinking Settlement and Integration Strategies," *Integrating Diversity*, Working Paper 15 (CERIS-Toronto, 2000).

About the Contributors

Jeanne Batalova is a Ph.D. candidate in the Department of Sociology at University of California, Irvine. Her research interests include skilled and professional migration, and impacts of immigration on social structures, labor markets, and multiracial identification. She is currently working on her dissertation, which concerns the labor market implications of highly skilled migration in the United States. In addition, her research deals with gender inequality at home and work. Her recent article (with Philip Cohen) on cohabitation and division of housework in twenty-two countries appeared in *Journal of Marriage and the Family*.

Frank D. Bean is professor of sociology and co-director of the Center for Research on Immigration, Population and Public Policy at the University of California, Irvine. Prior to 1999, he was professor of sociology and public affairs at the University of Texas at Austin, where he also served as director of the Population Research Center and chair of the Department of Sociology. From 1988 to 1990, he served as the founding director of both the Program for Research on Immigration Policy and the Population Studies Center at The Urban Institute in Washington, D.C. He has published numerous research articles in such scholarly journals as *Demography*, *Population and Development Review*, the *American Sociological Review*, and *Social Forces*, as well as written for the *New York Times* and the *Houston Chronicle*. He is the author or editor of sixteen books, including *The Hispanic Population of the United States* (with Marta Tienda), *At the Crossroads: Mexico and U.S. Immigration Policy* (with Rodolfo de la Garza, Bryan Roberts, and Sidney Weintraub), *Help or Hindrance? The Economic Implications of Immigration for African Americans* (with Dan Hamermesh), *Immigration and Opportunity: Race, Ethnicity, and Employment in the United States* (with Stephanie Bell-Rose), and *America's Newcomers and the Dynamics of Diversity* (with Gillian Stevens). His current research focuses on various determinants and consequences of U.S. immigration patterns and policies and on the implication of immigration for changing race/ethnicity in the United States.

Vernon M. Briggs, Jr. is a professor of economics at the New York State School of Industrial and Labor Relations at Cornell University. He specializes in the area of human resource economics and public policy. In addition to numerous articles on immigration policy, he has authored or co-authored *Chicanos and Rural Poverty, The Chicano Worker, Immigration Policy and the American Labor Force, Immigration Policy and the U.S. Labor Market: Public Policy Gone Awry, Still an Open Door? Immigration Policy and the American Economy, Immigration and American Unionism,* and *Mass Immigration and the National Interest: Policy Directions for a New Century.* He has also been a frequent witness before various congressional committees on immigration policy issues.

Lisa Catanzarite received her Ph.D. in sociology from Stanford University and is currently senior research sociologist at the UCLA Chicano Studies Research Center. Her research focuses on labor markets and social inequality by race/ethnicity and gender, with a particular emphasis on occupational segregation. Recent articles concerned with Latino immigrants appear in *Social Problems, Work and Occupations,* and *Sociological Perspectives.*

Robert Cherry is a professor of economics at Brooklyn College of the City University of New York. His two most recent books are *Who Gets the Good Jobs? Combating Race and Gender Earnings Disparities* (2001) and *Prosperity for All? The Economic Boom and African Americans* (2000). His recent articles include "The Severe Implications of the Economic Downturn on Working Families," *WorkingUSA* (2002) and "Impact of Tight Labor Markets on Black Employment," *Review of Black Political Economy* (2000).

Gerald Jaynes is a professor of economics and African American studies at Yale University. He was study director for the Committee on the Status of Black Americans for the National Research Council in Washington, D.C. from 1985-89 and head of a research project on "Immigration, Blacks, and Race Relations" sponsored by the Mellon Foundation. He is the author of *Branches Without Roots: The Genesis of the Black Working Class* (1986), the co-editor of *A Common Destiny: Blacks and American Society* (1989), and the editor of *Immigration and Race: New Challenges to American Democracy* (2000).

Hannes Johannsson is a senior financial economist in the Risk Analysis Division at the Office of the Comptroller of the Currency (OCC). At the OCC, Dr. Johannsson provides technical support to national bank examiners in evaluating the statistical soundness and regulatory compliance of banks' credit scoring systems. Dr. Johannsson also maintains an active research agenda on issues related to discrimination in the financial markets and immigration. His research papers have been published in journals such as *Research in Labor Economics* and *Growth and Change.*

Jennifer Lee is associate professor of sociology at the University of California, Irvine. She is author of *Civility in the City: Blacks, Jews, and Koreans in Urban America* (2002) and co-editor of *Asian American Youth: Culture, Identity, and Ethnicity* (forthcoming in 2004). In 2003 she received the Robert E. Park Best Scholarly Article Award from the American Sociological Association's Community and Urban Sociology Section and Honorable Mention for the Thomas and Znaniecki Distinguished Book Award from ASA's International Migration Section. She has recently been a fellow at the Center for the Advanced Study in the Behavioral Sciences. Her current research focuses on multiracial identification and identities, and immigrant and intergenerational mobility.

Enrico Marcelli is currently a 2003-2005 Robert Wood Johnson Health & Society Scholar at Harvard University's Department of Society, Human Development and Health, and has been an assistant professor of economics at the University of Massachusetts Boston since 2001. Most of his work focuses on how unauthorized Mexican and other Latino immigrants impact the labor market outcomes of members of other ethno-racial groups and how unauthorized residency status influences the integration of immigrants in the United States. He is currently investigating how individual behaviors and characteristics, social capital, and neighborhood environment influence various health outcomes (e.g., obesity, overall health, subjective well-being) among members of both foreign- and U.S.-born ethno-racial groups.

Frederick McKinney is an adjunct professor of business at the University of Connecticut, Stamford.

Manuel Pastor, Jr. is professor of Latin American and Latino studies and co-director, Center for Justice, Tolerance and Community, University of California, Santa Cruz. His current research focuses on community-based development strategies in metropolitan regions, specifically innovative efforts to address needs of low-income residents and immigrant workers. He also works on issues of environmental justice and has published widely in that area. His most recent book is *Searching for the Uncommon Common Ground: New Dimensions on Race in America* (co-authored with Angela Glover Blackwell and Stewart Kwoh; 2002).

Sabeen Sandhu is a Ph.D. candidate in the Department of Sociology at the University of California, Irvine. Her research interests include international migration, race and ethnicity, and Asian American studies. She is currently working on her doctoral dissertation, which explores high-skilled migrants' adaptive strategies to labor market inequality.

Steven Shulman is a professor of economics at Colorado State University. His current research focuses on the impact of family structure and immigration on ethnic inequality. His recent publications include "Immigration, African Americans, and the 'Rainbow Coalition,'" co-authored with Robert Smith (in *African Americans in the American Economy*, edited by Cecilia Conrad, John Whitehead, Patrick Mason, and James Stewart, forthcoming), "Right-to-Work Laws and Anti-Union Attitudes: Explaining the Variation in Union Density Among States," co-authored with Raymond Hogler and Stephan Weiler (forthcoming in the *Journal of Managerial Issues*), and "Immigration and the Labor Force Participation of Low Skill Native Workers," co-authored with Hannes Johannsson and Stephan Weiler (*Research in Labor Economics*, 2003).

Index

Affirmative action, xii, 13, 88, 94-95, 104, 121, 124, 130, 152, 153, 156
AFL-CIO, 71, 138
African American, or black
  Activism, or activists, 94, 154
  Attitude toward immigrants, 108, 109, 119-121, 124, 126, 127, 131, 139
  Birth rates, 129
  Capitalism, 153
  Codes, 7
  Community, 22, 94, 107, 120, 128, 130, 131
  Earnings, 77, 108, 109, 110, 111, 116, 118, 138, 140, 141, 146
  Economic gap with whites, 28, 141
  Education, or students, 7, 84, 87, 89, 150-153, 156
  Employees, or workers, 6, 7, 10, 13, 23, 78, 83, 85, 87, 88, 89, 98, 100, 101, 102, 104, 105, 115, 116, 118, 139, 141, 143, 144-148, 154, 156
  Employment, xi, 1, 5, 13, 20, 22, 23, 79, 83, 85, 86, 87, 93, 94, 95, 100, 101, 102, 108, 109, 110, 111, 116, 145, 146
  Entrepreneurship, or self-employment, 153-156
  Hiring, 85
  Job displacement, or job losses, 95, 118, 139, 145, 156
  Labor force, or labor force participation, 5, 13, 80, 81, 83, 84, 87, 111, 115, 144, 145
  Leaders, 9, 11, 23, 107-108, 119, 130-132
  Marriage, 37, 39, 84
  Migrants, or migration, 9, 10, 11, 13, 21
  Occupations, or occupational mobility, 1, 118
  Political power, 120, 132

  Politics, 108, 118
  Population, 3, 5, 6, 7, 9, 11, 13, 16, 18, 20, 21, 22, 23, 87, 100, 101, 152
  Rights, 94
  Segregation, 131
  Unemployment, 84, 144
  Wages, xi, 60, 66, 68, 70, 116, 118
Asian
  Businesses, 153
  Employees, or workers, 104
  Population, 18, 29, 41, 43, 151
  Proposition 187, 120
  Refugees, 148
  Wealth, 104

Bean, Frank D., 88, 139-141, 143-144, 148-149, 157-158
Bell-Rose, Stephanie, 88
Betts, Julian R., 89, 151
Bilingual, 104, 139, 156
Blacks, *see* African American
Bonacich, Edna, 154
Borjas, George, 59, 77, 84, 127, 138, 139, 141-143, 148-150, 153, 157
Bound, Richard, 142
Bouvier, Leon, 153
Briggs, Vernon, ix, x, xi, xiii, 108, 133, 137-138, 140
Butcher, Kristin, 141, 142
Butler, Richard, 83

Catanzarite, Lisa, xi, 133
Celler, Emanuel, 16
Chavez, Ceasar, ix
Cherry, Robert, xii
Chinese, 9, 32
Civil rights
  Act, 11, 12, 13, 21, 94
  Coalition, ix
  Leaders, 119

Legislation, 12, 28, 104
Movement, x, 9, 11, 94, 103, 104
Period, x
Policy, 11
Values, 126
Color line, 27, 28, 33, 36, 37, 43, 50, 51
Commission on Immigration Reform, or
 Jordan Commission, 19, 23, 108
Congressional Black Caucus, 23, 108
Congressional Hispanic Caucus, 23, 108
Cornelius, Wayne A., 110

Discrimination, 8, 11-14, 16, 21, 27-30,
 32, 35, 42, 43, 51, 85, 87, 102, 103,
 105, 129, 143
Diversity
 Ethnic, or racial, x, xii, 29, 43, 44-50,
  52, 89
 Goals, 104, 152
 Policies, 102
 Population, 102
 Socioeconomic, 33
 Workforce, or workplace, 94-95, 100
Du Bois, W.E.B., 27, 28

English-only movement, ix, x, xi, xiii
Equal Employment Opportunity Com-
 mission, or EEOC, xii, 96-97, 99,
 100, 105, 142
Espenshade, Thomas, 140
Ethington, Philip J., 131
Ethnicity, x, 29-31, 34, 35, 47, 50, 60,
 146
European Americans, or whites
 Attitudes, 128
 Birth rates, 129
 Community, 127
 Earnings, or wages, 60, 61, 66, 68, 69
 Education, or students, 150, 153
 Employees, or workers, 6, 7, 10, 70,
  78, 83, 87, 145, 146
 Job displacement, 146
 Immigrants, 10
 Indentured servants, 3
 Power structure, 129
 Settlers, 2
 Unemployment, 144
 Women, xii, 94-96, 98, 99, 101-103,
  105

Fairlie, Robert, 155
Fix, Michael, 151, 156

Fosset, Mark, 144
Freeman, Richard, 142, 144, 156
Frenette, Marc, 142
Frey, William H., 131, 143
Friedberg, Rachel, 139
Frost, Raymond, 9

Germans, 9
Globalization, xiii, 19, 143
Group position theory, 31, 36-37, 47, 49-
 51
Gurcak, Jennifer, 152
Gustman, Alan, 149

Hamermesh, Daniel, 139, 141, 143
Heckman, James, 83
Heer, David M., 110
Hindus, 9
Hispanics, or Latinos
 Businesses, 153
 Community, 153
 Congressional Caucus, 108
 Employees, or workers, 138-140,
  143, 145-147
 Marriage, 38-39
 Native born, 141, 146
 Population, 18, 29, 40, 41, 43, 48,
  49, 151, 153
 Students, 151-152
Howell, David, 146-147
Hoxby, Caroline M., 89, 151-152
Hunt, Jennifer, 139

Immigrant
 Advocates, or immigration advocates,
  x, 132
 African, 18, 22, 85, 87
 Asian, 8, 14, 33, 34, 35, 51
 Attitudes of, 139
 Caribbean, 138
 Central American, 148
 Cuban, 138
 Education of, or human capital of, or
  skills of, 19, 23, 59, 138, 139-140,
  142, 156-157
 European, 3, 5, 6, 8, 18, 28, 30, 32,
  33, 34, 138
 Illegal, or undocumented, or unautho-
  rized, 19, 111, 112, 113, 118, 120,
  138, 140
 Incorporation, 30, 31, 33, 36, 50
 Involuntary, 3, 9

Korean, 88, 138
Latino, or Hispanic, xi, 33-35, 51, 70,
    108, 111, 120, 133, 140
Legal, 19, 28
Mexican, 110, 111, 112, 113, 118,
    127, 143, 148, 149
"Nation of," x, 78
Networks, 21-22, 86, 129, 145, 147
New, or recent, 21, 28, 29, 33, 34,
    35, 37, 47, 51, 62, 108, 130, 131,
    140, 141, 142, 149
Perception of, 85
Population, or number of, 3, 6, 7, 8,
    9, 11, 13, 14, 16, 17, 18, 20-23,
    28, 33, 137
Immigration
    Act of 1965, 14-17, 137
    Benefits of, ix, 77, 89, 137, 139
    Costs of, ix, 69, 77-78, 89, 137
    Economic effects of, xi, xii, 59, 70-
        71, 77, 83-89, 108, 110, 126,
        138
    and Education, 151-153
    and Employment niches, 87-89, 144-
        148
    and Ethnic relations, or ethnic diver-
        sity, 28, 29, 31, 47-52
    and Family reunification, 15-16, 18,
        21
    First wave, 5
    Fourth wave, 9, 17, 18, 20-22
    History, 5-11, 28
    Illegal, or undocumented, or unautho-
        rized, 18, 105, 108, 110, 111, 112,
        115, 116, 118, 129
    Impact on African Americans, 17-20,
        68-71, 77-79, 85-89, 93, 104-105,
        107, 109, 116, 120, 140-144
    Impact on Latinos, 68-71
    and Job competition, x, xi, 20, 22,
        23, 59, 60, 69, 71, 82, 85, 86, 88,
        89, 93, 108, 109, 111, 118, 127,
        128, 133
    and Labor supply, or labor force, 78-
        84
    Legal, xiii
    Limit, or reduction, or restriction, ix,
        x, xii, 8, 107, 120, 127-130, 133,
        142, 156
    Mass, 1, 5-10, 17-23, 25, 137
    National Origins Act, 8
    New, 29, 30, 137

Policy, ix, x, xii, xiii, 1-2, 12, 14, 23,
    108, 109, 126-132, 137, 156-157
    and Population growth, ix, 69, 89
    Reforms, xiii
    Second wave, 6
    and Taxpayer burdens, 148-150, 157
    Third wave, 6, 8, 20
    and Unions, 138, 140
Intermarriage, xi, 29-31, 33, 35-41, 47,
    48, 50-52
Irish, 31, 32
Italians, 9, 31, 32

Jaeger, David, 150, 158
Jaynes, Gerald, xii, 138-139, 153
Jews, 31, 32, 154, 157, 160
Joassart, Pascale M., 110
Johannsson, Hannes, xi, 141-142, 156
Johnson, George, 141
Johnson, James H., 132
Johnson, Lyndon B., 12, 14, 15
Jordan, Barbara, 19, 108

Katz, Lawrence, 21
Kennedy, Edward, 16
Kennedy, John F., 12, 14
Kessler, Alan, 121, 124, 130, 132
Kim, Claire Jeanne, 153-154
King, Mary, 148

Latinos, see Hispanics
Lee, Jennifer, xi
Lim, Nelson, 86-87
Link, Arthur, 9-10
Lo, Lucia, 157
Loury, Linda Datcher, 152

Marcelli, Enrico, xii, 110, 111
Martin, John, 153
Massey, Douglas, 142
McKinney, Frederick, xii
Meyer, Bruce, 155
Mexicans, 34, 116, 132, 147
Models of ethnic assimilation
    Pluralist, 34-35
    Straight-line, 33-35
Multiculturalism, x, xii
Muller, Thomas, 87, 144
Multiracial identification, 30, 31, 35-37,
    40, 41, 43, 45-52
Myers, Dowell, 131
Myrdal, Gunnar, 138

National Academy of Science, or NAS, 137, 139-140, 150
National Advisory Commission on Civil Disorders, 13-14, 24
Native workers
  Competition with immigrants, 84
  Earnings, or wages, 60, 69, 70, 72, 77, 78, 83, 85
  Employment, 81, 84, 86, 157
  Labor force participation, or labor force withdrawal, or labor supply reduction, 78, 79, 82-83, 87
  Low-skill, or low wage, 11, 59, 78, 83, 85, 86, 88, 89
  Migration, 77, 82
Nixon, Richard, 153
North, David, 23, 153

Occupations
  Blue collar, 142, 147
  Brown collar, xi, 60, 61, 62, 65, 66, 68-72
  Service, 20
  White collar, 19, 87, 142
One-drop rule, 27, 33, 42

Park, Kyung Tae, 144
Pastor, Manuel, xii, 110
Portes, Alejandro, 153, 155
Proposition 187, 120, 129, 130
Proposition 209, 130
Public services, ix, 120, 140, 148-151

Race relations
  and Immigration, 28, 31
  Black-white model of, 37, 50, 51
Racism, or racist, xi, xiii, 2, 12, 15, 43, 78, 89, 103, 107, 124, 126, 127, 139, 143
  Laissez-faire, 37
  Declining significance, 30, 31, 35, 37, 50-51

Rainbow coalition, 23, 88, 108, 126, 127, 128, 131
Randolph, A. Phillip, ix, 9, 11
Reimers, Cordelia, 140-141
Riot, 10, 13, 88
Roosevelt, Franklin, 11
Rosenfeld, Michael, 87, 147-148
Rusk, Dean, 12, 24

Segregated, or segregation, 1, 7, 12, 33, 35, 59, 61, 64, 65, 66, 70, 71, 72, 94, 131, 142, 143, 158
Shulman, Steven, xi, 108, 131, 133, 141-142, 156
Slave, or slavery, xi, 1-7, 14, 23, 27, 33, 42, 43, 51, 94, 121
Smith, Robert C., 108, 131
Srivastava, Siddharth, 156
Steinmeier, Thomas, 149
Stevens, Gillian, 139-141, 143, 148-149, 157-158

Tienda, Marta, 87, 143, 147-148

Unions, or labor movement, 129, 137-138, 140, 156, 157
U.S. Immigration and Naturalization Service, 111

Van Hook, Jennifer, 144

Washington, Booker T., 7
Waters, Mary, 145-146
Weiler, Stephan, 141-142, 156
Welfare, 13, 83, 138, 145, 148-150, 156, 157, 159
Wilson, Franklin D., 86, 148
Wilson, Pete, 129
Wilson, William Julius, 35-36

Zhou, Min, 131, 153, 155
Zimmerman, Wendy, 151, 156
Zlolniski, Christopher, 140